GOFFMAN UNBOUND!

Advancing the Sociological Imagination

A Series from Paradigm Publishers

Edited by Bernard Phillips and Harold Kincaid

Goffman Unbound! A New Paradigm for Social Science
By Thomas J. Scheff (2006)

The Invisible Crisis of Contemporary Society: Reconstructing Sociology's Fundamental Assumptions
By Bernard Phillips and Louis C. Johnston (2007)

Understanding Terrorism: Building on the Sociological Imagination
Edited by Bernard Phillips (2007)

Struggles before Brown: *Early Civil Rights Protests and Their Significance Today*
By Jean Van Delinder (2008)

GOFFMAN UNBOUND!

A NEW PARADIGM FOR SOCIAL SCIENCE

Thomas J. Scheff

Paradigm Publishers

Boulder • London

Copyright © 2006 by Paradigm Publishers

Published in the United States by Paradigm Publishers, 3360 Mitchell Lane, Suite E, Boulder, Colorado 80301 USA

Paradigm Publishers is the trade name of Birkenkamp & Company, LLC, Dean Birkenkamp, President and Publisher.

Library of Congress Cataloging-in-Publication Data

Goffman unbound! A new paradigm for social science / Thomas J. Scheff.
    p. cm.
  (Advancing the sociological imagination)
  Includes bibliographical references and index.
  ISBN: 978-1-59451-195-0 (hc)
  ISBN: 978-1-59451-196-7 (pbk)
  1. Goffman, Erving.   2. Emotions—Sociological aspects.   3. Interpersonal relations.   4. Microsociology.   I. Title.   II. Series.
  HM479.G64S34 2006
  301.092—dc22

                                                                    2005027188

Printed and bound in the United States of America on acid-free paper that meets the standards of the American National Standard for Permanence of Paper for Printed Library Materials.

Designed and Typeset by Straight Creek Bookmakers.

10 09 08 07

Contents

Preface

Erving Goffman, Norbert Elias, and Harvey Sacks may have been the three most gifted sociologists of the twentieth century. Goffman's work, however, has been little used as a resource, unlike that of Sacks and Elias. There has been substantial commentary, but no body of Goffmanian work has resulted. Not ignored, to say the least, but at this writing its meaning and usefulness have not been established.

This book has three main goals. First, to explicate Goffman's achievements more clearly and directly than has been the case so far. Second, to show how some of them might be extended or modified to be of greater use. Finally, to discuss some of the gaps and shortcomings, and what might be done about them. The three parts of this book undertake these three goals.

To carry out this plan, I have called upon my earlier sketch of a part/whole approach (1997c), and the framework developed by Bernard Phillips (2001; Phillips et al. 2002) that emphasizes the use of interrelated concepts. Part/whole analysis focuses on the need to link what Spinoza called "the least parts" to the "greatest wholes." Spinoza's point was that human beings are so complex that we have no chance to understand them unless we link the smallest parts and the largest wholes. For my purposes I have identified the least parts of human conduct as the words, gestures, thoughts, and feelings in particular social interactions, and the greatest wholes with social institutions and abstract theories.

Phillips's Web of Concepts approach overlaps to some extent with the part/whole idea, but has a somewhat different emphasis. His approach, like mine, puts human complexity in the forefront, and also emphasizes, like mine, the need to shuttle up and down the concrete/abstract ladder. Phillips also urges an aspect of research that has not been explicit in my earlier work, the need for reflexiveness, for including the researcher her- or himself in the overall picture. Phillips's approach differs from mine in proposing the use of many conventional concepts as the basis for scholarship, such as stratification, personality, social structure, etc. My own approach has been to develop new concepts for each study, and to attempt to integrate disciplines, sub-disciplines and levels of analysis.

The feature that Goffman, Phillips, and I share is the attempt to get outside the box, beyond the conventions of our society and of social science. Although Goffman cited other scholars, most of his work was fully original. He eschewed conventional approaches, seeking rather to reground social science in a new language with new concepts. How did he embark on such an odyssey?

Goffman's main focus was what might be called the microworld of emotions and relationships (ERW). We all live in it every day of our lives, yet we have been trained not to notice. Since Goffman noticed it, he was the discoverer of a hidden world. His work, if properly construed, provides a window into that otherwise invisible place. It is important for many reasons. For brevity I will mention only two obvious ones: First, it is important in its own right, since it constitutes the moment-by-moment texture of our lives. Second, it is intimately connected to the larger world; it both causes and is caused by that world. If we are to have more than a passing understanding of ourselves and our society, we need to become better acquainted with the emotional/relational world.

A *New Yorker* cartoon conveyed the idea that we avoid knowledge of this world. A man lying on the analyst's couch is basically saying: "Call it denial if you will, but frankly I think that my personal life is none of my own damn business."

Although humor is often based on exaggeration, the idea that our personal lives are "none of our own damn business" comes close to the truth of the matter, or at least more truth than poetry. The patient in the

"Look, call it denial if you like, but I think what goes on in my personal life is none of my own damn business."

cartoon being a man, rather than a woman, is also significant. Men, more than women, are trained to ignore the details that reveal the nature of emotions and relationships. Their attention is diverted elsewhere. But both women and men know much less about this world (for short, the ERW) than the larger one.

Our obliviousness could be a creation of the modern urban/industrial society. In traditional societies, the ERW was virtually the only world there was. In modern societies there are so many duties, distractions, and diversions that most of us learn to ignore the ERW, except when in crisis.

Conventional social science mostly ignores emotions and relationships in favor of behavior and cognition. Goffman's recognition of the existence of an ERW is the foundation of his whole approach. He realized, at some level, that conventional social and behavioral science was blind to the ERW, and might as well be blind in many other arenas as well.

Following Goffman's lead, if we are going to advance in our understanding of the human condition, we need to build a new approach. This approach would not only include the ERW, but other hitherto unrecognized structures and processes as well, such as the filigree of emotions and relationships that underlies large-scale behavior, as in the case of collective cooperation and conflict.

Limitations of Goffman's Work

Goffman's work is a wholesale attack on this problem: how can we make the invisible, the backstage he sometimes called it, visible? Not that he had all the answers. His work provides pathways for approach to only some of the facets of the problem.[1] His treatment of emotions, for example, is crucial on embarrassment and shame, and to a much smaller extent, disgust, but he has almost nothing to say about other important emotions, such as fear, pride, and love. Similarly, his approach to relationships is inspired on loneliness, disconnectedness, and alienation, but omits the opposite pole: solidarity, secure bonds, and moments of profound unity.

Another significant problem with Goffman's approach is his writing. It is brilliant, suggestive, and entertaining, but also playful and teasing, revealing and concealing. Furthermore, he never steps back to summarize the implications of what he had to say, let alone to get very far in systematizing any of it. His style violates what might be considered the first rule of scientific and scholarly writing: the thesis should be stated clearly, and more than once, so that there can be no mistake about the main goal. It is customary to invoke the basic thesis at various levels of specificity five times: in the title, abstract, first paragraph, text, and conclusion. Much of Goffman's writing provides either no thesis at all or one that is so elliptic as to be virtually useless, if not misleading.

There is another problem with understanding Goffman's work that is somewhat unusual: his reputation as a "character" among people who knew him, and even among those who didn't. Although he died in 1982, his reputation as a character continues, and casts something of a shadow over his work. This issue will be considered in several chapters.

The main emphasis will be to use Goffman's approach to the ERW as a starting point. The introduction summarizes the primary features of Goffman's work, and shows some links to his life. The chapters in Part I seek to derive, and state outright, flatfootedly if necessary, some of Goffman's main theses, particularly with respect to the ERW as he saw them. Part II shows some of the implications of his ideas for future research. Part III outlines my modifications, extensions, and supplements to the framework that Goffman provided.

In my own work I have, at times intentionally, but usually inadvertently, dealt with gaps in Goffman's approach, both in the microworld, and in linking this world to large-scale social change. Just as Marx was the discoverer of the vast world of political economy and its effects on civilizations, Goffman discovered the empire of the ERW, which complements and extends Marx's analysis of feast and famine, peace and war, and many other aspects of the human condition.

Marxian and Goffmanian analysis provide vistas for exploring two basic dimensions of societies. The first focuses on political/economic structure/process, especially power and ranking of groups. Social integration, on the other hand, concerns solidarity and alienation, independently of power and rank. In the last section of this book, I link the ERW to social change in the larger world, particularly to the processes that lead to war and peace.

The last section outlines some of the most important implications for a new microsociology and its links to the larger world. In particular, this section connects Goffman's work to his life, and to extensions of Phillips's Web approach and to part/whole analysis. This book will foster complexity rather than simplification, argue concept development preliminary to systematic studies, and show paths between least parts and greatest wholes.

Part I

The first chapter is an introduction to Goffman's life and work. It provides an overview of scholarly commentary on his work, and biographical material about his life, including some of my own encounters with him. Although there is considerable appreciation of Goffman's work among scholars, it is mixed with, and much outweighed by, criticism. Similarly, Goffman's reputation as a person was quite mixed, with many people considering him to be, at best, an odd character. This chapter evaluates both the appreciative and critical sides, seeking to show links between his life and work. This issue is taken up again in Chapter 10, on hypermasculinity.

Chapter 2. Goffman's greatest achievement seems to have been the creation of a vocabulary that enabled him to see the human condition in a new way. He was able to deconstruct not only specific conventional ideas of the self, mental illness, and, to some extent, gender, but also the whole conventional schema in modern societies, what has been called "the assumptive world." In this respect he came nearest to carrying through the program of deconstructing/reconstructing the world of everyday life.

Chapter 3. Goffman's best known work was *Presentation of Self in Everyday Life.* This chapter shows first that this book contains two somewhat conflicting theses, the more explicit one structural, the more hidden one, social psychological, spelling out in detail the ramifications of Cooley's idea of the looking-glass self. The chapter's main thrust is that contrary to most of the comments on this book, it focuses not only on embarrassment, but also on shame, either real or anticipated, as the basic emotions of most social transactions. The relationship between embarrassment and shame is further explored in this chapter, because Goffman's work implies a close link, but doesn't comment on it directly. Goffman's treatment of the looking-glass self suggests that shame/embarrassment is the master emotion of social life.

Part II

Chapter 4. This chapter takes a broad look at Goffman's treatment of emotions, comparing it with other writers like Freud, Elias, and the psychoanalyst Helen Block Lewis. There turns out to be considerable overlap in their approaches to emotion, in that all four place considerable emphasis on the role of shame/embarrassment in human conduct. What has made this emphasis problematic to this point is what might be called a taboo on shame in Western societies. The chapter proposes that this taboo makes the emotional/relational world all but invisible in modern societies.

Chapter 5. Goffman's longest, most difficult and enigmatic book is *Frame Analysis.* What is the purpose of this book, and what is its main point? In this chapter I propose an answer to the problem: Although Goffman doesn't say it, this book takes a long step toward describing the structure of *context.* That is, the subjective and intersubjective context or background is often so complex that it requires an assembly of premises. Goffman himself, and others, have hinted that this structure might require mathematical notation, which this chapter explores. This chapter also links frame analysis to earlier studies of the intersubjective structure of consensus, suggesting a model of social facts.

Chapter 6. Goffman's book *Asylums* had considerable impact both on the mental health system and on the public at large. His critique of existing psychiatry is clear and passionate. However, his attempt to provide an alternative to the medical model is much less clear. One of the problems is that Goffman avoided any involvement in psychology, picturing himself as a structuralist. This chapter proposes a systems approach to mental illness, one that might encompass physical, psychological, and social aspects of the problem.

Part III

Chapter 7. As already indicated, love is one of the emotions that are absent in Goffman's work. This chapter proposes an explicit definition of genuine love, both the romantic and non-romantic kinds. One facet of this definition rests on further elaboration of the idea of intersubjectivity proposed by Cooley and Goffman, along with two other facets. Attachment is a component of both romantic and non-romantic love, but (sexual) attraction is involved only in romantic love. Using the word attunement to mean balanced intersubjectivity between self and other, non-romantic love can be defined as being made up of two A's, attachment and attunement. Romantic love has three: attachment, attunement, and attraction. This definition serves to differentiate genuine love from look-alikes, such as infatuation, heartbreak, and lust alone, and to connect it to theories of social integration.

Chapter 8. Ordinary language serves to hide the meaning of both love and hate, particularly the processes that increase or decrease their intensity. This chapter proposes a conceptual definition of hate that parallels the definition of love in Chapter 7. The basic structure of hate, it is proposed, involves a shame/anger sequence that goes unacknowledged. The proposed definitions of love and hate link both concepts to a theory of the social origins of pride and shame and therefore to a theory of social integration.

Chapter 9. Analysis of the emotional/relational world provides a path toward understanding the variety of human relationships, the various kinds of bonds that unite and divide individuals and groups. Using reports on dialogues in their families by students, this chapter shows the way in which the management of pride and shame both reflects and generates different kinds of bonds at the interpersonal level. This kind of analysis on a small and intimate scale provides the basis for applying ideas about social integration to large-scale cooperation and conflict between groups.

Chapter 10. One of the enigmas of the modern world is the way in which social groups seem to act against their own political and economic interests. Present-day examples are working-class support for a tax structure that benefits the wealthy, and gratuitous wars for which the working-class provides the cannon fodder. This chapter proposes one component of the solution to this enigma, the way in which hypermasculinity results in mass support for destructive policies and warfare. In his lengthy essay "Where the Action Is," Goffman inadvertently contributed to a model of hypermasculinity and its links to the ERW. This chapter uses Goffman's idea of "character contests" as a way of explaining the link between the ERW and both interpersonal and group conflict.

Chapter 11. Particularly in issues of peace and war, the exact nature of nationalism may be crucial. This chapter continues the analysis in the last chapter by examining the emotional/relational bases of blind patriotism, my country right or wrong. This kind of nationalism is only part of the explanation of the actions of leaders of large groups, since warfare is usually in their economic and political interests. However, blind patriotism in public support for war is difficult to explain in this way, since it doesn't seem to be in the public interest. This chapter outlines how the interaction between alienation and unacknowledged emotons might explain the puzzle.

Chapter 12. Identifying and exploring the ERW and its links to the macroworld makes for a new approach to human conduct. The last chapter reviews the main points of the book as a whole, and examines their implications for social and behavioral science. It shows how these considerations further extend the usefulness of part/whole analysis and Phillips's Web of Concepts. The new approach requires research beginning with the development of at least one clearly defined concept through the careful examination of many and varied concrete instances.

Acknowledgments

This project nearly ended after I had written about half the draft chapters. Many years of struggle had led to what seemed to be a period of terminal stuckness. Luckily for me, Bernard Phillips was willing to read the chapters. With his encouragement and quite detailed suggestions, I was able to finish. I am also indebted to Randall Collins and Arlie Hochschild, both for their work and their advice. From his comprehensive knowledge of Goffman's work, Greg Smith also provided crucial answers to my questions. Further acknowledgments are made in the chapters themselves. Once again I have found my colleagues to be an invaluable source of help and inspiration.

Note

1. For an early and still useful analysis of the limitations of Goffman's work, see Hochschild (1983).

CHAPTER 1

Introduction

The Life and Work of Genius

> On First Looking into a Manuscript by Goffman
> ... You sloughed
> Methodologies, set out to tell what oft
> Is done, but ne'er well expressed. And until
> Well expressed, well christened, ill seen. Gentle
> GOFFMAN, so much of such seeing we owe, we know,
> To thy quick quirky quizzing of our status quo.
> Dell Hymes (1984)

THIS CHAPTER BEGINS WITH A REVIEW of the scholarly response to Goffman's work, and also considers his personal reputation. I include his life for two reasons. First, because I think one part of that reputation, as an obnoxious character, casts a shadow on his work. Second, because I believe that a dispassionate consideration of links between an author's life and work can be valuable in themselves. In earlier studies, I have tried to show that the work of a brilliant author, Goethe, for example, can be used to understand his or her own life, and that knowledge of the author's life can help us better understand the work.[1] It can also help us understand an author's reputation among his colleagues.

Goffman's work has a large and appreciative following among scholars. Many of them seem to believe, as I do, that his work bears the stamp of genius, and that it contains a legacy that could lead to revolutionary changes in social science. However, there is also a mass of critical opinion, some of which finds its way into the commentary of even his most loyal admirers.

1

As with his work, there are also two distinct representations of Goffman's life. In addition to published reviews, mostly favorable, there is also a shadow life that might be called the Goffman legend: stories and gossip about oddness. Although he died over twenty years ago, his behavior is still much referred to in private; there exists, at least among sociologists, what might be called an urban legend, Goffman the Character. Here I will attempt to make sense of the two versions of his life, and to relate them to his work.

Responses to Goffman's Work

The last line of the witty poem (1984) by Hymes, above, miraculously implies much of what is to be said, at, alas, great length in these chapters. However, for the sake of argument, I will quibble with one of Hymes's three q's: that Goffman's work is "quirky." The idea that his approach is at least odd or weird is shared by a virtual army of commentators. At its most extreme, as in the case of Scheibe (2000), the widespread critique says that Goffman's approach is "cold-eyed and sour" and other similar epithets. I will argue that Goffman's work is extremely unusual because of its originality, but not ever "quirky," once we understand the direction that it takes. That is, if one were to set out to reach what I think might be the main goals and consequences of Goffman's work, one would be advised to follow an approach quite similar to his.

Erving Goffman is probably the most widely read sociologist in the history of the discipline. I say that not to take away from Durkheim, but to call attention to the diversity of his audience, which includes vast numbers of laypersons. Perhaps almost as widely cited, his work has been noted throughout the social sciences and humanities.

But the meaning of his work and therefore his legacy is by no means clear. In the 23 years since his tragically youthful death at 60, eight valuable monographs and edited volumes interpreting his work have been published in English.[2] Many further mentions, some of them chapter length, can be found in other volumes. But even a quick reading suggests that there is no consensus. As a review of one of the volumes (Smith 1999) suggests (Toiskallio 2000), the contributors view Goffman's writings with "simultaneous irritation and fascination."

One can go further if one compares the offerings in these books. There is agreement between the authors about Goffman's felicitous style and stimulus value. But there are also grave doubts about the nature of his legacy. Most of those reviewing Goffman's work, even the most appreciative, are at best ambivalent. Although they find much to praise, there are also many irritations, and considerable confusion.

Goffman's critics are not ambivalent. Even though they find positive features, critics like Gouldner (1970), Psathas (1980), and Schegloff (1988) are largely dismissive. Gouldner was repelled by Goffman's miniature scale, and by what Gouldner thought was his disinterest in power and hierarchy. Psathas and Schegloff, like many of the commentators, critics and admirers alike, found Goffman unsystematic to the point of chaos. Goffman's approach to the main elements in social science is, to say the least, not clear.

An extended exchange on this issue can be found in the first of the four Fine and Smith (2000) volumes. Posner (Ch. 9), like many others, finds Goffman's work enigmatic. To back up this claim, she cites several of his critics, and considers several readings of his work that she finds to be outright misunderstandings. She concludes that although often cited, Goffman's work has little status, and even less application in the academic community.

But Oromaner (Ch. 10) challenges Posner. He argues that not only is Goffman's work massively cited, but that he also received many honors from the academic community, and that even his critics offer praise. Posner's response (Ch. 11) is blunt. The crucial point that Oromaner missed, she insists, is that even the praise Goffman received consisted of "left handed compliments." Even more to the point is Posner's argument that most of the commentary shows that his work is either not understood or misunderstood. Many reviews of Goffman's work agree: they see his work as virtually impossible to understand or apply.

There seem to be several reasons for the problem. For one, Goffman's prose style is incredibly involuted and complex. It is dense with meaning, innuendo, impromptu classifications, qualifications, and expansion. It is also humorous, ironic, and witty in ways that both entertain and irritate, reveal and conceal. Winkins's (2000, 206) comment on his epistolary style is also applicable to most of his writing: "sharp, full of humour, and yet circumvoluted, ever *precieux.*"

As with most readers, I want to agree that Goffman's style is "ever precious." Yet I have a reservation that can be expressed by a passage from Auden's poem "The Truest Poetry Is the Most Feigning":

> What but tall tales, the luck of verbal playing,
> Can trick his [human beings'] lying nature into saying
> That love or truth in any serious sense,
> Like orthodoxy, is a reticence.

Goffman's style was reticent. He seemed to sense how far he could go with an idea without completely losing the reader. Perhaps instead of blurting out everything he knew, he went only as far as he thought the reader would be ready for. In my view, this might be a valuable aid to communicating new ideas.

But there is also a difficulty more fundamental than mere style. Goffman seemed to revel in complexity. Not only ordinary people, but also most social science assumes that human conduct is simple enough that it can be understood in commonsense terms. For that reason, key concepts are often expressed in ordinary language, using vernacular words rather than concepts.

For example, there have been a large number of studies of alienation, and many more mentions, that have not provided a clear definition of the concept itself. Although there are standardized alienation scales, there have been few attempts to decide, conceptually, what it is that these scales are supposed to be measuring.

In 1975, Seeman reviewed studies of alienation based on standardized scales. His analysis revealed that the scales involve six different dimensions.

1. Powerlessness
2. Meaninglessness
3. Normlessness
4. Cultural estrangement
5. Self-estrangement
6. Social isolation: exclusion or rejection

Each of these categories, in turn, is also somewhat ambiguous. Powerlessness, for example, can mean a relational element, lack of actual power relative to other people, and a dispositional element, the feeling of powerlessness, whether grounded in comparison to others or not. Five of the six dimensions can refer to relational elements, but one, self-estrangement, cannot, since it is solely intrapersonal.

Furthermore, at least two of the six meanings imply emotional components: the exclusion or rejection of social isolation is a correlate of shame, as is the feeling of inadequacy that may accompany powerlessness. Seeman's study demonstrates both kinds of confounds: dispositional vs. relational, and cognitive vs. emotional.[3]

It may be significant that although Seeman's study was published over thirty years ago, no real inroads seem to have been made on clearly defining alienation, or creating specialized scales that measure only one of the six dimensions. Nor did his study slow down the creation of new, general alienation scales, or studies using standardized scales. For all practical purposes, his study has had no impact at all. The idea of alienation is quite central in sociology, yet when we use this word, we still don't know what it is we are talking about.

Many key concepts in social science are ambiguous in a similar way. Self-esteem—easily the most studied topic in all of social science, with at least *fifteen thousand* studies—seems to have a similar problem. A well-known study by Leary and Baumeister (2000) implies that self-esteem scales confound dispositional and relational dimensions. And I have shown, with David Fearon (2004), that these scales also confound cognitive and emotional dimensions. There are now well over 200 standardized scales for measuring self-esteem reliably. Yet there is still no agreed-upon definition of the concept. What that means is that although all the scales are reliable, there is no way of checking their validity, since we haven't agreed upon the meaning of what it is that is being measured. The tail is wagging the dog.

Some key concepts, such as alienation and self-esteem, involve potentially orthogonal meanings (such as individual, relational, cognitive, and emotional dimensions) confounded in what is usually thought of as a single idea. Emotion words, especially in English, are notoriously confusing. As indicated in Chapter 3, below, Goffman offered a carefully thought through and precise definition of embarrassment. Other important ideas, such as irrationality, and, as indicated in Chapter 5, context, are mere residual categories, conceptually empty boxes, because they encompass an enormously wide variety of different kinds of things. Goffman's favorite target was the idea of an individual self, standing alone, as if there were no social context. Assumptions of simplicity hide these confusions. Goffman seemed to be trying to at least expose these basic problems, and in some cases, begin the search for remedies, as will be further discussed in the next chapter.

But introducing complexity into modern social science leads to trouble with reviewers, at least in Goffman's case. Even his most loyal fans have complained. Two of the most detailed and appreciative commentators are Lofland (1980), reviewing the work up to and including *Stigma* (1963), and Manning (1980), the whole *oeuvre,* with special attention to a later work, *Frame Analysis* (1974). The overall tone of both Lofland and Manning is strongly appreciative. Yet their systematic reviews unearth features that give them pause. One that is also noted by most of the essayists is that Goffman started afresh in each book, not only not relating his new ideas to his old ones, but not even taking note of them. This practice gives rise to some confusion as to Goffman's intent.

In his highly appreciative essay, Lofland (1980, 29) has also pointed out that the first three pages of Goffman's article on face work contain:

3 types of face
4 consequences of being out of or in the wrong face
2 basic kinds of face work
5 kinds of avoidance processes
3 phases of the corrective process
5 ways an offering can be accepted (1955, pp. 213–15).

Manning (1980, 270) notes that later, in *Frame Analysis,* the following concepts "at least" are found in a nineteen-page span:

4 kinds of playful deceit
6 types of benign fabrications
3 kinds of exploitative fabrications
5 sorts of self-deception (1974, 87–116).

Perhaps Lofland and Manning are implying that so many partridges and pear trees suggest a Christmas carol more than a sociological theory.

Manning (1980, 270) goes on to complain explicitly:

> Such lists of items do not always fall out so neatly in a text, they may accrue in an almost shadowy fashion. The purpose of these lists is unstated and often elusive. He does not infer or deduce from them, does not claim that these types are exhaustive, explicate the degree of kinds of possible logical interconnections between them, nor does he always relate his current efforts to previous ideas of himself or others.

It is clear from such observations that Goffman's work does not make much, if any, contribution to theory. Other commentators have unanimously agreed that Goffman has not contributed to method or empirical evidence as these categories have come to be understood in social science. If not to theory, method, or data, where could his contribution lie? Chapter 2 proposes three vitally important contributions, all necessary *before* conventional science and scholarship can be applied.

Personal Reputation

Because I have been speaking for many years about Goffman's work, formally and informally, I have heard many opinions expressed about both his work and his behavior. It often turns out that those who tell me about his behavior usually don't have firsthand information; they are merely repeating what they heard. I won't repeat these stories because I can't establish the extent that they are true or false. My version of his behavior will be based on publications by Lofland and Winkin, my own encounters with Goffman, and three interviews I conducted with persons who knew him well.

In including Goffman's life within my purview, I am following Phillips's idea that self-reference or reflexiveness is an important part of all scholarship. Since Goffman himself did not self-reference at all, to the point of secrecy, perhaps I can remedy in part that omission.

Another inclination to include Goffman's life comes from the tradition of the most skillful of all biographers, James Boswell. He apologized for including Samuel Johnson's tics and odd behaviors, pleading, "Let me not be censured for mentioning such minute particulars. Everything relative to so great a man is worth observing" (1961, p. 4 of the dedication). I am happy to follow in Boswell's footsteps.

The information about Goffman's personal life that I have found most helpful, all things considered, has been provided by John Lofland (1984), John Irwin (personal correspondence), and Yves Winkins (2000). Lofland, like me, studied with Goffman in graduate school at Berkeley, but knew him longer and better than I did. Lofland's article, written after Goffman's death in 1982, provides a very favorable summary of his legacy and his life. However, it repeats some of the stories that suggest that much of Goffman's behavior was at the very least odd or challenging, and at times cruel and wounding. Irwin's account of the long and close relationship that he and his wife, Marsha Rosenbaum, had with Goffman makes a very similar point. Winkins published a biography in French in 1988, and is preparing an English translation and extension.

After noting that Goffman's remarks were often quite humorous, including humor directed against himself, Lofland interprets stories of Goffman's oddness or hostility as follows:

> A theme of his behavior that was broader and more encompassing than his humor was his desire for candor and the use of penetrating remarks to cut through the banal and false surfaces in order to touch truth ... Moreover, in encounters and in relationships he was carrying on a type of testing or even hazing. (1980, 21)

The part about testing and hazing seems particularly important in general, and especially for me, since it helps me understand my own encounters with Goffman.

It seems clear that Goffman did test and/or haze, but it was possible to pass Goffman's tests, and thereby stop most of the hazing, as suggested in my interview of Arlene Daniels. This incident occurred at a cocktail party after Arlene, a graduate student at the time, had encountered Goffman only once before, and then only briefly.

Goffman opened the conversation by saying, "I see you have gained weight, Mrs. Daniels. What do you think your husband will think about that?" Arlene responded: "I understand that your wife wants you back, Professor Goffman. Do you think that would be wise?" At this point, Goffman laughed, put his arm around Arlene's shoulders, and said, "Come on, kid, I'll buy you a drink."

Arlene passed Goffman's test; they became friends, with little further testing/hazing. In my own encounters with Goffman, I didn't stand up to him like Arlene did, so he continued to haze. Arlene gave as good as she got, trading insult for insult. I tried to ignore them, so I continued to be their butt. Perhaps Goffman saw himself as a street fighter in his encounters, looking for those worthy to be members of his gang.

But as my teacher and mentor, Goffman was generous and helpful, if somewhat abrupt. He got me my first job, at a time when jobs were scarce, by little more than a wave of his hand. When Robert MacGinnis was a visiting professor at Berkeley, he asked Goffman if he could recommend an advanced graduate student who had a mathematical background. Since he knew I had been a graduate student in physics before switching to sociology, Goffman told him my name, resulting in my first job (assistant professor at the University of Wisconsin, Madison).

Soon afterwards, Goffman gave me advice that enabled me to finish the research project that resulted in my dissertation. Without his advice, I might have been unable to write it. My project began when another of my mentors, Tom Shibutani, obtained a six-month research fellowship for me at Stockton State Hospital, as it was called at that time (1958). I believe that Dorothy Smith and several others also had the same kind of fellowship.

Although I knew nothing at all about mental hospitals or mental illness, I needed money and I needed data for my dissertation. I was contracted to teach at Wisconsin after I finished my fellowship at Stockton. But after spending a month observing in various units of the hospital, I was in a muddle. Most of my observations confused me. I had no problem during my first week, because I spent all of my time in the front end of the hospital, the two admittance wards, one for men, one for women. The procedures there were understandable: physicians and nurses interviewing and treating patients.

But if the patients didn't respond to treatment in a week or ten days, they were sent to the other units that comprised the bulk of the hospital. My trouble started when I ventured into these other units. As far as I could tell, what went on there had little or nothing to do with the practice of medicine. For one thing, I hardly ever saw doctors or nurses. The units were run by "psychiatric technicians." That meant, it seemed to me, persons with no training whatsoever. But my clock was ticking: I had to be in Wisconsin in five months, bringing with me at least the data for my dissertation, if not the dissertation itself.

So I made my way to an appointment with Goffman in his office in Berkeley. He cut me off abruptly after hearing only a few minutes about my observations and confusion. He said "Read Lemert." I said "What?" He said "Read Edwin Lemert. It's a book called *Social Pathology.*" It was off-putting to drive sixty miles for a consultation that lasted five minutes, but Goffman's advice turned out to be exactly what I needed to hear. One of the chapters in Lemert's book outlined an early version of the labeling theory of mental illness. Reading this chapter gave me the framework I needed to understand what I was seeing at Stockton. I finished my dissertation during my second year at Wisconsin.

It was odd, but somehow Goffman-like, that he made no reference to his own experiences as a participant-observer at St. Elizabeth's Hospital in

Washington, D.C., which led to the publication of *Asylums* in 1961, but referred me to Lemert instead. By the time I spoke to him in 1958, he already had a relevant chapter and an article at least in process, if not in print. Indeed, his essay on total institutions (1958) would have been even more relevant to my study than Lemert. Many of my observations turned out to parallel his. Perhaps he treated encounters with me as "character contests," as will be suggested below. In not revealing his own work, he was maintaining his poise and composure in the face of my ignorance, obliviousness, and general straightness.

Another consultation in regard to my work at Stockton also proved to be helpful, at least in the short run. After several months at the hospital, I begin to suspect that there were ongoing patterns of abuse of the patients by the staff. Many abuses were only negligent, but some might have been criminal. For example, although never an eyewitness, I was told by several patient informants about one practice that could have resulted in serious illness and/or death, and on one occasion, I believe, actually did.

Patients who had been unruly or violent in those days were often sequestered in solitary rooms to cool off. In the unit that I was most familiar with, a back ward for women I called E-5 in my dissertation, there was a whole row of such cells. My informants told me that if techs wanted to punish a patient, they would remove mattress and bedclothes from the bed, so that the patient would be lying on bare bedsprings. Then they would remove the patient's clothes and strap her to the bed. Finally they would open the window and douse the patient with water, leaving her overnight so that she would really cool off.

After learning about this practice, I was not surprised when a patient who had been in solitary overnight developed pneumonia and was shipped off to the medical ward of the hospital, where she died. At this point I became agitated about my presence in the wards. I didn't report my suspicions to the superintendent, so I felt complicit with this abuse and several others I suspected.

Once more I resorted to my mentor. When I reported to Goffman, his advice was terse, as usual. He told me to be a *lammelke* (Yiddish for "little lamb"). That is, he advised me to keep my mouth shut. Because, he said, as I already knew, that if I ratted on the techs, they would, at the very least, give me the cold shoulder, and worse yet, might make it difficult to observe on the wards at all.

So I kept my mouth shut through the end of my six-month term. Since my dissertation recorded my suspicions, I sent copies to the officials in charge of the hospital and the California system as a whole. As it happened, my moral dilemma about one of the abuses was resolved quickly during my stay without help from me. A patient on E-5 who had challenged the techs' authority had been strapped to a post in the lounge, and reviled there by some of the techs and patients. No one objected. I was appalled, silent, and near the bursting point.

I felt that I could delay telling about the pneumonia case because I hadn't seen any of the incidents myself, and only guessed at the consequences. But the abuse of this patient was going on before my eyes every day. The patient had been free of her symptoms (delusions) for many weeks before undergoing public humiliation. On the second day she began to be deluded again and to hallucinate. When I listened to what she was saying it broke my heart. She said at first that she was Jesus on the cross, sacrificing herself for others. But before long she was saying that she was Jean Valjean (the hero of the novel *Les Misérables*), being imprisoned for stealing a loaf of bread to feed her starving children. What should I do?

Although as a rule, social workers and psychologists didn't enter back wards, during the third day of punishment a social worker (Jean Norwood) somehow found out. Without hesitation, she reported the episode to the superintendent. The patient was unchained from the post, but the absentee doctor who was supposedly in charge of the unit, and the tech supervisor who actually was, received only verbal reprimands, a slap on the wrist. I saw no indications of change in the other abuses.

Goffman's advice enabled me to finish the research leading to my dissertation. But following his advice left me with bad dreams for years, and with a lifelong feeling of guilt. Of course it is not Goffman's fault that I followed his advice, entirely my own.

In most of my direct encounters with Goffman, it seems to me now that I failed his tests, so I usually felt like I was being hazed. At one point he asked me where I grew up. I told him in small rural towns in Texas and Louisiana. He laughed, saying: "That explains you without remainder. A Jew from the rural South." Never mind that I later found out that Goffman himself was a Jew from a small rural town in Canada (Dauphin, Manitoba). At the time I felt I had been diminished, if not dismissed, by his remark.

An incident on an airplane was worse. When I was still a graduate student in Berkeley, Goffman had arranged a flight from Oakland to Los Angeles to see Harold Garfinkel and Harvey Sacks, who had only recently become Garfinkel's student. I think that Garfinkel was proud of Sacks, and wanted to show him off to Goffman. For reasons that I have either forgotten or didn't know in the first place, Goffman arranged for me to go with him.

The flight was extremely turbulent from beginning to end. The sudden falls, jerks, and bouncing got me to the point that I was nauseated. I put the bag provided for just such a moment up to my mouth in the nick of time. But as I vomited, Goffman was laughing and narrating a blow-by-blow description of my behavior, describing my attempt to be polite as I was overcome by an irresistible impulse. I felt doubly humiliated, not just because of my behavior, but also because I felt Goffman had mocked me.

One final hazing incident occurred in an exchange of letters. Sometime in the late seventies, I had written to Goffman that I was completing a book on catharsis (1979). He replied in exasperation that "I could always find a wall to be off of." Since he hadn't seen any part of the manuscript, his reply was prejudicial. He was simply confirming his allegiance to the standard sociological stereotype of psychology as irrelevant. Once again, he was hazing me in his partly humorous, partly hostile way. To be fair to Goffman, once I told him by letter about the part that "distancing" played in my manuscript, a dramaturgical idea, he offered useful advice on citations. Not every encounter was hostile.

In considering the way Goffman treated me, I think I can add a further aspect to Lofland's analysis. It is clear from the accounts by Lofland and others that although many of Goffman's encounters and relationships involved testing and/or hazing, this was not always true. For example, my impression is that Lofland himself was not treated in this way.

Nor were Jane and Irving Piliavin, who had a close, long-term relationship with Goffman beginning when all three were undergraduates. In my interview with them, there was no mention of testing or hazing: their account was of a good friend whose behavior was unexceptional. I have already mentioned how Arlene Daniels solved the hazing problem. Finally, although I haven't interviewed them, my guess is that Goffman was a good father, that he didn't test or haze either his son Tom or his daughter Alice. Goffman had introduced me to Tom when he was a child of six or seven in Berkeley. My impression, based solely on a single brief meeting, was that he adored his dad.

An incident from some of my earliest contacts with Goffman might provide another reason that he hazed me, in addition to my not standing up to him. During the second semester of his first year (1958) at Berkeley, I was one of Goffman's teaching assistants in a large undergraduate class. For reasons that will become clear below, I don't remember much of the content or even the title, which might have been something like "Interpersonal Relationships" or "Social Interaction."

There must have been at least five hundred students in the class, because there were five teaching assistants. I can identify only two of them: Isadora Ding and Leonard Lieberman. We were all advanced graduate students, but none of us, I now believe, had the slightest clue as to what the class was about. Goffman had little published work at that time, but even if we had tried to read it, we probably would not have understood. I say that not only because of my later difficulties with Goffman's writings, but because I clearly remember an incident at the last meeting of the class, even though it occurred almost fifty years ago.

As is the custom, when Goffman bade the class farewell on the last day, the students applauded. To the surprise of us TAs, sitting together in the last row, making snide comments, the applause became a standing ovation. We looked at each other: had we missed something? It seems to me now that in our function as discussion leaders, we probably had all been more critical of Goffman's lectures than understanding. Apparently the undergraduate students had understood the class far better than we had, and were now giving Goffman his due, and us our comeuppance.

What I think had happened is that all of the teaching assistants had already been indoctrinated by the time we got to Goffman's class. He was offering a radically new approach that we could not absorb for that reason. I was by that time committed to social psychology, but to the more conventional version offered by Tom Shibutani. Compared to us, the undergraduates were less doctrinaire, and could appreciate what Goffman had to offer. Later, in my work on shame, the importance of Goffman's emphasis on embarrassment finally dawned on me. I have been struggling with Goffman's work ever since, trying to catch up. Like the proverbial son's father, Goffman seems to me to get smarter every year.

My guess is that Goffman hazed me not only as a test, but also because he sensed that I didn't understand. As it happened, the first time I saw him was a chance encounter in a university hallway. We had narrowly missed colliding, and we both mumbled apologies. What I saw was a quite small, dapper, boyish-looking male with a crew cut. Assuming that he was an undergraduate, I quite literally didn't know who he was, prophetic of my later relationship with him.

Goffman had what amounts to X-ray vision in social transactions; he could see much of what was going on backstage. It must have been very frustrating to have a student like me, without a clue. Perhaps he defended against feelings resulting from my obliviousness and disconnection from him by hazing me. He was rejecting the rejector.

This explanation doesn't contradict Lofland's idea (Goffman's search for truth), but supplements it. There are many paths to truth: why, with students at least, did Goffman often pick the hazing one? My guess is that because of his exquisite sensitivity, he usually felt alone and disconnected from other people, like an alien from outer space. Still, the question of the path he chose goes unanswered. He could have employed his advanced knowledge of others to help them with their difficulties in understanding, rather than hazing, advancing toward mutual discovery of truth in that way. Why hazing?

Goffman's own work offers what might be a clue in this regard. In his 1967 book on interaction ritual, the last chapter, "Where the Action Is," stands out because of its length. This book contains many of Goffman's other important essays, such as the chapters on embarrassment and on deference and demeanor. Yet the last chapter is by far the longest, with almost as many pages (122) as all of the other chapters put together (149). Indeed, it may be the longest essay in his entire oeuvre. As far as I know, the length of this chapter has not been commented on, nor its structure much discussed.

Late in the chapter, Goffman reveals that the kind of "action" (risky behavior) he is talking about occurs primarily inside of what he calls "the cult of masculinity." I believe that this idea might help to understand some of his personal life. Goffman seems to have treated his contacts with me and with many others as "action." His persona in these encounters, maintaining "composure, poise, and control of his emotions," was not just masculine, but hypermasculine. After my discussion of the relationship of masculinity to emotions in Chapter 10, I will return to this issue at the end of this book, in the concluding chapters.

Notes

1. As in my discussion of the emotional roots of Goethe's genius in Chapter 9, Scheff 1990.

2. Ditton (1980), Drew and Wootton (1988), Riggins (1990), Manning (1992), Burns (1992), Smith (1999), Fine and Smith (2000), and Trevino (2003). The Fine and Smith publication is virtually a monument. In four volumes, it contains most of the chapters from the earlier seven books as well as a very large sampling of every other evaluation of Goffman's work. There are also several volumes in other languages devoted to Goffman.

3. Heinz (1992) also criticizes alienation studies for confounding individual and relational elements, but doesn't note the emotion/cognition confound. Nor does Gergen (1996), who has proposed giving more emphasis to the relational aspect of alienation, in line with his more general interest in bringing relational elements into individual psychology.

CHAPTER 2

The Goffman Style

Deconstructing Society and Social Science

IN MY VIEW, GOFFMAN'S WORK as a whole is so incredibly insightful that it could become an impetus for a new social science. In itself it sought to bring into focus the microworld, the domain of interaction, emotions, and relationships. In this way it could serve as a tonic, correcting for excessive emphasis on the macroworld and most of the quite abstract ideas that are used to describe it. Goffman's vision could also make a starting point for further development of interdisciplinary and interlevel social science, an approach that would unify most of the disparate and separate points of view that now rule the roost.

As indicated in the last chapter, Goffman's work has been the subject of many, often conflicting, interpretations. It seems clear from the widespread criticism that his work makes little or no contribution of theory, method, or systematic data, that is, to conventional social science as it is practiced. Assuming that this is the case, what contributions did he make? I propose that his work cleared the way for wholesale changes in social science in three different ways:

1. Goffman was an incredibly perceptive observer of the microworld of social interaction. He created a vocabulary for uncovering this world, otherwise virtually invisible in modern societies.

2. Most of Goffman's descriptions of interaction represented emotions as well as thought and action. In this respect they were three-dimensional,

arousing the reader's emotions, sympathy, and understanding. This approach remedies a great failing of current social science, which tends to be two-dimensional at best.

3. Trope-clearing: (a) The trope that he most often attacked was the Western conception of the self as an isolated, self-contained individual. He offered an alternative conception: the self as an aspect of social and cultural arrangements. (b) His attack on individualism is one example of his deconstruction of basic tropes in our society: mental illness, gender, language, and many of the conventions of current social science.

Goffman's deconstructions made his work controversial, but also gave it revolutionary potential. He followed the tradition of Whitehead, Koestler, Schutz, and Mannheim, in order to create a new social science culture. In this respect, I propose that his work might serve as a model not only for the study of his field, the interaction order, but for all of social science.

Goffman dealt with tasks more primitive, preliminary to theory, method, and evidence that clear the way for social science. Reading Goffman, as Lemert (1997, viiii) put it, "made something happen ... a shudder of recognition."

Lemert goes on to describe this quality of Goffman's work:

> The experience Goffman effects is that of colonizing a new social place into which the reader enters from which to exit never quite the same. To have once, even if only once, seen the social world from within such a place is never after to see it otherwise, ever after to read the world anew. In thus seeing differently, we are other than we were ... (xiii)

This is a strong claim: our vision of the world, and even of ourselves, is transformed by reading. But it is a claim with which I agree. My question is, how did Goffman do it? I propose that his work had three qualities that arouse readers out of their slumbers: he provided a vocabulary for describing the microworld; his portrayals of human beings usually included emotions, as well as thoughts and actions; and his method of investigation was to undercut the assumptive reality of our society, with his deconstruction of conception of the self as an isolated individual being the most prominent example.

A Vocabulary for the Microworld

The first gift, widely agreed upon by commentators, is that Goffman was an incredibly perceptive observer of the microworld of social interaction. He saw and called to our attention a world that surrounds us, but that we usually do not notice. As implied in the *New Yorker* cartoon referred to earlier, in daily life, and in most social science, the details of the microworld of interaction go unmarked and disregarded.

Goffman, however, noticed the riches of activity in the microworld, and invented a panoply of terms and phrases to describe them. Certainly the idea of impression management is one such invention. Also frequently quoted are: situational improprieties, face-work, the interaction order, cooling the mark, frames (in the special sense in which Goffman used the term), role distance, alienation from interaction, footing, and many others. These terms have come to be irreplaceable for those who want to understand mundane experience in everyday life. Since there is almost unanimous consensus on this point among his commentators, I will not elaborate on it further.

Emotions in the Microworld

There is a second feature of Goffman's work that is less obvious: unlike most social scientists, he often included emotions as well as thoughts and actions in descriptions of his actors. However, this feature is more difficult to establish than the first one. An immediate sticking point is that most of Goffman's explicit treatment of emotions concerns only one emotion, embarrassment. This emotion plays an important part in his studies, especially the earlier ones, both explicitly, and in a much larger scope, by implication. But why only one emotion? What about other primary emotions, such as love, fear, anger, grief, and so on? To the average reader, the exclusive focus on embarrassment might seem arbitrary. Schudson (1984) has devoted an entire article to Goffman's concern with embarrassment, and argued that it is, in part, misleading.

Explicitly, Goffman gave only one justification. He argued that embarrassment had universal, pancultural importance in social interaction:

> Face-to-face interaction in any culture seems to require just those capacities that flustering seems to destroy. Therefore, events which lead to embarrassment and the methods for avoiding and dispelling it may provide a cross-cultural framework of sociological analysis. (1956, 266)

Heath (1988, 137) further justifies Goffman's focus:

> Embarrassment lies at the heart of the social organization of day-to-day conduct. It provides a personal constraint on the behavior of the individual in society and a public response to actions and activities considered problematic or untoward. Embarrassment and its potential play an important part in sustaining the individual's commitment to social organization, values and convention. It permeates everyday life and our dealings with others. It informs ordinary conduct and bounds the individual's behavior in areas of social life that formal and institutionalized constraints do not reach.

Beyond these considerations, there is another, broader one that is implied in Goffman's ideas, particularly the idea of impression management. Most of his work implies that every actor is extraordinarily sensitive to the exact amount of deference being received by others. Even a slight difference between what is expected and what is received, whether it be too little or too much, can cause embarrassment and other painful emotions.

In an earlier article (Scheff 2000), I followed Goffman's lead by proposing that embarrassment and shame are primarily social emotions, because they usually arise from a threat to the bond, *no matter how slight.* In my view, the degree of social connectedness, of accurately taking the viewpoint of the other, is the key component of social bonds. A discrepancy in the amount of deference conveys judgement, and so is experienced as a threat to the bond. Since even a slight discrepancy in deference is sensed, embarrassment or the anticipation of embarrassment would be a virtually continuous presence in interaction.

In most of his writing, Goffman's Everyperson was constantly aware of her own standing in the eyes of others, implying almost continuous states of self-conscious emotions: embarrassment, shame, humiliation, and in rare instances, pride, or anticipation of these states. Their sensitivity to the eyes of others make Goffman's actors seem three-dimensional, since they embody not only thought and behavior, but also feeling ("hand, mind, and heart," in Phillips's [2001] phrase).

This is probably one of the aspects of Goffman's writings that makes them fascinating to readers, as suggested by Lofland's (1980, 47) appreciative comment:

> I suspect I am not alone in knowing people who have been deeply moved upon reading *Stigma* [1963b] and other of his works. These people recognized themselves and others and saw that Goffman was articulating some of the most fundamental and painful of human social experiences. He showed them suddenly that they were not alone, that someone else understood what they knew and felt. He knew and expressed it beautifully, producing in them joy over pain understood and appreciated, an inextricable mixture of happiness and sadness, expressed in tears.

Although Lofland doesn't name specific emotions, his reference to "the most fundamental and painful of human social experiences" might be taken to imply the emotions of embarrassment, shame, and humiliation. Goffman's inclusion of embarrassment as a key component of his writing could lead to the type of empathic identification described by Lofland, since most social science writing is unemotional.

Deconstructing the Self

Goffman's basic method was to deconstruct the assumptive reality of our society, as will be described under the heading "Deconstructing Social Reality" below. The most prominent example of this method was his attack on the social institution of the self-contained individual. This institution was also repeatedly challenged by Elias throughout his writings, but especially in his essay (1998) on "homo clausus" (the myth of the closed, self-contained individual). Sociological social psychology, insofar as it is derived from the work of George H. Mead (1934), also challenges this conception. Blumer (1986) was particularly forceful in this regard.

Goffman challenged any perspective that isolates individuals from the social matrix in which they are embedded. This challenge was not limited to psychiatry and medicine, its most obvious targets; it pervades virtually all of his writing. Although Goffman allowed some freedom to the individual through role-distance, his basic theme was that the self was more or less an image cast by social arrangements:

> The self ... is not an organic thing that has a specific location, whose fundamental fate is to be born, to mature and die; it is a dramatic effect arising diffusely from a scene that is presented ... (1959, 252–53)

> The self ... can be seen as something that resides in the arrangements prevailing in a social system for its members. The self in this sense is not a property of the persons to whom it is attributed, but dwells rather in the pattern of social control that is exerted in connection with the person by himself and those around him. This special kind of institutional arrangement does not so much support the self as constitute it. (1961a, 168)

> ... the proper study of interaction is not the individual and his psychology, but rather the syntactical relations among acts of different persons mutually present to one another ... not, then, men [sic] and their moments. Rather, moments and their men [sic]. (1967, 2, 3)[1]

Smith (1999) comes close to the view that Goffman's main target was Western individualism:

> The pursuit of a sociological decimation of conventional Western liberal notions of the individual is an analytic impulse animating much of Goffman's sociology. (10)

However, the implication that Goffman was challenging only liberal notions of the individual misses the mark. His attack ranges over the entire political, psychological, and philosophical spectrum: radical, liberal, conservative, and reactionary. Although political conservatives may occasionally sound the note of community, they are easily as adamant as liberals in their insistence on rugged individualism. Goffman was an affirmative-action deconstructionist; he didn't discriminate according to political persuasion.

Deconstructing Social Reality

There is another, broader dimension to Goffman's legacy, one at the most elemental level. I propose that the central thrust of Goffman's method was toward creating free-floating intelligence in social science. Although Goffman himself made no such claim, it seems to me that that his work sought to demonstrate, each time anew, the possibility of overthrowing cultural assumptions about the nature of reality.

Gronfein (1999, 83) reminds us, early in his review of Goffman's many articles and chapters on mental illness, that Goffman clearly indicated that he was not a sociologist of any particularly substantive area. This is an important point with reference to mental illness not only because of the large number of his essays on this topic, but also because of the extraordinary vehemence of his attack. As Manning suggests:

> … Goffman reserves his most cutting ironies and examples for the most legitimate of social institutions, medicine. Psychiatrists and psychiatry merit even more severe condemnation through incongruity. Goffman, in a series of [seven] papers … has ridiculed and indignantly criticized the assumptions and operation of conventional medicine and psychiatry. (1980, 265)

Goffman referred to psychiatrists as "tinkers" and to psychiatry as "the tinkering trade" and in many other ways, heaped ridicule on the profession. Manning (1980, 267) goes on to note the effect:

> Such harshness, when combined with the brilliant metaphoric work that accompanies it, has the intended effect of producing a sense of shocked disbelief in the reader. More significantly, it acts to corrode the authoritative hegemony of meanings wrapped around their conduct by members of powerful institutions.

This comment, in passing, proposes that Goffman's purpose was to attack powerful institutions. But first we must deal with a seeming inconsistency. Both Gronfein and Manning make the point that the institution of psychiatry and mental illness was one of Goffman's main targets. How can this point be reconciled with Goffman's assertions that he was not a sociologist of any particular area? I want to second the proposition, made by several commentators, that although mental illness was important for Goffman, it was nothing but the telling topic or case for him. I think that the idea that Goffman was not interested in any of the phenomena he studied for its own sake, but only as a topic for his particular mode of investigation, makes a first step into the Goffman enigma. But what was his mode of investigation?

Goffman's primary goal may have been the development of a reflexive social science. Most of the appreciative reviews of Goffman's work invoke the idea of reflexiveness, but only in passing. These commentators do little to explain what they mean by the term, nor its implications for current social science. Those who do explain what they mean by reflexiveness usually ignore or even dismiss Goffman. Alvin Gouldner provides an example. He proposed *reflexivity*, self-awareness, as a *sine qua non* of social science. He argued for the need

> ... to *transform* the sociologist, to penetrate deeply into his daily life and work, enriching them with new sensitivities, and so raise the sociologist's self-awareness to a new historical level. (Gouldner 1970, 34)

In a later comment, Gouldner explained that current social science was deeply mired in everyday language and understanding:

> The pursuit of hermeneutic understanding, however, cannot promise that men [sic] as we now find them, with their everyday language and understanding, will always be capable of further understanding and of liberating themselves. At decisive points the ordinary language and conventional understandings fail and must be transcended. It is essentially the task of the social sciences, more generally, to create new and "extraordinary" languages, to help men [sic] learn to speak them, and to mediate between the deficient understandings of ordinary language and the different and liberating perspectives of the extraordinary languages of social theory ... To say social theorists are concept-creators means that they are not merely in the *knowledge*-creating business, but also in the *language*-reform and language-creating business. In other words, they are from the beginning involved in creating a new *culture*. (Gouldner 1972, 16, quoted in Phillips 1988)

Was Goffman attempting a reflexive sociology, one that would create a new culture for social science?

Unfortunately, Goffman never clearly explained the overall point of his studies. His descriptions of the meaning of his work were almost comically laconic. He and others have clearly made the point that he was trying to achieve "perspective by incongruity." To find more substantial ground, one needs to look at some of his statements about actors in general. In one of his early (1961a) statements, he said:

> ... any accurately improper move can poke through the thin sleeve of immediate reality.

Although this passage is not self-referential, it could also be applied to Goffman's own basic method if we can understand what he meant by an "accurately improper move" and "the thin sleeve of immediate reality." The meaning of an improper move is easy: one that violates the assumptions of one's audience. The idea of improper moves that are accurate is harder to pin down.

To explain this idea, I draw upon Whitehead, a philosopher of science who stated:

> A clash of doctrines is not a disaster—it is an opportunity ... In formal logic, a contradiction is the signal of a defeat; but in the evolution of real knowledge it marks the first step in progress toward a victory. (Whitehead 1962, 266-67)

Goffman's method of investigation was to engineer a continuing clash between the taken-for-granted assumptions in our society and his incongruous metaphors and propositions. Most improper moves merely embarrass the actor and/or those near her. But by framing a viewpoint that exactly contradicts commonly held assumptions, Goffman was developing what Koestler (1967) called *bisociation*: seeing phenomena simultaneously from two contradictory viewpoints. Like Whitehead, Koestler thought that all creativity arose from the collision of contradictory viewpoints.

Devising a phrase or sentence that is "accurately improper" in this sense would seem to be a formidable task. One must first seek out an important, commonly held assumption, then exactly counter it with an equally plausible assumption. It would depend, like writing poetry, on deep intuition rather than logical analysis. Goffman was awash with this kind of intuition.

Goffman's idea of "alienation from interaction" similarly helps explain what he meant by an improper move. Once again, he did little to apply this idea to his own work. What he meant was that those actors who behave improperly, breaking the rules, not only become alienated from whatever transaction they are involved in, but also might catch an enlightening glimpse of the nature of that transaction, that is, a glimpse of another reality behind the conventional one. Manning (1980, 263), in passing, makes a similar point:

> His [technique] is not simply a matter of convenience or artifice. It would appear to be a deliberate choice of weapons by which to assail the fictional facades that constitute the assumptive reality of conventional society.

Goffman seems to have been trying to free himself and his readers from the culturally induced reality in which he and they were entrapped, by making "accurately improper" moves.

Manning's usage, "assumptive reality," is a necessity for understanding Goffman's approach. This phrase stands for the total perspective on what is real that is held in common in each society. As it happens, there is no generally agreed-upon term for this perspective. Durkheim's usage, "collective consciousness," comes close, but it seems to leave out the collective unconscious, and it does not give enough emphasis to the substantive content. Similarly, the term used by mystics, "the great cloud of unknowing," is evocative, but it is also partial. It leaves out the "knowing" part of assumptive realities. As Geertz (1983) points out in his description of the different cultural versions of common sense, it is a great repository both of wisdom and of error.

Pace postmodernity, one can never be completely free of cultural perspectives. There is no place to stand that does not require linguistic and cultural assumptions. Mannheim's (1951) point about free-floating intellectuals was that they were not completely free, but free relative to the attitude of everyday life, which is completely entrapped, like the great majority of the members of any society. Being able to see any phenomenon from more than one perspective is a great advantage for innovators of any kind, but it is also fairly rare.

Reflexive Social Science in Theory and in Practice

As already indicated, Gouldner (1970) issued a forceful call for a reflexive social science, one that would free social scientists from the trap of "everyday language and understanding." But it didn't occur to him that Goffman might be actually doing what Gouldner was calling for. Instead, Gouldner was repelled by what he thought of as Goffman's lack of attention to power, and his lack of a strong political stance. In a very detailed rebuttal, Rogers (1980, Ch. 4) clears Goffman of the charge of ignoring power. She shows how Goffman did indeed analyze power, and went further than Gouldner into the corollary spheres of influence and control. Like most of the rest of us at the time, Gouldner didn't understand who Goffman was, nor what he was about.

Rogers goes on to characterize Gouldner's critique of Goffman's work as inappropriate and even careless (1980, 128). In what may be another, but less direct rebuttal to Gouldner, she wrote that Goffman was interested in power, but not obsessed with it. This statement may have been Rogers's delicate way of implying that whereas Goffman was not obsessed with power, Gouldner was. Touché!

Her comment may help explain not only Gouldner's dismissal of Goffman, but also the resistance of most social scientists to his work. The reason that Goffman was not obsessed with power is that he might be seen to treat power, hierarchy, and authority as only one of two key dimensions of social organization. The other key dimension was what might be called social integration (alienation/solidarity—Scheff 1997a, Ch. 4). Goffman's analysis of power, influence, and control was integral to his examination of the extent to which actors were alienated or solidary with each other.

Classical sociology was formulated around this latter dimension: the way in which urbanization and industrialization lead to increasing alienation. Marx was the first theorist who gave more emphasis to power than to alienation. In his early writing, both dimensions were represented: balancing his attention to economic and political power were his writings on alienation. However, Marx went on from this balance point to develop and elaborate his analysis of power/authority, but left the complementary analysis of social integration behind. Modern social science has taken the same path, concentrating, for the most part, on power in politics and economies at the macrolevel, with less concern for social integration, especially at the microlevel. Rogers's reply to Gouldner has hit upon one reason that Goffman irritates his commentators.

However, the basic source of irritation, it seems to me, does not concern topic or level, but Goffman's basic method, making "improper moves so as to poke through the thin sleeve of immediate reality." All of his work, virtually every sentence, is an attack on what Gouldner referred to as ordinary language and conventional understandings. Goffman's main target of attack, moreover, is not only the language and understandings that obtain in our society as a whole. Perhaps the primary source of irritation for academics is that Goffman was also attacking their own language and assumptions. His method of investigation pointed toward a radically new social science.

Deconstructing Social Institutions

To appreciate the savage force of Goffman's method, it will be necessary to digress for a moment into the nature of social institutions. George H. Mead (1934) defined an institution as a system of beliefs and practices in which each participant incorporates not only her own attitude and role, but also the attitudes and roles of all the other participants. Mead used the example of the institution of private property. The pickpocket knows what to expect not only from the victim and the onlookers, but also from the police, judges, jailers, etc. Private property is an institution in a society in which each member knows and expects their own role and the roles of others, and the accompanying attitudes, but knows that virtually everyone else knows and expects them.

One crucial element that is not developed in Mead's account is what has come to be called the greediness of institutions. Manning (1980, 267) referred in passing to this quality with his comment that Goffman attacked hegemonic institutions. The attitudes and expectations that make up an institution are held in common with fervor; any violation is apt to be experienced as a shockingly personal attack because it shatters participants' sense of possibility, decency, and reality. The God of all major institutions, not only religious ones, is a jealous God: "Thou shalt have no other gods before me."

Although there may be individuals and even segments in a society that do not participate in a basic institution, the overwhelming majority does. Because of the vehemence with which the majority upholds an institution, and the large size of the majority, the institution's demands are experienced by most persons as imperative. In Durkheim's phrase, they are felt to be external and constraining. But Durkheim's phrase doesn't quite do justice to the greediness of institutions, since it leaves out the fervor of attachment to them. Durkheim's language, external and constraining, is too gentle to catch the violent passion behind our attachments to institutions.

The dominant reality in any society is socially constructed, to use postmodern language. But this formulation has become a cliché because it is usually stated only abstractly. Considering the dominant reality as a system of interlocking social institutions may help flesh out the abstract idea.

Geertz's (1983) "common sense" can be taken as an illustration of a particular dominant institution. He makes the point that what is considered common sense in any particular society is culturally constructed, giving many examples showing how the common sense of one society contradicts that of another (Scheff 1990, 137–42).

A crucial point implied by Geertz's consideration of common sense is that it is always anti-reflexive no matter what culture it occurs in:

> Common sense represents matters ... as being what they are by the simple nature of the case. An air of "of-courseness," a sense of "it figures" is cast over things ...They are depicted as being inherent in the situation, intrinsic aspects of the situation, the way things go. (1983, 139)

The idea that common sense is anti-reflexive is a crucial point for understanding not only this particular instance, but also all other social institutions. What gives institutions their enormous power is that they are seen as self-evident, and therefore not available for inspection or questioning. If one does not even have that option, conformity is more or less automatic.

Geertz's comments on common sense can be applied intact to any dominant social institution. The attitude of the simpleness of reality that he says is characteristic of cultural systems of common sense applies equally well to all hegemonic institutions:

> The world is what the wide-awake, uncomplicated person takes it to be ... the really important facts of life lie scattered openly along its surface ... (1983, 139)

To give an example, it is my experience that the attitude of simpleness described by Geertz obtains for the large majority of persons in Western societies toward psychotherapy. Their attitude is not necessarily contemptuous, although it often is. But it is dismissive. A relative of mine, a very intelligent person, recently told me that what goes on in psychotherapy is mostly navel-gazing. Except for a fairly small, psychologically minded, middle-class group in the United States, this attitude is nearly universal in modern societies. It is a spin-off from the more formidable institution in Western societies, the myth of the self-contained individual.

If, as I have suggested, everyday reality is made up of a system of interlocking institutions, than a reflexive social science would challenge all of them. As Schutz (1962) pointed out, the smooth functioning of the status quo of a society requires in its members a virtually identical set of presuppositions, "the attitude of daily life." This attitude is accepted totally and without question. Those that accept it are seen as normal, sane, regular persons. They are thought of as "fitting in," as "our sort." They are *gleigeschalten* (meshing smoothly like the gears of a perfectly engineered machine). Not only do their thoughts, actions, and feelings mesh with those of others, but the enmeshment is perfectly aligned: there is no friction.

But Goffman's writing shatters the calm surface of everyday life, it notices and comments upon what is to be taken for granted by members in good standing. It therefore challenges the sanctity of daily life by implying that it, like other any other social institution, is constructed. Goffman's writing is not radical in a political sense; it is more elemental than that. What it points toward is not only a political/economic revolution, but a revolution in culture.

It was Goffman's challenge to all dominant institutions that confused Gouldner and other reviewers who criticized Goffman's politics, or lack of politics. His method of investigation was more fundamental than the politics of left and right, which is highly conventional compared to Goffman's incursions.

Before Science

The grip that established institutions have even on science has been nicely caught by the philosopher Quine (1979):

> The neatly worked inner stretches of science are an open space in the tropical jungle, created by clearing tropes [*metaphors*] away. (1979, 160, quoted in Manning 1992, 147)

That is to say, it often happens that *before* scientific procedures are applicable, an obstructive metaphor has to be overthrown. Manning applies Quine's dictum to Goffman's metaphors (drama, games, ritual, etc.), suggesting that in the course of his career, Goffman made progress toward clearing away or at least qualifying his own metaphors. But Manning doesn't give full weight to what to me is the more significant point, the importance of Goffman's metaphors in clearing a way for social science itself.

The history of the physical sciences is full of examples of the clearing away of obstructive tropes. Progress in the astronomy of planetary motion was delayed for over a century because of the trope that the earth was the center of the universe. This idea is a correlate of a social institution that might be called universal ethnocentrism: we human beings are the center and purpose of the cosmos. Astronomers, like everyone else, took for granted that the planets circled around the earth. In the sixteenth century, Tycho Brahe had made a very accurate charting of the transit of Venus. But he could not plot the shape of the orbit because he assumed Venus was orbiting around the earth. Johannes Kepler, who obtained the data after Brahe's death, was equally puzzled for many years.

The idea of a logocentric universe was so ingrained that Kepler hit upon the solution only inadvertently. In an attempt to get past whatever it was that was obscuring the solution, he devised a geometric model of the planetary orbits based on solid figures representing polyhedrons. The model was ridiculous except for one feature; Kepler had inadvertently placed the sun, rather than the earth, at the center.

Similarly, Einstein began work on the theory of relativity with a joke concerning persons passing each other on trains, trying to determine their speed relative to each other. He realized intuitively that this situation challenged the ruling trope that time and motion were absolute. Although he had a doctorate in physics, Einstein knew little mathematics. He had to get help to put his anti-trope into mathematical form.

Quine's formulation captures the primitive, intuitive element necessary for scientific advance. Goffman's work seems to have made the deconstruction of ruling tropes its main goal. This goal would explain why he seemed to start afresh with each work. He was not trying to establish a theory, method, or evidence. "Look," he might have said, "it's easy to construct an alternative universe. It's so easy I can start anew with each book, ignoring even my own earlier work."

Freud and Goffman's Challenge to Institutions

Freud's work can be used to provide an example of another writer who seemed to have an instinct for challenging dominant institutions. Like Goffman, his principal attack was on the myth of the rational individual. His attack concerned a different component than Goffman's, the idea of rational self-control. Freud sought to show that most human behavior is compulsive, determined not by rational self-control, but by one's past.

Freud's early studies challenged another dominant institution of his era, male superiority. When he reported a case of male hysteria to his local medical society, he was surprised by the vehemence and disgust of the response. A much wider shock was caused by his study that suggested that neurosis was caused by child molestation, usually in the form of father/daughter incest. Freud quickly recanted from this thesis, perhaps because of the hostility of his colleagues. The institution of male superiority was so powerful that Freud's challenge led his colleagues to threaten expulsion.

Toward the end of his life, Freud took on the institution of organized religion, which in his time was still one of the dominant institutions. In *The Future of an Illusion* (1927), he had the temerity to argue that religion acted as a mechanism of defense, warding off not only pain and suffering, but also reality.

Like Goffman, Freud's main substantive challenge was to the core social institution of Western societies, the belief in the individual. The basic premise of Freud's work was that unconscious thoughts, motives, and feelings formed the core of the self—a premise from which he never recanted. The idea of the unconscious has not only not been accepted in Western societies, it is usually not even seriously considered. The average layperson, and perhaps even the average academic, simply dismisses this idea out of hand, as in one of Geertz's examples of the attitude of common sense. Certainly the premise of rational choice is far more prevalent in current social science, and is accepted with little critical evaluation. The idea that psychotherapy involves little more than navel-gazing, mentioned earlier, is one of many corollaries of the institution of individualism.

Unlike Goffman, Freud was emotionally committed to the substantive areas he investigated, since they were closely connected to his work as a practitioner. Goffman, on the other hand, was free to enter and leave substantive areas at will. Perhaps that is one reason he was better able than Freud to maintain a reflexive stance with respect to his own work.

Goffman's primary interest was not in deconstructing the institution of the self-contained individual. Rather his focus was always on deconstructing all taken-for-granted conventions in social science, of "unmasking vested orthodoxies wherever they were encountered" (Travers 1997). A clear example is Goffman's attack on the social institution of gender (1979). Long before it was stylish for men to do so, he discovered the subordination of women implied in ads about women. West (1996) has shown how correct, by current feminist standards, his analysis was. But he wasn't a feminist, just a hell-raising social scientist. His legacy is one of intellectual revolution, undermining the status quo, that is, the dominant social institutions in Western societies.

Was Goffman a Free-floating Intellectual?

I think it was Goffman's challenge to the assumptive grounds, the overall foot-ing, of social science that was most irritating to those who have commented on his work, even the most appreciative of them. In one of the broadest of reviews, Collins appreciates and criticizes simultaneously:

> Goffman seems hyper-reflexive; he himself manifests an extreme form of role-distance, separating himself from any clear, straightforward posi-tion, be it theoretical or popular. In this sense, he appears as the epitome of the 1950s intellectual; hip to the point of unwillingness to take any strong stance, even the stance of his own hipness. (1980, 206)

On the one hand, Collins has alluded to what I take to be the central feature of all of Goffman's writing; it is "hyper-reflexive." On the other hand, to accuse him of a pose (hipness) seems not only misguided, but also suggests irritation.

Lemert, perhaps the most appreciative of all of the commentators, suggested that as with his contemporaries—Riesman, Mills, Whyte, etc.—a critique of contemporary society could be found in Goffman:

> ... contrary to the impression that he lacked a social consciousness, he actually worked out his own, admittedly perverse and muted, social cri-tique of American society in the 1950s. (Lemert 1997, xxiv)

As in the Collins passage, there is a slap mixed in with the praise, in "perverse and muted." The idea that Goffman's social critique was "muted" is like Collins's complaint that Goffman "separat[ed] himself from any clear, straightforward position." As already indicated, I think that there is some justice to the charge that Goffman's position is muted or not clear, because he didn't adequately explain his intent. But another reason might have to do more with us readers than with Goffman: that his work is so advanced that we haven't yet understood it.

The surprising part of the Lemert passage is the choice of the word *perverse*. It seems to me that a more appropriate word would have been *subversive*. As suggested, Goffman's work pulls the rug from under everyone, including his most insightful and appreciative commentators. The implication I draw is that none of us, not even his fans, is yet as free of the assumptive world as Goffman. We haven't caught up with him yet.

Does that mean that I think that Goffman was indeed a free-floating intellectual in all areas? By no means. I think he went further than anyone in social science, but he himself had at least one area in which he was as entrapped as anyone else. Giddens (1988) has pointed out that Goffman's interaction order, his arena of supreme competence, can be seen as a link between two other crucial arenas: the psychology of the individual, and macrosystems of the larger society—political, economic, linguistic, and so on. Giddens went on to say that Goffman did little in exploring such links, largely because he ignored both macrosystems and individual psychology.

I think that Goffman wasn't prejudiced against studying macrosystems. In his early work, he was too busy charting the interaction order. But even in that early work, some of his ideas pointed toward larger systems, e.g., the concept of the total institution. Later he was clearly moving toward such systems, the institutions of gender and of language (Goffman 1979; 1981). One of the concepts from his later work, "footing" (the presuppositions held in common by persons engaged in dialogue), can be extended from the microworld setting he intended to the macroworld. In this world, the footing becomes the set of presuppositions held in common by all persons in dialogue in a given society. Goffman's use of the term *footing* seems to be an application of Schutz's idea of the attitude of everyday life applicable not only to specific interactions, but to the assumptive worlds of entire societies.

I think that Goffman was prejudiced toward individual psychology, entrapped in a way that is conventional in most of our society. One early indication is his omission of the experiential side of embarrassment in the article in which he sought to provide an explicit definition of that emotion. He also seemed overly ready to criticize psychology as a discipline as in this comment (1983, 2):

> ... we (sociologists) haven't managed to produce in our students the high level of trained incompetence that psychologists have achieved in theirs, although, God knows, we're working on it. (quoted in Lemert 1997, xvii)

In my own contact with him, he often expressed reservations about my interest in connecting individual and social psychology with societal process. It was not the societal part he objected to; he never complained about my interest in large-scale process. It was only the psychology part.

I dwell on Goffman's prejudice against individual psychology because I think it illustrates an important general point. An intellectual can be free-floating in some arenas, as Goffman was with respect to the interaction order, but entrapped in others. Mannheim (1936) had distinguished between two kinds of rigid assumptive worlds, *ideology* and *utopia*. He used the word *ideology* in a much broader sense than it is ordinarily used: he meant the entire assumptive world that underlies the status quo in a given society.

In Mannheim's sense, a utopia was a reaction against the prevailing ideology, a counterculture. Initially it may liberate creative forces in the rebels, when they are still capable of seeing the world both in the old and in the new way. But over time, as the utopians lose touch with the old ide-ology, the utopia degenerates into an institution as restrictive as the status quo that was rejected. The utopians reject the holders of ideology as much as those holders reject them. Psychoanalytic theory, offering a binocular vi-sion (Koestler 1967) in its early days, now has its own cultural status quo. On a grander scale, Western individualism stands as a rigid utopia toward the rigid social enmeshment of traditional and Asian societies. Goffman rebelled against most of the dominant institutions, but not against the bias in social science and society against the psychology of individuals.

Conclusion

Is there any remedy for social science? Mainstream social science, for the most part, continues to ignore the basic implications of Goffman's substan-tive work. One example would be the methodological individualism upon which most social science research is based. Sample surveys, for the most part, still use individuals as their basic sources. Those parts of self that Goffman suggested are reflections of social arrangements are automatically ignored. Most psychological scales have the same limitation. Even that research which seeks only to explore the psychology of individuals seems unaware of Goffman's approach to interaction, particularly on the large and subtle effects of the subject's relationship with the interviewer or test administrator, and the larger social context in which the data is gathered.

Since there don't seem to be any new Goffmans on the horizon, perhaps we all need to practice his art of deconstructing taken-for-granted assumptions in social science, not just the Western fascination with the individual. To be as effective as Goffman, we all need to be marginal persons, like him. Any exposure to new perspectives can open the door: partaking of a culture new to us, as in participant observation, and not just in foreign countries; learning a new language; reading fiction that serves as entrance to new and different worlds. Living in a new town or country, or undertaking psychotherapy, can also serve as gateways to bisociation, having binocular vision.

In terms of substantive issues, I think that linking the macroworld, interaction order, and individual psychology is the most pressing need in social science, as Giddens (1988) suggested. An example is provided by the extraordinary book *Freudian Repression: Conversation Creating the Unconscious* (1999) by Billig. He arranges a collision between dis-course analysis and psychoanalytic theory by using dialogue from Freud's cases and from his life. As a result, Billig is able to modify the theory in a way that grounds it in actual instances. The way he gets to institutional anti-Semitism in the Vienna of Freud's time from the dialogue between Freud and his patient known as Dora is nothing less than inspired.

In my own work I made a halting step toward connecting the three arenas in my analysis of emotions in the origins of the two World Wars (Scheff 1994). It is little more than a sketch, but I show how various texts suggest that in the period 1871–1914 France and Germany were entangled in a collective spiral of shame/rage, and how Hitler's appeal to the German people was based on shame/rage. If anyone knows of other attempts, I would like to hear about them.

In the meantime, since Goffman went further in freeing himself from the restrictions of our assumptive reality, perhaps we should hew to the lines that he was establishing. Several of Goffman's reviewers have suggested directions that could systematize his work as a tool for further research (see Williams, particularly, on Goffman's methods: Ch. 4 in Drew and Wooton [1988]; and Manning [1992] on combining Goffman's ideas to construct a viable theory). Until we have a new Goffman, perhaps we still have to make the most of the old one.

I propose that Goffman's method of the development of concepts based on making "accurately improper moves" should be applied not only to his own field, the interaction order, but to the two other fields to which it is linked: the study of individual psychology and of social institutions. That is to say that Goffman's approach could be the model for the development of a new social science.

Note

1. This last passage, because of its inclusion of the idea that the social scene involves persons mutually *present* for one another, invokes the kind of social sharing of consciousness central to Goffman's focus on embarrassment, described above. The idea of selves arising out of the social sharing of consciousness has been presaged by literary masters, such as Henry James and Virginia Woolf: "... [James and Woolf's] basic assumption [was] that the individual's identity is gained only through participation in a complex field of other individuals' consciousnesses ... " (Oates 1974, 33).

CHAPTER 3

Looking-Glass Self

Goffman as Symbolic Interactionist

GOFFMAN'S MOST BASIC WORK can be seen as closely related to "the look-ing-glass self" (LGS). This idea is of great interest because it connects two vast realms, the social nature of the self, on the one hand, and the intense emotional life that results, on the other. Charles Cooley, who invented the phrase, proposed first that the self is social, that we "live in the minds of others without knowing it." He went on to say that living in the minds of others, imaginatively, gives rise to real and intensely powerful emotions, pride and shame (Cooley 1922).

The importance of Cooley's idea is not immediately apparent in Goffman's writing. As already indicated, although seemingly clear on the surface, there are many twists and turns. Read with care, the structure of his most popular work, *Presentation of Self in Everyday Life,* reveals what seems to be two different authors. The first half of the book deals with performances and dramaturgical staging, rituals of theatre (Goff-man the Structuralist). Behavior is scripted by the social situation, mo-tives are not important. The first act lulls the sociological reader into the Durkheimian fantasy.

However, beginning with Chapter 4 on discrepant roles, the thesis begins to drift toward the motives of the actors. By the sixth and most substantial chapter on "impression management," the other Goffman has virtually disappeared. This chapter instead concerns actors' motives, their harried attempts to stave off, or at least manage, embarrassment and related emotions. Without a word of warning, Goffman the Sociological Social Psychologist has reared his head, shape-shifting. The reader has been conned.

The idea of impression management underlies many of the examples that enliven Goffman's work, and makes it understandable and entertaining. One manages one's image in the eyes of others in order to come to terms with the basic social emotions, pride and shame. This idea is stated in Cooley's (1922) evocation of the looking-glass self:

> A self-idea of this sort seems to have three principal elements: the imagination of our appearance to the other person; the imagination of his [sic] judgment of that appearance, and some sort of self-feeling, such as pride or mortification. (184)

Compared to Goffman, Cooley was relatively direct in naming pride and shame (considering mortification to be a shame variant). For him these two emotions both arose from self-monitoring, the process that was at the center of his social psychology. To be sure, in his discussion of what he called the "self-sentiments," pride and shame are mentioned only as two of other possible emotions.

But in his definition of the looking-glass self, he referred exclusively to pride and shame. And to make sure we understand this point, he mentions shame three more times in the passage that follows (184–85, emphasis added):

> The comparison with a looking-glass hardly suggests the second element, the imagined judgment, which is quite essential. The thing that moves us to *pride* or *shame* is not the mere mechanical reflection of ourselves, but an imputed sentiment, the imagined effect of this reflection upon another's mind. This is evident from the fact that the character and weight of that other, in whose mind we see ourselves, makes all the difference with our feeling. We are *ashamed* to seem evasive in the presence of a straightforward man, cowardly in the presence of a brave one, gross in the eyes of a refined one and so on. We always imagine, and in imagining share, the judgments of the other mind. A man will boast to one person of an action—say some sharp transaction in trade—which he would be *ashamed* to own to another.

Although Cooley is explicit in suggesting that pride and shame are social emotions, he makes no attempt to define either emotion. Instead he uses the vernacular words as if they are self-explanatory.

But the meanings of vernacular words for emotions are usually quite ambiguous. For example, in current usage in English, the word *pride* used without qualification usually has an inflection of arrogance or hubris

("Pride goeth before a fall"). In order to refer to the kind of pride implied in Cooley's analysis, the opposite of shame, one must add a qualifier like *justified* or *genuine*. And usage of the word *shame,* especially in English, is even more confusing, as will be indicated below. Using undefined emotion words is an invitation to the Tower of Babel.

However ambiguous, Cooley's analysis of self-monitoring clearly suggests that pride and shame are the basic social emotions. Goffman was the first social scientist to follow up on Cooley's idea, fleshing it out with a large number of refreshingly varied examples of everyday behavior.

Goffman's Version of the Looking Glass

In Goffman's basic work, *Presentation of Self in Everyday Life,* the looking-glass self is not mentioned explicitly. There are three references to Cooley, but none concern the looking glass. Yet Cooley's idea can be seen to form the basic structure of all of Goffman's earlier writings, especially *Presentation of Self,* some of the chapters of *Interaction Ritual,* and several other books that were published before *Frame Analysis* (1974). The latter book is entirely cognitive, and so marks a departure from Goffman's concern with emotions.

Like Cooley, Goffman's elaboration on the theme of the looking glass is ambiguous but in an entirely different way. Cooley's prose is simple and unassuming, only slightly removed from ordinary language. But Goffman's, besides being dazzlingly brilliant, is also incredibly involuted and complex. It is dense with meaning, innuendo, impromptu classifications, qualifications, and expansion. It is also humorous, ironic, and witty in ways that both entertain and irritate, reveal and conceal.

Emotions and shared awareness are basic components in much of Goffman's thought for most of his career. Unlike most social scientists, Goffman explored emotions as well as thoughts and actions. However, there is an immediate sticking point: most of Goffman's treatment of feeling concerns embarrassment, and less prominently, its two cousins, shame and humiliation. These emotions play an important part in many of his early studies, both explicitly, and in larger scope, by implication. Why only these three emotions? What about other primary emotions, such as love, fear, anger, grief, and so on?

To the average reader, the exclusive focus on shame/embarrassment seems arbitrary. An exception is the great English comic writer Allan Bennett, who appears to take Goffman's emphasis in stride. He sums it up: "We must love one another or die—of embarrassment"(2001, 353). This short sentence packs a lot of information: what Goffman has left out (love) and what he has included (embarrassment). It also wittily alludes to a 1960s song by Crosby, Stills, Nash, and Young: "We Must Love One Another or Die." But Schudson's reaction (1984) is more typical. He devoted an entire article to questioning what he sees as Goffman's exclusive concern with embarrassment.

As indicated in the last chapter, Goffman offered only a single and somewhat unclear justification. He argued that embarrassment had universal, pancultural importance in social interaction, but he didn't bother to explain why. His examples, however, suggest that every actor is extraordinarily sensitive to the amount of *deference* being received by others. No matter how slight the difference between what is expected and what is received, embarrassment and other painful emotions may result. We are social creatures to the core.

Durkheim, the French sociologist who was the founder of modern sociology, provided only hints along these lines. His theory depended on the idea of a *social emotion* that held societies together, but the word he used for it, *respect*, is not an emotion. He also pointed to what he called "collective consciousness" as a necessary prerequisite for a society, but went no further than describing it abstractly. Before reviewing Goffman's treatment of shared awareness, it is first necessary to further explore his treatment of emotions.

The Emotion Lexicon in *Presentation of Self*

This section explores the density of emotion words in *Presentation of Self in Everyday Life* (PSEL). As noted above, several readers of PSEL concluded that Goffman dealt extensively with embarrassment, but only this emotion. Some, like Bennett and Heath, didn't mind, but most others, like Schudson, did. In this section I want to further clarify the extent and nature of Goffman's treatment of embarrassment and related emotions, since his usage in this respect is central to my thesis. For this purpose, I will focus, for the most part, on PSEL since I consider it to be his most fundamental statement, at least for the major part of his career.

First, as already indicated, in this book he not only dealt extensively with embarrassment, but also with its two relatives, shame and humiliation. To get an idea of the attention he gave to these and other emotions, I made a count of the various emotion words it contains. With 36 occurrences, *embarrassment* is far and away the most frequent. But the word *shame* and its derivatives, such as *shamed* and *ashamed,* are also frequent, with 22 occurrences. The other member of this family, *humiliation,* occurs 5 times.

Even the least frequent of these three words, humiliation, occurs more frequently in the text than any other emotion word. Fear, with 4 occurrences, is next, followed by love, with three. The words naming the other major emotions such as pride (3), anger/rage (2), and grief (1) are still less frequent.

Indirect References to Shame/Embarrassment

Although the word count of the shame triad in PSEL is helpful, it fails to capture the extent of Goffman's treatment of embarrassment and its close relatives. First, Goffman used many words that convey shame or embarrassment without naming them explicitly. Many of his quotes are of this nature. For example, "his pride is deeply wounded" (50) conveys shame indirectly.[1] Another instance occurs in his discussion of the difficulty faced by the person in the role of the go-between:

> When a go-between operates in the actual presence of the two teams of which he is a member, we obtain a wonderful display, not unlike a man desperately trying to play tennis with himself ... As an individual, the go-between's activity is bizarre, untenable, and *undignified,* vacillating as it does from one set of appearances and loyalties to another. (149, emphasis added)

The idea that the activity of a go-between caught between conflicting audiences is "bizarre, untenable, and undignified" is an indirect referral to embarrassment, especially the use of the word *undignified.* The idea of dignity and its lack, almost always a cognate or pride and shame, occurs very frequently in PSEL. Goffman's references to dignity or its derivatives (17 times) always imply pride or, much more frequently, shame.

Another obvious instance occurs in a by now well-known quote from Simmel that Goffman has included:

> An ideal sphere lies around every human being. Although differing in size in various directions and differing according to the person with whom one entertains relations, this sphere cannot be penetrated, unless the personality value of the individual is thereby destroyed. A sphere of this sort is placed around man by his "honor." Language very poignantly designates an insult to one's honor as "coming too close": the radius of this sphere marks, as it were, the distance whose trespassing by another person insults one's honor. (69)

The idea of honor, especially insulting it or having it destroyed, might as well be expressed in pride and shame language.

Many passages indicate *embarrassment* or *shame* without using either word explicitly. Here is a virtuoso instance that involves two direct and two indirect referrals:

> Knowing that his audiences are capable of forming bad impressions of him, the individual may come to feel *ashamed* [1] of a well-intentioned honest act merely because the context of its performance provides false

impressions that are bad. Feeling this unwarranted *shame* [2], he may feel that his feelings can be seen; feeling that he is thus seen, *he may feel that his appearance confirms these false conclusions* concerning him [3]. He may then add to the precariousness of his position by engaging in just those defensive maneuvers that he would employ were he really guilty. In this way it is possible for all of us to become fleetingly for ourselves *the worst person we can imagine that others might imagine us to be* [4]. (236, emphasis added)

Following the logic of the looking-glass self, the clause "he may feel that his appearance confirms these false conclusions concerning him" implies at least the possibility of shame or embarrassment. The final sentence in this passage goes much further: "In this way it is possible for all of us to become fleetingly for ourselves the worst person we can imagine that others might imagine us to be."

This last haunting line implies a shame state, brief though it may be, that is extremely intense. More than any other passage by Goffman, perhaps, this one takes us on a jolting roller-coaster ride through all three steps of the looking-glass self: the imagination of the other's view of self, the imagined judgment of the other of self, and, with powerful impact, the actual, not imagined, feeling about self that is the result. For Goffman's actors, social interaction, if not a vale of embarrassment, is a slippery slope because of the constant anticipation of the possibility of embarrassment or even more painful variants.

In addition to finding many instances in which embarrassment or shame are implied but not stated directly, another unexpected result of my count of emotion words in PSEL is the large number of direct references to shame and humiliation. Together the count of these two words (27) is almost as great as that for the word *embarrassment* (36). The ratio between these three words brings up a new issue.

The Taboo on Shame in Modern Societies

The response of readers like Schudson, Heath, and Bennett has led us to expect that Goffman's focus was overwhelmingly only on a single emotion, embarrassment. Indeed, Goffman himself contributed to this expectation, since his one essay on emotion concerned embarrassment (1956). In this article, and in the later reprinting of it in 1967, Goffman provides no link to shame or humiliation. Indeed, he makes no reference to either emotion. The word *ashamed* occurs once, in a quote from another author. Furthermore, his study of stigma (1963b), whose central topic might be seen as shame, uses that word only twice, and only in passing.

How are we to understand the single-minded focus on embarrassment by Goffman in all but one of his works, and by readers even of that work? Attempting to answer this question requires reference to cultural influences on emotion discourse in Western society. As indicated in the Preface, I propose that there is a *taboo* on shame in modern industrial societies (Scheff 2003a). One indication is that studies of shame by Cooley, Freud, Elias, Lynd, Lewis, and Tomkins, like Goffman's, have been largely ignored. The taboo on shame in English still holds: current usage, for the most part, assigns a singular meaning that is intense and narrow. This meaning offends, on the one hand, and, on the other, misses the everyday function of shame.

The aspect of the taboo that is most relevant to the argument here is that unlike traditional societies, Western culture makes a firm distinction between shame, humiliation, and with great force, embarrassment. When I ask students if shame and embarrassment are close relatives or distinct emotions, there is virtual unanimity of opinion: distinct emotions. If I perchance suggest that embarrassment might be a mild version of shame, their eyes glaze over.

Usage in traditional societies makes no such distinction. In Spanish, for example, the word *verguenza* means both shame and embarrassment. Languages of traditional societies, such as Arabic, are the same. In Western culture, embarrassment, usually a less intense form of shame, is less taboo. Embarrassment is speakable, shame is unspeakable, in ordinary conversation.

In the twentieth century, an increasing taboo on the shame word has been especially clear in English (Scheff 2003a). There has also been, as noted above, an ambiguity in using the word for pride: is it a positive or a negative emotion? Surprisingly, a change in this respect seems to be taking place in the German language. Since the end of World War II, German speakers have been moving away from the tradition in European languages of having words for a positive shame (*scham*) and a negative, disgrace shame (*schande*). *Schande* is now seen as old-fashioned, and is seldom used. Like English, German now has a single word for shame (*scham*), and this word seems to be taking on at least some of the negative valence formerly reserved for *schande*.

Similarly, in German, the negative kind of pride (*hochmut*) is now also seen as old fashioned, and seldom used. The formerly positive word for pride (*stoltz*) is now taking on some of the negative valence of *hochmut*. In this sense, the pride/shame lexicon in German is being Anglicized.

As far as I can tell, however, the other European languages are not following suit. In French, for example, there continues to be a highly negative shame (*honte*) and an everyday shame (*pudeur*). Similarly, in French, there continues to be a highly negative form of pride (*orgueil*), and a less negative form (*fierté*).[2] It might be said that the pride/shame lexicon in English and German is becoming more taboo, but in the other European languages, such as French, Spanish, and Italian, it is not.

The idea of a taboo in Anglophone culture might explain why the readers of PSEL in English responded as if it dealt only with embarrassment, and also why Goffman himself emphasized embarrassment rather than shame and humiliation in his later work. My hypothesis is that like other scholars of shame, noticing that readers ignored it, he came to ignore it himself. With one exception, the other shame scholars mentioned above followed the same trajectory, especially Freud, Elias, Lynd, and Tomkins.

The exception was the psychologist/psychoanalyst Helen Lewis. Her principal empirical study, an analysis of shame and guilt in psychotherapy transcripts (1971), was published early in her career, and she continued shame studies for the rest of her life. She told me (correspondence, 1991), however, she had noted that although many people praised her book, no one seemed to have read it. If my argument is correct, she might have had many more readers if she had used the phrase "Embarrassment and Guilt" rather than "Shame and Guilt" in the title. In any case, like Lewis and the other scholars of shame named above, Goffman appeared to consider shame and its close relatives like embarrassment the *master emotion* of everyday life.

Mindreading (Intersubjectivity/Attunement)

The Cooley/Goffman emphasis on the shame triad is a great deviation from the very foundations of Western thought. Western culture has at its center the embedded idea of the isolated, self-contained individual. Since the shame triad implies that our self-feelings are dependent on other people, it violates the principle of Western culture. For this reason, discussions of shame and its relatives are usually avoided, both in lay and social science discourse.

The second component of the Cooley conjecture, shared awareness, also involves violation of the canon of individualism. Intersubjectivity, living in the minds of others, implies that individuals, as well as being separate units, may be joined together as components of larger units, such as pairs, threesomes, and still larger groups. Although the idea of shared consciousness is a staple in Eastern cultures, it is unacceptable in Western thought. The Cooley/Goffman conjecture, linking a taboo emotion, shame, and a taboo idea of unity, is infinitely unacceptable in the West.

The focus on embarrassment/shame as a response to the views that others have of the self forces us to entertain the second component of the Cooley/Goffman analysis, intersubjectivity. They suggest that we spend much of our life living in the minds of others. In this respect, the conjecture follows in the footsteps of Mead (1934) and Blumer (1986). What might be called "mutual mindreading" was central to their perspectives.

Mead's description of taking the role of the other initially gives the impression that he is referring to role *behavior.* Indeed, he sometimes uses the phrase in that way: in order to coordinate one's actions with another, say in dancing a tango, one needs to learn not only one's own role, but also the role enactment of one's partner.

But in reading further, it becomes clear that Mead is referring not only to behavior, but also, more frequently, to the perspective and thoughts of others as well. The concept of "taking the role of the generalized other" clearly means that one takes on the perspective of an imagined person or group of persons, even a fictitious group. Similarly, his definition of a social institution involves each participant knowing not only her own perspective, attitudes, and actions, but also those of the other participants. Mead's theory of role-taking clearly involves the concept of intersubjectivity, the sharing of subjective states by two or more individuals.

Is Intersubjectivity Invisible?

Cooley's idea of social life was also built around intersubjectivity. But he carried the implications of the idea an important step further than Mead, Dewey, or any of their followers. Cooley argued that intersubjectivity is taken completely for granted to the point of invisibility:

> As is the case with other feelings, we do not think much of it [that is, of social self-feeling] so long as it is moderately and regularly gratified. Many people of balanced mind and congenial activity scarcely know that they care what others think of them, and will deny, perhaps with indignation, that such care is an important factor in what they are and do. But this is illusion. If failure or disgrace arrives, if one suddenly finds that the faces of men [sic] show coldness or contempt instead of the kindliness and deference that he is used to, he will perceive from the shock, the fear, the sense of being outcast and helpless, that he was living in the minds of others without knowing it, just as we daily walk the solid ground without thinking how it bears us up. (Cooley 1922, 208)

The idea that we are "living in the minds of others *without knowing it*" is profoundly significant. Intersubjectivity is built into human nature, yet Western culture makes it invisible. As small children we learn to go back and forth between our own point of view and that of the other(s). By the age of five or six, children have become so adept that they forget they are doing it. Using a variation of Cooley's words, it's like "the ground that bears us up when we walk," it is taken for granted. The intersubjective bond to others becomes invisible, at least in Western societies.

Although human communication is built upon intersubjective accord, it is learned so early it goes unmarked in most discourse. Occasionally it will be referred to, but only casually and in passing. For example, one might say to a friend,"We both know that.... " The idea occurs much more elaborately in the popular song (from the 1930s?) whose lyrics were something like:

> I know that you know that I know that you know ... [that we're in love?]
> (Note: I recall this song from my childhood, but so far have been unable to locate it.)

The reference in the song to the cascading levels of reciprocating min-dreading is mostly comical. Goffman's *Strategic Interaction* (1969) took this issue seriously. When persons accurately assess each other at all the levels of cascade, they arrive at a sharing of experience so deep that one can well say that they become as one, if only momentarily.

But as Cooley noted, we usually ignore this fact. An example of scholars taking mindreading in humans for granted occurs in a treatise by O'Connell (1998). The author reviews a large body of experiments that show that small children, animals such as primates, and autistic persons are very poor at reading the minds of others. But neither O'Connell nor any of the studies she reviews acknowledge one implication of the findings: children, primates, and the autistic are poor at mindreading, but *normal human adults are good at it.* No studies are reported which test the accuracy of normal adult intersubjectivity. Even studies of mindreading seem to take for granted Cooley's idea that human adults spend much of their life living in the minds of others.

A flagrant instance involves one of the central doctrines in post-modern theory, Derrida's proposition that the meaning of all texts is fundamentally undecideable. At the most atomic level, this proposition is true, since all commonly used words, in all languages, have more than one meaning. Multiple meanings lead to inescapable ambiguity in the meaning of individual words, whether spoken or written.

But the leap to the idea of universal undecideability is erroneous. The meaning of individual words is undecideable only if the *context* is shorn away. Consensual meanings are arrived at by referring to the context in which words occur, both the local context and the extended context. To be sure, interpretation in context is a complex process, fraught with the risk of error. For this reason, there is considerable misunderstanding in communication, even when messages or texts are skillfully constructed.

But, by the same token, there is also considerable consensual under-standing about the meaning of messages and texts, even complex ones. Otherwise the social order would immediately collapse. The idea of unde-cideability seems to be based on a mechanical model of the communication of meaning, as if it were determined by rote responses to individual words. In particular, undecideabilty ignores the possibility that communication involves at its very core the process of taking the role of the other, of understanding the meaning of messages or texts not only from the receiver's point of view, but also from the sender's (compare Donald Davidson, "The Very Idea of Conceptual Schemas," in Davidson 2001).

Another example is what is called the Problem of Other Minds in the discipline of philosophy. Like much of postmodern theory, it is built entirely upon abstract reasoning rather than on systematic observation. Given this approach, it is not surprising that the contributors to this field have decided that no one can ever really know the mind of another person. This belief reflects the Western insistence on individualism, that each of us is essentially alone. But it seems bizarre in Eastern cultures, with their insistence on the group over the individual. In these settings, each mind is thought to be a fragment of one supermind, the Great Cloud of Unknowing. The concept of intersubjectivity offers a middle ground, in that one can evaluate the accuracy of mindreading without automatically assuming or rejecting the idea.

Beginning in the 1980s, there has been an expanding literature on what is called "mutual knowledge" in philosophy and economics (Clark and Marshall 1981; Sperber and Wilson 1986). These ventures do not mention the earlier explorations of the looking glass, consensus, or Goffman. They also have a quirk: the possibility of cascades of mutual mindreading, "I know that you know that I know ... ," seems to cause panic reactions in the authors. As Goffman and others have hinted however, the number of levels of mutual awareness is surely an empirical problem, not a conceptual one.

A final and arguable example is the work of Cooley, Mead, and Blumer themselves. Although role-taking is central to their visions of human nature, they deal with the concept only in the abstract. Goffman's treatment of concrete episodes of intersubjectivity (and its correlate, the pervasiveness of embarrassment or anticipations of embarrassment) begins to fill in the interstellar void between the abstraction and its omnipresent everyday meaning in human conduct.

Goffman's treatment fleshes out the idea of role-taking itself, and just as importantly, its close kinship to emotion, in a way that Mead, Blumer, and even Cooley never did. To be sure, Cooley clearly states the linkage to embarrassment/shame in his discussion of the looking-glass self, but he doesn't give enough varied examples that would allow one to see implications. Cooley's few examples also tend to the melodramatic. Goffman uses many, many everyday examples that bring the ideas to life in living color. In this sense, the earlier writers found a vast, unknown continent, the emotional/relational world, without leaving their ships. Goffman, along with the more cunning novelists, explored the interior.

Emotion Management

Goffman went beyond Cooley in another way also. Cooley stopped at three steps of the looking-glass self, with the experience of pride or shame.

But Goffman's exploration of impression management implies a fourth step, the management of emotion.[3] Although Goffman had nothing to say about the pride option, his examples suggest that actors usually do not accept shame/embarrassment passively. Instead they try to manage it, by avoidance, if possible. Most of the embarrassment/shame possibilities that Goffman's examples explore are not about the actual occurrence of emotions, but anticipations, and management based on these anticipations. (In European languages other than English, the anticipation of shame/embarrassment is taken to be a shame variant, such as *pudeur* [modesty]. This same idea is expressible in English as "a sense of shame.")

Goffman's examples further imply that if shame/embarrassment cannot be avoided, then his actors actively deny it, attempting to save face, on the one hand, and/or to avoid pain, on the other. The idea of shame management connects Goffman's work with that of Lynd (1958) and Lewis (1971). Lewis (1971), specifically, showed that in sessions of psychotherapy, shame/embarrassment occurs with greater frequency than any other emotion, but is almost never acknowledged, either by therapist or patient. Like shared awareness, it is largely invisible, at least in modern Western societies.

Goffman's drift into instances of emotion avoidance provides yet another example of contradiction between what he said and what he did. Ideologically, Goffman was dismissive of psychoanalytic and psychodynamic formulations. But his portrayals of emotion management cross over, however inadvertently, into the psychodynamic realm of Freud and of Lewis. These cases strongly support their psychodynamic formulations, and importantly, also broaden them.

Almost all of Freud's and Lewis's cases were patients in psychotherapy, leaving the reader free to infer that avoidance/denial of emotion occurs for the most part only in neurosis. Like Lynd (1958), however, Goffman's everyday instances suggest that they occur not only in psychotherapy, but are a basic part of the human condition.

However, Goffman's actual language implies an important difference between his use of the looking-glass model and Cooley's conception. In his straightforward and unassuming way, Cooley strongly implied that the looking-glass process was outside of awareness ("we live in the minds of others *without knowing it*"). As far as I have been able to tell, Goffman doesn't consider this issue: to what extent are his actors aware of their more or less constant impression management?

I have been unable to find any explicit consideration of this issue, but Goffman's language seems to imply awareness:

> When an individual's projected self is threatened during interaction, he may with poise suppress all signs of shame and embarrassment. No flusterings, or efforts to conceal having seen them, obtrude upon the

smooth flow of the encounter; participants can proceed as if no incident has occurred. (Goffman 1967, 110)

This passage seems to imply awareness, as do many others. Here is another example:

... preventive practices are constantly employed to avoid ... embarrassments and ... corrective practices are constantly employed to compensate for discrediting occurrences that have not been successfully avoided. (Goffman 1959, 13)

Although the matter is by no means clear, these passages and other similar ones seem to suggest that Goffman's version of the looking-glass process was mostly conscious. One consequence is that it gives many readers the impression that his actors are cynical and self-centered. If we take the Cooley line that they are often not aware of the looking-glass process, they might somehow seem less repulsive. It's a tradeoff, because at the same time they are also less aware. This latter interpretation seems to me much more preferable, because it is less morally rejecting about the nature of human nature.

There are other aspects of the looking-glass process that both Cooley and Goffman omitted entirely in their consideration of the second step, imagining the other's view of self. First, there is the degree of *accuracy* in our image of how the other sees us. The extent to which they actually see us the way we imagine makes a great deal of difference in real life. Neither Cooley nor Goffman, nor Mead or Dewey for that matter, discusses this issue. Mead, especially, since he is concerned with cooperation and rational reflection, seems to take accuracy for granted.

There is also another part of the second step which is somewhat more subtle than accuracy. It involves the *weight* the actor gives to the point of view of the other, relative to one's own point of view. Does one assign more value to one's own point of view, to the other's, or balance the two as equally valuable? This issue arises again in Chapter 7 in defining genuine love, and by implication, true solidarity.

To understand another person in any way, the comparison of the other person's view of you needs to be weighed against your own view. This is not a static matter, but seems to involve moving back and forth between one's own view and that of the other. Even something as simple as understanding the meaning of the other's words and their importance involves this back and forth process, which has been called *pendulation* (Levine 1997). In social interaction, we move swiftly and unself-consciously between the viewpoints of self and other, as a pendulum swings, back and forth. By the time we are adults we have been doing it so long and so well that we are completely unaware that it is happening. The process of pendulation is the real meaning of Cooley's idea that we live in the minds of others without knowing it; we are in and out. This dynamic is the key for understanding many important issues about human relationships.

Pendulation starts out, in early childhood, as movement between self and other's viewpoint. But after we have mastered that process, we are able to perform a parallel internally, back and forth between self and an imagined external other. This dynamic lies at the heart of what is called distancing of emotion: feeling an emotion, then seeing oneself externally feeling it. As proposed in my earlier book (1979), true catharsis occurs only at optimal distance, that is, balancing between being in and out of the emotion.

As will be discussed in Chapter 12, distancing of this kind is also a key issue in creative writing. The best of the creative writers, like Goffman, often have insufficient distance from their own work. They can't see it objectively because most of their effort is involved in creating it in the first place. Most writers have the opposite problem, continually worrying about the viewpoint of the other, what others will think of their writing. All writers face the problem of finding the right distance.

In the larger scheme of things, Goffman's forceful treatment of the major role that intersubjectivity and embarrassment continually play in social interaction gives credence to Cooley's version of the looking-glass self. Goffman was very clear on this point:

> ... embarrassment is not an irrational impulse breaking through socially prescribed behavior but part of this orderly behavior itself. (1967, 111)

Even Simmel, who was aware of intersubjectivity and of shame, didn't link them, and gave few concrete examples. Goffman stands alone. In my opinion, it was he, and not any of his antecedents, who discovered the emotional/relational world. We all swim in this world all day, every day, but Goffman was the first to notice and describe it. For this service alone, I believe that we should award supreme honor to his memory.

Goffman and Positive Science

Unlike most analysts of interior life, Goffman was not content to leave his basic concepts undefined. Although he casually uses metaphors like everyone else (the term "mystic union" several times to refer to speakers who are talking to each other), he also offers a fairly elaborate and complex definition of "being in a state of talk." Since his definition requires an entire page of text, I will not repeat it all here. Suffice it to know that it contains phrases that imply mutual mindreading: "An understanding will prevail [among the speakers] as to how long and how frequently each speaker is to hold the floor ..." (1967, 35; a similar formulation occurs earlier, on p. 34). The definition comes closest to explicitly describing intersubjective accord in this line:

A single focus of thought and attention, and a single flow of talk, tends to be maintained and to be legitimated as officially representative of the encounter. (Goffman 1967, 34, emphasis added)

The significance of the phrase "a single focus of thought and attention" becomes more apparent if it is compared to a similar phrase, "joint attention," used by the psychologist Bruner (1983) when he is explaining how an infant learns to become *attuned*[4] to its caretaker. The mother, he says, is only trying to teach a new word. She places an object (such as a doll) in her own and the baby's line of gaze, and shakes it to make sure of the baby's attention, saying, "See the pretty *dolly.*" In this situation, the baby is likely to learn not only the meaning of a word, but also, since both parties are looking at the same object, how to have, jointly with the mother, "a single focus of thought and attention" to use Goffman's phrase.

A conceptual definition of intersubjectivity is as far as Goffman goes in attempting to explicate this idea; he doesn't provide objective indicators. Perhaps Goffman was uncomfortable about the implications of flatly stating and following up an idea that is anathema in individualistic modern societies, that we are all "members one of another." Although church members recite this idea every Sunday, most would be loath to take its meaning literally, as Cooley and Goffman did.

But with the other interior strand of Goffman's work, embarrassment, he was not content to give only a conceptual definition, but also followed up, offering elements of an operational definition:

An individual may recognize extreme embarrassment in others and even in himself by the objective signs of emotional disturbance: blushing, fumbling, stuttering, an unusually low- or high-pitched voice, quavering speech or breaking of the voice, sweating, blanching, blinking, tremor of the hand, hesitating or vacillating movement, absentmindedness, and malapropisms. As Mark Baldwin remarked about shyness, there may be "a lowering of the eyes, bowing of the head, putting of hands behind the back, nervous fingering of the clothing or twisting of the fingers together, and stammering, with some incoherence of idea as expressed in speech." There are also symptoms of a subjective kind: constriction of the diaphragm, a feeling of wobbliness, consciousness of strained and unnatural gestures, a dazed sensation, dryness of the mouth, and tenseness of the muscles. In cases of mild discomfiture, *these visible and invisible flusterings occur but in less perceptible form.* (Goffman 1967, 97, emphasis added)

This definition links an interior emotion with surface observables. With his usual uncanny instinct, in the last sentence he even seems to hint at the need for further elaboration of the operational definition: "these visible and invisible flusterings [that accompany embarrassment] occur but in less perceptible form."This clause seems to point toward the development of more elaborate coding systems for the verbal and gestural indicators of shame and embarrassment, such as the one by Retzinger (1991; 1995).

Goffman's attempt at defining embarrassment is even more extraordinary in the context of contemporary social science. The few social science theorists who emphasize emotions seldom define them, even conceptually.[5] An example would be Elias's masterwork, *The Civilizing Process* (1939). His proposition that the threshold for shame is advanced in the civilizing process is the central thread of the entire work. In a later work of Elias's, *The Germans* (1996), shame is again frequently evoked, though not explicitly as in the earlier study.

Yet Elias offered no definition of shame in either book, seeming to assume that the reader would understand the concept of shame in the same way that he did. The absence of any definition of shame and a systematic way of identifying it is particularly glaring in *The Civilizing Process*. This study entails an extensive analysis of shame in many excerpts from advice and etiquette manuals in five languages over six centuries. The analysis of the excerpts is completely intuitive, and in most cases, highly inferential. That is, the word *shame* is sometimes used in the excerpts that he selected, but much more frequently it is not.

Elias relied on intuitive and unexplicated interpretations of what Retzinger would call cue words, phrases, and sentences, in context. Even if his interpretations were fairly accurate, which they might be, he still gave little direction to future research on the subject. Unlike Elias and most other analysts of emotion, Goffman took at least the initial step toward overcoming this problem. By explicitly defining his concepts, he attempted to link interior variables with observable indicators. Perhaps the secret for success in social science is not only to study both surface and interior, but to also provide links that connect them.

Conclusion

This chapter has inferred two basic propositions about self and society from an analysis of the work of Cooley and Goffman. These propositions link two concepts: intersubjective attunement on the one hand, and shame and its close relatives on the other. (1) To the extent that two parties are intersubjectively attuned, both parties will be in a state of authentic pride. (2) To the extent that they are not attuned, one or both will be in a state of embarrassment, shame, or humiliation. Like Cooley, Goffman's approach implied that mutual awareness, along with pride and shame, is the glue that holds not only relationships, but whole societies, together.

In this respect, Goffman turns out to be not a follower of Durkheim, the founder of modern sociology, but a step beyond him. Durkheim alluded to both mutual awareness and the social emotion, but only abstractly and in separate compartments of his work. By bringing the two realms together, and profusely illustrating their linkage in concrete examples, Goffman took a giant step forward with ideas that in Durkheim, and even in Cooley, were quite abstract and unclear.

The Cooley/Goffman approach could open up a whole approach built around the dynamics of the looking-glass self, and Goffman's extension of it into a fourth step, the management of the resulting emotions. Exploration of this type could mean a new understanding of human relationships.

Notes

1. Retzinger (1991; 1995) has provided a lengthy list of these words.

2. I am indebted to Simon Gottschalk for calling my attention to the positive and negative pride words in French.

3. Arlie Hochschild, who was Goffman's student, has made emotion management a central topic in her work.

4. Attunement is Stern's (1977) term for intersubjective accord.

5. However, in her extensive treatment of shame, Lynd (1958) also took a step toward explicit definition. In a rare miss, Goffman did not reference Lynd's work.

CHAPTER 4

Goffman's World of Emotions

THIS CHAPTER FURTHER CONSIDERS Goffman's treatment of emotions. As indicated earlier, Goffman followed Cooley's lead into the looking-glass self. One difference is that Cooley dealt with both pride and shame, but Goffman didn't provide examples of pride. He considered embarrassment, shame, and humiliation, closely related emotions, and also disgust, a separate emotion. In this respect, Goffman's approach was similar to Freud's and Elias's early work. All three began their careers with studies that gave shame and other emotions considerable attention. Their work needs to be considered in light of a taboo on emotions in modern society. In order to understand Goffman's achievement, it will be necessary to consider the meaning of shame, how it has been dealt with, and ignored, in modern social science. Both Goffman and Helen Lewis implied that shame was fundamental to understanding human relationships.

Many social science theorists have implied that emotions are an important force. Although Weber didn't refer to emotions directly, his emphasis on values implies it, since values are emotionally charged beliefs. Durkheim implicated collective sentiments in the creation of solidarity through moral community. Parsons and Shils (1955) made emotion a component of social action in their AGIL scheme. Even Marx and Engels involved emotions in class tensions and in the solidarity of rebellious classes.

But the classic formulations have had little influence, because they concerned emotions in general. Our knowledge of emotions is not generalized but particular. For example, we believe we know a great deal about anger: sources from which it arises, different forms it can take, and some of its outcomes. We also have similar kinds of beliefs about other primary emotions, such as fear, grief, shame, contempt, disgust, love, and joy.

Our shared beliefs about specific emotions allow us to communicate with each other on this topic, and restrain flights of fancy. The different emotions may have several underlying similarities, but more obvious are the differences in origins, appearance, and trajectories. It is for this reason that general statements have so little meaning. Some of what Durkheim, Mead, and Parsons said about emotion might appear plausible when applied to one emotion, say anger or fear, but not to others.

In any case, most theorists who dealt with emotions implicitly or explicitly did not develop concepts nor explore how they might appear in real life. In this respect Goffman, along with Freud and Elias, was quite distinct. Goffman usually identified his central emotion as embarrassment, even though his exploration, as already indicated, is broader than it seems. If we call Goffman's emotion *embarrassment/shame,* as proposed below, then there are many parallels between his treatment and the way in which Freud and Elias explored the emotion they called *shame.*

Goffman's very detailed exploration of embarrassment was extraordinary in many ways, as was Freud's and Elias's work on shame. With increasing industrialization and urbanization in the nineteenth century, modern societies began to retreat from acknowledging the emotional/relational world. With very few exceptions, not only modern sociology, as indicated above, but also psychiatry, psychology, and the other social sciences mostly ignored emotions.

To understand Goffman's breakthrough, it will first be necessary to review the repression of emotions, especially shame, in modern societies.

A Taboo?

As already suggested, urban/industrial societies seem to taboo emotions. The psychologist Gershen Kaufman has argued that shame is particularly taboo in U.S. society:

> American society is a shame-based culture, but ... shame remains hidden. Since there is shame about shame, it remains under taboo ... The taboo on shame is so strict ... that *we behave as if shame does not exist.* (Kaufman 1989, 24, emphasis added; see also Kaufman and Raphael 1984; Scheff 1984.)

In this section, I review studies of embarrassment and shame by Goffman, Freud, and Elias, showing that the response to them has been, for the most part, that shame doesn't exist. A large part of the cultural defense against shame is linguistic; the English language, particularly, disguises shame.

According to one current definition, a taboo involves:

> The prohibition of an action or the use of an object based on ritualistic distinctions of them either as being sacred and consecrated or as being dangerous, unclean, and accursed.(*Encyclopedia Britannica Online*)

Shame is not consecrated in modern societies. Perhaps "unclean" comes closest to catching the flavor. Kaufman's idea that there is shame about shame
explains, more precisely, why shame seems to be taboo in modern societies.
Because there is usually shame about shame, one risks offense by referring
to it. Defining taboo as an institution that evokes shame, because it points to
an identifiable process, may be an improvement over other definitions.

The encyclopedia definition goes on to note a very general point
about taboos that will also be emphasized here:

> There is broad agreement that the taboos current in any society tend to relate
> to objects and actions that are significant for the social order and that belong
> to the general system of social control. (Encyclopedia Britannica Online)

Although Elias (1939) didn't use the term *taboo,* his study of manners
through hundreds of years of European history offers an explanation of
Kaufman's idea in terms of social control. Elias found that the civilizing process in Europe was built on two contradictory movements: increasing use
of shame as an internal control, on the one hand, and increasing repression
of shame, on the other. Elias's findings will be further discussed below.

To understand the crucial function played by shame in systems of
social control, it will first be necessary to define it in a way that is broader
than current usage. The narrowest conceptions are found in vernacular English, orthodox psychoanalytic theory, and experimental social psychology.
A broad conception is found in qualitative and micro-linguistic research,
and in vernacular usage in traditional societies.[1] It is also implied in theories
developed by Mead, Cooley, and Goffman, as discussed in Chapter 3.

European languages other than English identify two kinds of shame.
In German, for example, there is *schande* (disgrace shame) and *scham*
(everyday shame). French makes exactly the same distinction, *honte* and
pudeur. With the exception of English, the languages of all modern societies have a word for everyday shame, and another word for disgrace shame.
Everyday shame usually carries no offense; a tacit understanding of everyday
shame (a sense of shame) is usually treated as a necessary part of one's
equipment as a proper person. Since English has no word for everyday
shame, one cannot discuss shame in English without risking offense. In
this way, English, uniquely among all languages, blocks off a whole area of
personhood and social interaction from discussion.

One way around the taboo is, rather than referring to shame, to use
a softer, less offensive member of the same family of emotions. Goffman
usually took this route. The books from the first three quarters of his career imply that embarrassment is the key emotion in social interaction, as
Goffman himself stated explicitly in his essay on embarrassment (1967).
Brown and Levinson (1987) observed the centrality of embarrassment in
Goffman's work, but only in passing. Schudson (1984) noted this emphasis

but made an issue of it. This chapter proposes a comprehensive answer. Building on the work of earlier theorists, I offer a definition of shame (in its broad sense) that can be used to understand Goffman's interest. The first issue to be faced is that shame is both a social and a psychological phenomenon.

Shame Arises Because the Self Is Social

Social conceptions of the self can serve as the background for a broad definition of shame. Mead (1934) proposed that the self is a social phenomenon as much as a biological one. His fundamental insight into consciousness was that it arose out of role taking, of seeing things from the point of view of the other(s), as well as from one's own point of view. This idea is central to the social psychology of Mead, Cooley, and Goffman.

Mead himself gave very little attention to shame or any other emotion. The problem that he attacked was the basis of reflective intelligence. He needed the idea of role-taking to explain the origins of intelligence and objectivity. However, a contemporary of Mead's, Charles Cooley, in his version of role-taking, noted that reading the mind of the other would usually generate emotions.

For Cooley (1922), shame and pride both arose from seeing oneself from the point of view of the other. In his discussion of what he called the "self-sentiments," pride and shame are mentioned as two of the emotions possible. But his concept of "the looking-glass self," which implies the social nature of the self, refers directly and exclusively to pride and shame. As discussed in Chapter 3, Cooley saw self-monitoring in three steps (184):

> A self-idea of this sort seems to have three principal elements: the imagination of our appearance to the other person; the imagination of his judgment of that appearance; and some sort of self-feeling, such as pride or mortification.

It is clear that "mortification" means shame, since Cooley mentions shame three more times in the passage that follows (184–85).

The way in which Cooley linked intersubjective connectedness, on the one hand, with pride and shame, on the other, could have been the basis for a general social psychological theory of bond affect. Even though the looking-glass self was appreciated and frequently cited in mainstream sociology and social psychology, the part involving pride and shame was simply ignored. Why?

Like most of the pioneers in the study of emotions, Cooley didn't attempt to define what he meant by pride or shame. He simply used these words as if their meaning were simple and singular. But in Western societies, the meaning of pride and shame is neither simple nor singular.

The meaning of these words is complex, and laden with emotion. Unless prefaced by an adjective like *genuine* or *justified,* the word *pride* carries a strong connotation of arrogance and selfishness, the kind of pride that "goeth before the fall." The unadorned word *pride,* that is, is usually taken to mean false pride or vanity.

As already indicated, the word *shame* also has negative connotations to the point that it is taboo. Perhaps because he was born in the nineteenth century, when these words may have been less weighted with feeling, Cooley seems to have been unaware of the problem. But it appears that his readers didn't know what to make of his emphasis on pride and shame. In any case, his insights into the relationship between attunement and emotion were ignored until my review (Scheff 1990), a hiatus of 68 years.

Goffman also pursued the idea of emotions arising out of role-taking, but formulated it less directly than Cooley, dealing with embarrassment more than with the whole shame triad. But more than Cooley, and much more than Mead, Goffman fleshed out the link between embarrassment and role-taking by providing many examples (1959; 1963a; 1963b; 1967). These examples allow the reader concrete understanding of ideas that are only abstractions in the work of Mead and Cooley.

The idea of impression management, crucial in most of Goffman's writing, made the avoidance of embarrassment a central motive of interpersonal behavior. Goffman's Everyperson is always concerned about her image in the eyes of others, trying to present herself with her best foot forward. Goffman's work vivifies Cooley's abstract idea of the way in which the looking glass generates emotion, giving the idea roots in the reader's imagination.

Goffman also made the key sociological point about embarrassment: it arises out of slights—real, anticipated, or just imagined—*no matter how trivial* they might appear to the outside observer. Everyone is extremely sensitive to the exact nuance of deference they receive. This is Goffman's key contribution to emotion knowledge.

There is a vast difference between Goffman and Cooley in this respect, because the few instances of shame-bound situations that Cooley provided were extreme, melodramatic situations of crisis and disgrace. This implication reinforces the repressive treatment of shame in modern societies, that it is extreme and unusual. Goffman's bold insistence on the ubiquity of emotion in normal, everyday social relationships is unique. In Goffman's language:

> One assumes that embarrassment is a normal part of normal social life, the individual becoming uneasy not because he is personally maladjusted but rather because he is not ... [E]mbarrassment is not an irrational impulse breaking through social prescribed behavior, but part of this orderly behavior itself. (1967, 109 and 111)

This idea is also implied in the work of Freud and Elias, but not stated as forcefully and explicitly: shame/embarrassment is the master emotion of everyday life.

Goffman on Embarrassment and Shame

It was fortunate, perhaps, in terms of the size of his readership, that Goffman chose to focus on embarrassment, without explicitly connecting it to shame. It doesn't appear that Goffman chose that strategy intentionally. On the one hand, there is lack of attention to shame in his book *Stigma* (1963b). Since shame is the central topic of this work, it provided him with ample opportunity to explore the relationship between embarrassment and shame. But he did not: shame is mentioned only a few times, and in passing.

In fairness to Goffman, although he emphasized embarrassment in his work before 1974, he didn't exactly avoid shame. In the thirty pages of Chapter VI of PSEL (1959), he mentioned *shame* or *ashamed* 4 times, *guilt* and *humiliation* once each, and *embarrassment* 7 times. But this count underplays his consideration of everyday bond affects, because there are many more images that imply them.

One example from the many in the same chapter should be enough to make this point:

> He may ... add to the precariousness of his position by engaging in just those defensive maneuvers that would employ if he were really guilty. In this way it is possible for all of us *to become fleetingly for ourselves the worst person we can imagine that others might imagine us to be.* (236, emphasis added)

This image of seeing one's self negatively in the eyes of others was perceived as the origin of shame or embarrassment by Darwin, Cooley, and Goffman himself. Although I haven't made an actual count, I propose that it is invoked constantly by Goffman, particularly in his most popular work. As indicated in Chapter 3, Goffman doesn't credit Cooley directly; the central theme of *Presentation of Self,* and much of Goffman's later writing, is an elaboration on Cooley's thesis: since we live in the minds of others, shame (in its broad sense as bond affect) is the master emotion of everyday life.

As indicated in Chapter 3, Goffman attempted to define embarrassment operationally, which implies his theoretical and methodological sophistication. In opposition to Cooley and Goffman, Jack Katz (1999, Ch. 3) offers a complex but narrow definition of shame with no attempt made at an operational definition:

> ... an [1] eerie revelation to self that [2] isolates one [3] in the face of an sacred community. What is revealed is a [4] moral inferiority that

makes one [5] vulnerable to [6] irresistible forces. As a state of feeling, shame is [7] fearful, [8] chaotic, [9] holistic and [10] humbling. (147)

The way these ten components are closely linked implies that there is only one type of shame, and each component also implies crisis and disgrace, as in vernacular usage, rather than a continuing presence in everyday life.

In contrast, Retzinger and I have defined shame broadly. Retzinger's central study concerned the exchange of feelings, second by second, in marital quarrels (1991). From her analysis of discourse in these quarrels, she developed a methodology for identifying shame and anger, even when the subjects are not aware of their own feelings. Retzinger also developed a theory of destructive conflict, based on a review of the social science literature on conflict, as well as her own findings. My own work on shame has relied on Retzinger's, both her methods for identifying shame and anger in discourse, and her theory of destructive conflict (Scheff 1994). Our work proposes that shame cannot be understood within an individualistic, asocial framework.

Social Definitions of Shame

There are also social definitions of shame in maverick psychoanalysis, sociology, and psychology that define shame broadly. The opening salvo was fired by Erikson (1950), who rejected Freud's assumption that guilt was the primary moral emotion for adults. He argued instead that shame was the more elemental in that it concerned the whole self, not just one's actions.

This idea was expanded by the sociologist Helen Lynd (1958), whose exposition of the importance of shame to the self and social life is remarkably clear. Her approach to shame did not test hypotheses, but used concrete examples to clarify the idea of shame. She was the first to recognize the need for a *concept* of shame that would be clearly defined, and that would differentiate it from vernacular usage.

Tomkins, who recognized the central role that shame plays in self-process, took the next step. In his volume on the negative affects (1963, vol. II) he devoted almost 500 pages to a very detailed and comprehensive discussion of shame and humiliation. Tomkins argued explicitly that embarrassment, shame, and guilt should be recognized as members of a single affect family, as I do here.

The work that Tomkins did on emotions was extensive and important, and has had considerable influence on emotion research. His idea that has had the most influence is that the seat of the emotions is in the face. There have been hundreds of studies of the facial expression of emotion. But these studies have contributed little to shame knowledge for two reasons.

First, the leaders in this approach, Ekman et al. (1972), decided that there was no consensus on the facial expression of shame, and therefore it

Table 4.1 Self/Other Relationship in Shame

Self (unable)	Other (able)
1. Object of scorn, contempt, ridicule; reduced little	1. The source of scorn, contempt, ridicule
2. Paralyzed; helpless; passive	2. Laughing, ridiculing; powerful; active
3. Assailed by noxious stimuli: rage Tears; blushing; fluster; blank	3. Appears intact
4. Feels childish	4. Appears adult; going away; abandoning
5. Focal in awareness; being looked at; split	5. Also focal in awareness; looking at
6. Functions poorly as an agent or perceiver; divided between imaging self and the other; boundaries are permeable; vicarious experience of self and other	6. Appears intact

Source: Retzinger (1991), adapted from Lewis (1991)

wasn't a genuine emotion. It is puzzling that Ekman thought he was following Tomkins, yet ignored the emotion to which Tomkins gave the most attention. The Ekman et al. studies, and those of most of the others who followed their lead, have ignored shame. Whatever Ekman's reasoning for excluding shame, the exclusion also suggests the working of the taboo on shame.

A second difficulty is that even the facial-expression researchers who study shame look only at still photographs, ignoring context and the sequencing of affects. For these reasons, Tomkins's work and the work of those who have followed him has had limited usefulness. Nathanson's (1992) work, for example, is based on Tomkins's affect theory, but like Tomkins, he fails to offer adequate conceptual and operational definitions of shame.

In contrast to Tomkins, the psychologist/psychoanalyst Helen Lewis (1971) developed an elaborate conceptual definition of shame and used an operational definition in her research. Her conceptual definition is suggested by one of her schematics.

Table 4.1 (Retzinger 1991, adapted from Lewis 1971) suggests the broadness of Lewis's shame concept. Unlike any other emotion, shame depends only on specific aspects of social relationships. As implied by the table, one can generate any specific bond affect by utilizing one or more of the six dimensions.

A second contribution by Lewis is the idea that shame is inherently a social emotion (1971). Her formulation was biopsychosocial. She asserted that human beings are social by biological inheritance. That is, she implied that shame is an instinct that has the function of signaling threats to the social bond. Just as the instinctual emotion of fear signals danger to life and limb, shame also signals a potential threat to survival, especially for an infant, threat to a social bond. In this same vein, Kaufman (1989) proposed that shame dynamics are part of the interpersonal bridge that connects individuals who would otherwise lead isolated existences.

On the basis of her empirical study of shame in psychotherapy, Lewis contributed to a broad definition of shame by proposing that most shame states seem to be outside of awareness. Her first book on shame (1971) was based on an analysis of verbatim transcripts of hundreds of psychotherapy sessions.

She encountered shame because she used a systematic method for identifying emotions in verbal transcripts, the Gottschalk-Gleser method (Gottschalk et al. 1969; Gottschalk 1995). This method involves long lists of key words that are correlated with specific emotions, such as anger, grief, fear, anxiety, and shame. This method forced Lewis to encounter shame as the dominant emotion in the sessions she analyzed. She found that anger, fear, grief, and anxiety cues showed up from time to time in the transcripts. What she was unprepared for was the massive frequency of shame cues. Her methodology was complex, in that once a shame episode was located by Gottschalk's method, Lewis also applied a qualitative method, analyzing each episode word by word.

The findings from her study most relevant to this chapter are:

1. Prevalence: Lewis found a high frequency of shame markers in all the sessions, far outranking markers of all other emotions combined. This finding alone suggests that shame was a dominant force in the sessions she analyzed.

2. Lack of awareness: Lewis noted that although shame markers were frequent in all of the sessions, both patient and therapist seldom referred to shame or its near cognates. Even the relatively mild word embarrassment was little used. In analyzing shame episodes, Lewis identified a specific context: situations in which the patient seemed to feel distant from, rejected, criticized, or exposed by the therapist, generated a cloud of shame markers. This context fits the proposition that shame arises from seeing one's self negatively from the point of view of the other (Darwin 1872; Cooley 1922).

3. However, patients showed two different, seemingly opposite responses in the shame context. In one, the patient seemed to be suffering psychological pain, but failed to identify it as shame. Lewis called this form *overt, undifferentiated shame*. In a second kind of response, the patient seemed not to be in pain, revealing an emotional response only by rapid, obsessional speech on topics that seemed slightly removed from the dialogue. Lewis called this second response *bypassed shame*. Identifying or calling shame by its right name seems to be an important aspect of understanding and managing it.

4. Finally, Lewis noted that there was an affinity between shame and anger. She found that anger markers in the patient's speech were always preceded by shame markers. Apparently one way of hiding shame is to become angry. This finding has implications for our understanding of affects like resentment and guilt, which will be discussed below.

Lynd, Lewis, Tomkins, Retzinger, and Scheff defined shame socially and broadly as all affects that arise from threats to the bond. They also compared the modern narrow treatment of shame to the broad usage in traditional societies. However, none of these researchers explored the history of shame, how its meaning has changed in the transition from traditional to modern societies. Although they report the repression of shame in modern societies, they do not explain how it has come to be. This is exactly the ground covered by Elias's study, the transition from the time of the Middle Ages to the beginning of modern societies in the nineteenth century.

Elias's History of Manners

Elias's analysis of the "civilizing process" (1978; 1982) shows how shame went underground in modern societies. He traces changes in the development of personality in the onset of modern civilization. Like Weber, Elias gives prominence to the development of rationality. Unlike Weber, however, he gives equal prominence to changes in the threshold of shame: "No less characteristic of a civilizing process than 'rationalization' is the peculiar molding of the drive economy that we call 'shame' and 'repugnance' or 'embarrassment'" (1982, 292).

Using excerpts from advice manuals in five languages from the Middle Ages to the nineteenth century, Elias outlined a theory of modernity. By examining advice concerning etiquette, especially table manners, body functions, sexuality, and anger, he suggested that a key aspect of modernity involves shame.

Although Elias's language differs from mine, his analysis parallels my own. His central thesis is closely related: decreasing shame thresholds at the time of the breakup of rural communities, and decreasing acknowledgment of shame, have had powerful consequences on levels of awareness and self-control. The following excerpt gives the flavor of Elias's study. He first presents an excerpt from a nineteenth-century work, *The Education of Girls* (von Raumer 1857) that advises mothers how to answer the sexual questions their daughters ask:

> Children should be left for as long as is at all possible in the belief that an angel brings the mother her little children. This legend, customary in some regions, is far better than the story of the stork common elsewhere.

Children, if they really grow up under their mother's eyes, will seldom ask forward questions on this point ... not even if the mother is prevented by a childbirth from having them about her ... If girls should later ask how little children really come into the world, they should be told that the good Lord gives the mother her child, who has a guardian angel in heaven who certainly played an invisible part in bringing us this great joy. "You do not need to know nor could you understand how God gives children." Girls must be satisfied with such answers in a hundred cases, and it is the mother's task to occupy her daughters' thoughts so incessantly with the good and beautiful that they are left no time to brood on such matters ... A mother ... ought only once to say seriously: "It would not be good for you to know such a thing, and you should take care not to listen to anything said about it." A truly well brought-up girl will from then on feel shame at hearing things of this kind spoken of. (1978, 180)

Elias first interprets the repression of sexuality in terms of unacknowledged shame:

In the civilizing process, sexuality too is increasingly removed behind the scenes of social life and enclosed in a particular enclave, the nuclear family. Likewise, the relations between the sexes are isolated, placed behind walls in consciousness. An aura of embarrassment, the expression of a sociogenetic fear, surrounds this sphere of life. Even among adults it is referred to officially only with caution and circumlocutions. And with children, particularly girls, such things are, as far as possible, not referred to at all. Von Raumer gives no reason why one ought not to speak of them with children. He could have said it is desirable to preserve the spiritual purity of girls for as long as possible. But even this reason is only another expression of how far the gradual submergence of these impulses in shame and embarrassment has advanced by this time. (1978, 180)

Elias raises a host of significant questions about this excerpt, concerning its motivation and its effects. His analysis goes to what I consider to be the central causal chain in modern civilization: denial of shame and of the threatened social bonds that both cause and reflect that denial. I concur with Elias's analysis of the causal process in repression, the arousal of shame and the denial of this arousal:

Considered rationally, the problem confronting him [von Raumer] seems unsolved, and what he says appears contradictory. He does not explain how and when the young girl should be made to understand what is happening and will happen to her. The primary concern is the necessity of instilling "modesty" (i.e., feelings of shame, fear, embarrassment, and guilt) or, more precisely, behavior conforming to the social standard. And one feels how infinitely difficult it is for the educator himself to overcome the resistance of the shame and embarrassment which surround this sphere for him. (1978, 181)

Elias's study suggests a way of understanding the social transmission of the taboo on shame and the social bond. The adult, the author von Raumer in this case, is not only ashamed of sex, he is ashamed of being ashamed, in accordance with Kaufman's analysis of taboo. The nineteenth-century reader, in turn, probably reacted in a similar way: being ashamed, and being ashamed of being ashamed, and being ashamed of causing further shame in the daughter. Von Raumer's advice was part of a social system in which attempts at civilized delicacy resulted and continue to result in an endless chain reaction of unacknowledged shame. The chain reaction is both within persons and between them, a "triple spiral" (Scheff 1990).

Elias understood the significance of the denial of shame: shame goes underground, leading to behavior that is outside of awareness:

> Neither rational motives nor practical reasons primarily determine this atti-tude, but rather the shame (*scham*) of adults themselves, which has become compulsive. It is the social prohibitions and resistances within themselves, their own superego, that makes them keep silent. (1978, 181)

Like many other passages, this one points not only to a taboo on shame, but at the actual mechanisms by which it is transmitted and maintained.

The translator of *The Civilizing Process* [TCP] from German into English made what I consider to be a gross mistake. He translated the word that Elias used, *scham,* into the word *shame.* Although technically correct, it is an error in terms of emotional content. Perhaps if he had used the word *embarrassment* instead of *shame,* the reception of the book in the U.S. might have been less tepid. Although one of the great landmarks of social science research in England and the rest of Europe, the book is still little known in the U.S.

Why was TCP well received in England? Because of the long hiatus between the original publication in German in 1939 and its first transla-tion into English in 1987, the scholars in England who became followers of Elias had read TCP only in German. Knowing German, they were able to accept Elias's emphasis on *scham.* Writing about the early reviews of TCP in Europe, Goudsblom (1977) noted that many of them were especially appreciative of the first part, the history of manners. Since French and Dutch each have a word that is the exact equivalent of *scham,* perhaps they were able to take his unusual emphasis on shame in stride. If Elias had used the word *schande* (the German equivalent of the word shame in English), rather than *scham,* the book might have gotten a less enthusiastic reception in Europe, paralleling its reception in the U.S.

In terms of taboo, it should also be noted that many years passed before reviewers or users of TCP referred to the central role of shame in Elias's study of manners. Goudsblom didn't note it in his 1977 review, nor did any of the reviewers cited by Goudsblom. The only researcher who made use of Elias's shame work was Sennett, who cited Elias in his own chapter on the way managers use shame to control workers (Sennett 1980). However, no reviewers or anyone else took note of that chapter. Perhaps both Sennett and Elias noted the lack of response, since neither gave a great deal of attention to shame in their subsequent work. The taboo on shame is maintained through silence, first by the readers of the books, then by the authors themselves. This taboo extends even into psychoanalysis and social psychology, disciplines in which emotion is a central concern.

Shame and Disgust in Psychoanalysis

Most writing in psychology ignores the social component in shame. Vernacular conceptions of shame in English and the European languages have a powerful hold on scholarly and scientific discussions. Even though Freud used the German term for everyday shame (*scham*), he still defined it narrowly, located within individuals. He assumed that *scham* arose out of a disparity between one's own ideals and one's actual behavior.

Because he saw so little evidence of shame in himself and in his male colleagues, Freud was dismissive of shame as an adult emotion in modern societies. He considered guilt to be the moral emotion of adults, being acutely conscious of it in himself and his male circle. Seeing little shame in himself and his friends, he found it, in his earliest work (1895), in his patients, all of whom were women. Reflecting the ageism, sexism, and racism of his time, Freud seemed to think that shame was the emotion of children, women, and savages. Following Freud's idea that guilt was the adult emotion in modern societies, the anthropologist Ruth Benedict (1946) proposed that traditional societies were shame cultures, modern societies, guilt cultures. As will be discussed below, this conception is misleading in several important ways.

Although in his later work Freud ignored shame, it had an important role in his first book. In *Studies on Hysteria* (1895), Freud and Breuer stated early on (p. 40) that hysteria is caused by hidden affects, and named the emotion of shame (*scham*) as one of these affects. Near the end of the book, this idea is urged more strongly:

> [The ideas that were being repressed] were all of a distressing nature, calculated to arouse the affects of shame, self-reproach and of psychical pain and the feeling of being harmed. (313)

Note that all of the affects mentioned can be considered to be shame derivatives, cognates, or a general name for emotional pain. Self-reproach is a specific shame cognate, the feeling of being harmed (as in rejection) somewhat broader, and finally, the quite abstract phrase "psychical pain," which like "hurt" or "emotional arousal" can be applied to any emotion. In this passage and several others, shame is given a central role in the causation of psychopathology.

In his early work, Freud named not only shame but also disgust as important. In his study of hysteria, and in *Three Essays on the Theory of Sexuality* (1905), Freud states that shame and disgust are the basis for repression. Elias seemed to have picked up this idea from his reading of early Freud. In TCP (1939), shame is the emotion that is most frequently invoked. However, in that book, Elias often mentions embarrassment and disgust (translated into English as "repugnance") along with shame.

In the excerpts chosen by Elias as illustrations of his theory, disgust often plays a role at least as important as shame. It is particularly important in his discussions of mealtime manners and the etiquette of the body and its products. For example, there are many excerpts concerning spitting and picking one's nose. These excerpts may actually evoke disgust in the reader. One fourteenth-century excerpt used by Elias warns the reader that if one is forced to blow one's nose in public, it should be wiped with a handkerchief, not on one's sleeve, and one should avoid looking at what comes out as if searching for treasure.

The idea that disgust can be an important force in social control is suggested in the work of the anthropologist Mary Douglas. In *Purity and Danger* (1966), she shows how the status quo in tribes and other groups is maintained by thoughts/feelings of clean and unclean. Surprisingly, although she does mention fear several times, she doesn't explicitly name disgust. But virtually all of her examples, coming as they do from the arenas of food, sex, and the body, evoke disgust rather than fear.

Under the heading of "bodily excreta," Goffman lists four types: "corporal excrete (or their stains) that contaminate by direct touch, odor, bodily heat (as on toilet seats), and markings left by the body in which excreta can be imagined, plate leavings are an example" (1971, 46–47). Goffman seems to have been particularly interested in the last category, since he goes on for another page about defilement fears connected with food (48). (I am indebted to Amelia George for calling these passages to my attention.) Miller (1997) is also very direct; he names disgust, as well as shame, as the crucial emotions in social control.

The idea that not only shame, but also disgust are major sources of social control suggests a link between Goffman and early Freud and Elias. Although Goffman didn't seem to be directly influenced by Freud, there may have been an indirect influence through Elias. Goffman had read Elias's TCP in its original German edition (1939). The idea that it is shame and disgust that cause repression would give these two emotions the leading role in the causation of all mental illness, not just hysteria. Oddly, in one of his statements many years later, Freud declared that repression was the central motor of human development and emotional illness, but psychoanalysis knew very little about it. Apparently Freud had forgotten his earlier discovery that shame was the agent of repression.

Current Psychoanalytic Perspectives

With the publication of *The Interpretation of Dreams* (1905), Freud permanently renounced his earlier formulation in favor of drive theory, especially the sexual drive. At this point, anxiety and guilt became the central emotions in psychoanalytic theory. Since 1905, shame has been ignored in orthodox formulations. Although psychoanalysts have made crucially important contributions to shame knowledge, these contributions helped make them marginal to mainstream psychoanalysis. Even in their own work, shame usually goes unnamed or undefined.

Alfred Adler, Abraham Kardiner, Karen Horney, and Erik Erikson provide examples of analyses that include or imply shame, yet fail to define it (Kardiner and Erikson) or even name it (Adler and Horney). Adler's formulation of the core position of prestige-seeking in human behavior, and his concept of the inferiority complex, are clearly shame-based ideas. To make the search for prestige and honor a central human motive is to focus on the pride/shame axis, as Cooley did. Similarly, the concept of an inferiority complex can be seen as a formulation about chronic low self-esteem, i.e., chronic shame.

Yet Adler never used the concept of shame. His theory of personality was that children deprived of love at key periods in their development would become adults with either a drive for power or an inferiority complex. This theory can be restated succinctly in terms of a theory of shame and the social bond: children without the requisite secure bonds will likely become adults whose affects are predominately bypassed (drive for power) or overt shame (inferiority complex, as in Lewis 1971).

Like Adler, Horney (1950) didn't name the emotion of shame. But her formulations implied it. Her theory of personality was based on what she called "the pride system." Most of her propositions imply that pride and shame are the keys to understanding both neurotic and normal behavior. Her concept of the "vindictive personality" implies shame/anger sequences as the emotional basis for vengeful behavior.

Kardiner was an anthropologist who applied psychoanalytic ideas to small traditional cultures. One of his studies (1939) compared the role of shame in four traditional societies. Unlike Adler and Horney, he named the emotion of shame, and stated, like Freud and Breuer, that shame is the emotion of repression. Like Adler, he also gave prominence to prestige as a fundamental human motive. Going further than Adler or Freud, he thought shame was the principal component of the superego, rather than guilt.

Like Kardiner, Erikson also named shame in his analysis of the relationship between shame and guilt (1950). In his discussion of these emotions, he proposed, contra Freud, that shame was the most fundamental emotion and that it had a vital role in child development. Like most theorists who discuss shame, neither Kardiner nor Erikson tried to define it. The work on shame by these four analysts was not recognized by the psychoanalytic establishment. Both Adler and Horney were excluded for their deviationism. Although neither Kardiner nor Erikson were excluded, there was no response by analysts, even their followers, to their work on shame.

Although there has been a reawakening of shame studies by current psychoanalysts, only a small minority of analysts are involved. Even in this group, converting from drive theory to a social affect language is a struggle. The work of Lansky (1992; 1995) on shame preserves drive theory. Morrison (1989) has translated drive theoretic formulations into shame dynamics, trying to bridge the two worlds. Only Broucek (1991) both rebelled against drive theory and attempted a social formulation of shame.

Experimental Social Psychological Studies of Embarrassment

The largest number of studies of embarrassment has occurred in experimental social psychology over the last twenty years. Sharkey (2001) lists almost 400 studies, most of which are experiments. Of those that consider the issue, all but one find embarrassment and shame to be different affects (e.g., Edelmann 1987; Miller and Tangney 1994; Lewis 1995; Tangney et al. 1996). Perhaps the key problem with these studies is that most of them use methods that rely on subjects' conscious classifications of affects. Since English-speaking subjects distinguish embarrassment from shame, that is what these studies find.

Keltner and Buswell (1997) mainly use facial expression to measure emotion, but conclude, like the studies above, that shame and embarrassment are distinct. They distinguish embarrassment from shame in two ways: (1) Difference in facial expression and (2) Source of the emotion. In terms of facial expression, they propose that embarrassment often involves a smile, where shame does not. However, that difference could be explained as involving only a difference in intensity. Their second difference: embarrassment is connected with breaking conventions, where shame is connected with moral lapses. Again, this could also be a matter only of intensity. Furthermore, as Sabini et al. (2001) show, the difference between convention and morality, in actual situations, can be unclear.

Sabini et al. (2001) measured subjects' emotion categories, but interpret their results as failing to support the distinction between shame and embarrassment. They conclude that shame and embarrassment belong to "a single affect system" (113). They do not name this system, but note that it is tied to what they call "breakdowns in self-presentation." Since self-presentation inevitably involves others' views of self, Sabini and his colleagues seem to be moving toward a conception of shame/embarrassment as a social affect.

Although they use subjects' emotion categories like most of the other experimental research on embarrassment, Sabini and his colleagues interpret their results in a way that contradicts the findings of the other studies. Why? A complete answer would involve a careful comparison of their methods and concepts to those of the earlier studies. But Sabini and his colleagues mention in passing an idea that might be the most crucial difference. They indicate "... we would distinguish what triggers an episode from the *totality of the episode*" (113).

Sabini et al. come closer to viewing the totality of the episodes they studied than the researchers in the earlier experiments. Edelmann, Miller and Tangney, and Keltner and Buswell focus only on the experimental variables. Sabini et al. consider these, but also other dimensions. Their study comes closest to what I call "part/whole analysis" (Scheff 1997c). As indicated in the preface, Spinoza proposed that human beings are so complex that we can understand them only by taking into account the least parts (words and gestures) in relationship to the greatest wholes (concepts, theories, contexts, etc.).

None of the experimental studies, moreover, explicitly consider the social dimensions of emotion. They fail to notice, for example, two social sources that are common to both shame and embarrassment. Most of one's personal ideals are held in common with other members of one's society. Personal ideals are largely social ideals. Second, and more subtly, the interior theatre of the self, in which both shame and embarrassment occur, is modeled on social interaction. One becomes ashamed by seeing one's self in the eyes of others, whether real or imagined. If shame in its broad sense is a continuous presence in human conduct we would need a new definition, a theory, and a method in order to study it.

Shame as Bond Affect

Shame has more functions than other emotions. First, shame is a key component of conscience, the moral sense: it signals moral transgression even without thoughts or words. Shame is our moral gyroscope.

Second, shame arises in elemental situations of threat to a bond; it signals trouble in a relationship. Since an infant's life is completely dependent on the bond with the caregivers, shame is as primitive and intense as fear. This idea subsumes the more usual one that shame arises when one feels one has failed to live up to one's standards, since these standards are, for the most part, held in common with the significant others in one's life. The sense that one has failed to live up to one's standards would usually also signal a threat to one's social relationships.

Finally, shame plays a central role in regulating the expression, and indeed, the awareness of all of our other emotions. Anger, fear, grief, and love, for example, are not likely to be expressed outwardly to the degree that one is ashamed of them. One can be so ashamed of one's emotions that they can be repressed completely. Although Freud later abandoned his finding, his discovery of shame (*scham*) as the agent of repression (Freud and Breuer 1895), discussed above, was not an error.

If shame in the broad sense is so central to understanding human conduct, it might be well to differentiate it from the narrow meaning in the vernacular. There are many words that are used as substitutes or cognates for the feeling that results from seeing one's self negatively in the eyes of the other, such as feeling self-conscious, rejected, unworthy, or inadequate. A first step toward a scientific definition is to use the term Shame as a *class name* for a large family of emotions and feelings that arise through *seeing self negatively, if even only slightly negatively,* through the eyes of others, or only anticipating such a reaction. This usage would therefore include all of Goffman's work on embarrassment. The complete definition will follow below.

A social definition is in conflict with vernacular usage, in which shame is defined narrowly, as *disgrace shame.* But most *Shame* does not involve crisis or disgrace. It is sometimes available in the interior theatre of the imagination as *discretion-shame,* but more often, Shame occurs out of awareness. Michael Lewis's contribution to our knowledge of the emotional/relational world was that Shame, or its anticipation, is a continuing presence in most social interaction. Because he made embarrassment central to social interaction, Goffman had made the same point on theoretical grounds. Shame is indicated at different levels of intensity and duration by the terms *embarrassment* (weak and transient), *shame* (stronger and more durable), and *humiliation* (powerful and of long duration). What these three terms have in common is that they all signal threat to the social bond. Many, many other terms are cognates or variants of Shame, each emphasizing one or the other aspects of the feeling or the situation. Self-consciousness, shyness, modesty, and conscience have already been mentioned in the discussion of discretion shame. Retzinger (1991; 1995) lists hundreds of such words.

Most of the words that reference social affect are codewords rather than cognates, because they have dual meanings. For example, the word *awkward* can mean physically clumsy, but it is also used as a codeword for embarrassment. The phrase "It was an awkward moment for me" is an indirect way of referring to embarrassment. It's not me that is embarrassed (denial), but the moment that is awkward (projection). Helen Lewis (1971) showed that even in psychotherapy sessions, references to Shame were usually in code.

There is a parallel between the concept of Shame and usage in reference to other emotions. The class name *anger,* for example, includes irritation, annoyance, frustration, being enraged, being pissed off, and many other words and phrases. As is the case with Shame, *anger* is the generic term for an elemental emotion class that includes many cognates. But since the word *anger* is not offensive, the class name can be direct.

In addition to being a class name for many social cognates and variants, Shame also combines with other emotions to form affects. Resentment and guilt may be the two most important examples. Resentment seems to be an affect of Shame and anger, with the anger pointed outwards. Insulted, one may mask Shame with anger by hostility. Guilt seems to have a similar makeup, but with the anger pointed back at self. One may address oneself angrily: "How could I treat my mother that way? She was only trying to help!"

To be sure, guilt serves a vital social function, leading one to make amends for one's trespass. But at the same time, it often serves to mask one's Shame, since it focuses on external behavior: one's trespass, and the amends one is to make. Benedict's (1946) idea that modern societies have a guilt culture is a gloss on the hidden relationship between guilt and shame. In the transition from traditional to modern societies, guilt arises in association with individualism. It does not so much replace Shame as serve as one of its many masks. Shame doesn't disappear, it goes underground. Elias traced this process in his study of the history of manners, as already indicated.

Formal Definition of Shame in Its Broad Sense

Drawing upon the work of the pioneers reviewed here, Shame can be defined as the large family of emotions that includes many cognates and variants, most notably embarrassment, guilt, humiliation, and related feelings such as shyness, that originate in *threats to the social bond.* This definition integrates self (emotional reactions) and society (the social bond).

If one postulates that Shame is generated by a threat to the bond, *no matter how slight,* then a wide range of cognates and variants follow: not only embarrassment, shyness, and modesty, but also feelings of rejection or failure, and heightened self-consciousness of any kind. A long list of gestures and codewords that can be used as indicators of shame has been provided by Retzinger (1991; 1995). A second operational definition is available from Louis Gottschalk, a professor of psychiatry at the University of California,

Irvine. His software deals with verbal texts only, but has been validated in 26 languages (Gottschalk 1995).

The social psychologist June Tangney and her colleagues have also developed a methodology to identify shame in discourse. They have developed a method based both on direct questions in interviews and an indirect method for coding answers to vignettes (Miller and Tangney 1994; Tangney et al. 1996; Tangney and Dearing 2002).

A Sense of Shame

Especially important for social control is a positive variant, a *sense of shame.* That is, Shame figures in most social interaction because members may only occasionally feel shame, but they are constantly anticipating it, as Goffman implied. Goffman's treatment continually points to the slightness of threats to the bond that lead to anticipation of embarrassment. As Darwin (1872) noted, the discrepancy can even be in the positive direction; too much deference can generate the embarrassment of heightened self-consciousness. This fact points to the intersubjective nature of the cause of shame. Receiving more deference than we expect is a threat to our sense of being connected to the other, of understanding them as they understand us. Even praise can be experienced as lack of attunement, giving rise to what Goffman called fluster.

If, as proposed here, Shame were a result of threat to the bond, Shame would be the most social of the basic emotions. Fear is a signal of danger to the body, anger a signal of frustration, and so on. The sources of fear and anger, unlike shame, are not uniquely social. Grief also has a social origin, since it signals the loss of a bond. But bond loss is not a frequent event. Shame on the other hand, since it can arise out of infinitesimal threats to the bond, is either present or anticipated in virtually every social interaction. Shame is the emotion that Durkheim could have named as the social emotion, had he named a specific emotion.

Given our extraordinary sensitivity to even minute differences between the deference we get and what we expect, virtually *every* social situation can arouse Shame or its shadow, either actual or anticipated. The ubiquity of Shame in social life obtains not only between individuals but also between groups. Not only duels, but also wars may be fought over greed and fear as well as over perceived slights to our individual or collective sense of self (Scheff 1994).

Conclusion

Why did Goffman and others make fundamental contributions to Shame knowledge, yet fail to explicitly name and define the emotion they studied as shame, or ignore it in their later work? Goffman was not alone in this respect. Mead and Dewey ignored the obvious importance of shame in Cooley's work; Brown and Levinson (1987) recognized the importance of Goffman's concept of face as the avoidance of embarrassment, but failed to utilize it. My description of the history of shame studies by psychoanalysts suggests similar questions, particularly Freud's early discovery of shame and his later disavowal.

These lapses can be explained in terms of Elias's idea of the advance of the shame threshold, and Lewis's work on unacknowledged shame. Elias's response to his data led him to an analysis that was too advanced for his audience. In Western societies, as Elias pointed out, the threshold for shame has been decreasing for hundreds of years, yet at the same time it has been becoming less and less visible. Similarly, Lewis's work suggests that the fate of shame in modern societies is to go unacknowledged. In our era the level of awareness of Shame is so low, especially in Anglophone societies, that unless it is at a very high level of intensity, it is virtually invisible.

This chapter has proposed that Goffman's treatment of embarrassment and shame was unique in many ways. Like Freud, Cooley, and Elias, his work implies that these are the master emotions of everyday life. But unlike them, his treatment boldly insisted that everyday life is rife with these emotions. Goffman's focus on embarrassment helped insure his wide readership, because embarrassment is much less taboo than shame. The choice of the word *shame* rather than *embarrassment* in the translation of Elias's magnum opus into English may have accounted, at least in part, for its tepid reception in the U.S.

Like all of his other work, Goffman's exploration of social emotions both reveals and conceals, so that it needs to be unpacked and clarified, line by line. Goffman's work on embarrassment/shame remains a powerful, but still largely unexplored resource for current social science. The next chapter provides a similar example, but from a later work, attempting to unpack and clarify Goffman's study of frame analysis.

Note

1. For the Maori case, see Metge (1986). The Maori word for shame is the exact equivalent of bond affect, as it will be discussed here.

CHAPTER 5

The Structure of Context
Deciphering *Frame Analysis*

THIS CHAPTER PROPOSES that Goffman's *Frame Analysis* can be interpreted as a step toward unpacking the idea of *context*. His analysis implies a recursive model involving frames within frames. The key problem is that neither Goffman nor anyone else has clearly defined what is meant by a frame. I propose that it can be represented by a *word, phrase,* or *proposition*. A *subjective* context can be represented as an assembly of these items, joined together by operators such as *and, since, if, not, then,* etc. Furthermore, this model can be combined with the recursive levels of mutual awareness in earlier approaches to consensus. The combination would represent the *intersubjective* context: it can be used to find the minimum amount of background that would allow consensual interpretations of discourse. It could also construct a chain that links discourse to the institutional level, the micro-macro pathway from word and gesture to social structure. Goffman hinted that mathematical notation might be used to represent a frame assembly. By adding levels of awareness to such notation, it could represent *social facts.* Because the use of vernacular words rather than concepts is a problem in social science, Goffman's approach has a general, as well as a particular significance.

Unlike most social science, Goffman's work complicates rather than simplifies. One of his signatures is the continuous creation of technical, rather than vernacular words. Most of his publications are rats' nests of elaborate schemes of definition and classification. Since these schemes go unused, for the most part, he apparently created terms on principle.

As indicated in Chapter 2, Goffman's basic approach seems to have been dedicated to deconstructing the *tropes* (metaphors) that rule both our society and social science. Many of our basic ideas about human conduct and experience are vernacular words, and therefore extremely vague and unclear. As already mentioned, Goffman frequently attacked the Western version of the self, implying that it was largely a social construction. He also proposed that the idea of insanity or irrationality was also only a trope, another construction of Western culture.

In the case of frame analysis, however, Goffman seems to have gone further than showing that the idea of context is merely a trope. I propose below that he also hinted at first steps toward a conceptual definition to replace the trope.

An adequate conceptual definition of context could reveal that it stands at the very center of a key problem in social science. How is it that conduct and subjective experience both reflect and generate the society in which they are embedded? How can we represent the reciprocal relationship between words and gestures in interaction, and the vast social structure/process of which they are a part? If discourse is the basement of a skyscraper, and social institutions the top floors, can one construct an elevator that goes up and down without having to get off at every floor? Goffman's *Frame Analysis,* and earlier work on consensus, suggest a step toward the solution of this core problem.

The Response to *Frame Analysis*

Frame Analysis generated an enormous response[1] (Benford and Snow 2000, 611). The *Social Science Citation Index* has more than 1800 references, making it one of the leading titles in social science. But a close reading of some of the citations suggests that Goffman's ideas have not fared well. Most of the responses have been of three kinds: paraphrase, harsh criticism, and adopting terms from frame analysis but ignoring or misconstruing Goffman's approach.

There have been many responses that go no further than paraphrasing:

> Frames are principles of selection, emphasis and presentation composed of little tacit theories about what exists, what happens, and what matters. (Gitlin 1980, 6)

Although this restatement casts the idea in different words, it is much like Goffman's definition in being a loose collection of abstract ideas with no clue as to how to organize them.

Some paraphrases seem to be misleading. As Koenig (2004) notes:

One response which seems particularly confusing is the conceptualization of frames as a metaphor, alluding to a picture frame ... While
I doubt that any metaphors are suitable for inclusion in sociological
theories, *picture* frames are definitely not a metaphor in Goffman's spirit.
His frames do not limit, but rather enable ... For Goffman and Gitlin ...
frames are indespensible for communication, they are the scaffolds for
any credible stories.

Koenig goes on to note that

Because frames consist of metaphors rather than overt conjectures, no-
torious difficulties to empirically identify frames arise ... [Koenig could
have noted that this was Gamson's (1975) chief objection also.] The
difficulty of measuring latent frames could partially explain the gradual
theoretical shift towards a conceptualization of frames as being more
actively adopted and manufactured. Entman, for example, clearly takes
this path ... [to] frame is to select some aspects of a perceived reality
and make them more salient in a communicating text, in such a way as
to promote a particular problem definition, causal interpretation, moral
evaluation, and/or treatment recommendation. (Entman 1993, 52)

Koenig's point is that, like this one, most responses to Goffman's book have
been misinterpretations, or at least, not constructive.

Critical responses are not hard to find. One reviewer complained that
Frame Analysis is too esoteric, obscure, and difficult (Davis 1975, 599-603).
Gamson (1975, 603-7) thought it was so inadequately systematized as to be
impossible to teach or research. Two of the six essays that concern frame
analysis in the Fine and Smith volumes (2000) are dismissive (Jameson;
Sharron). Both have arbitrarily decided that Goffman's scheme is static
(the title of Sharron's chapter is "Frame Paralysis!").

The other four chapters on frame analysis in the Fine and Smith
volumes (2000) are more appreciative. Maynard (Ch. 56) applies the idea
of framing to lawyers' discourse. Schmitt (Ch. 57) reviews applications of
framing ideas in many earlier studies, and suggests some new applications.
Bouissiac (Ch. 59) applies Goffman's idea of "negative experience" to the
faking of accidents in circus performances. Hazelrigg (Ch. 60) struggles
to make sense of Goffman's prose, but, it seems to me, with little success.
Indeed, none of these chapters succeed in clarifying the meaning of the
idea of frames, even the ones that apply it.

My own favorite criticism of the book is by an anonymous reviewer on
Amazon.com: "This book drove me crazy. It is repetitive and like a verbal
calculus problem that never ends." This comment struck a chord because
it pinpoints my own early reactions, and also because it notes an important

feature of Goffman's treatment, its iterative or recursive quality—boxes within boxes within boxes, etc.

I also find Goffman's verbal iterations oppressive, a kind of mechanical repetition that reminds me of some of my worst encounters with higher mathematics. Yet some type of iterative capacity might be necessary to represent the micro-macro pathway, and would be bearable in a highly compressed format. I will return to this issue below.

The Introductory Chapters of *Frame Analysis*

Goffman begins what is by far his longest (586 pp.), most complex and enigmatic book (1974) with his usual flurry of definitions and classifications.

> I assume that definitions of a situation are built up in accordance with principals of organization which govern events ... and our subjective involvement in them; frame is the word I use to refer to such of these basic elements as I am able to identify. (Goffman 1974, 10–11)

Just before this sentence, Goffman has also defined much more clearly another idea: "The term strip will be used to refer to any arbitrary slice or cut from the stream of ongoing activity ..." (10). So a strip is an excerpt from ongoing actions, but what is a frame?

One important idea is stated in the definition: frames are only a part of a still larger structure, the *definition of the situation*. The definition of the situation is the actors' largest subjective response; frames are a part of this subjective structure.

The definition above states that frames are the basis on which definitions of a situation are built, but doesn't explain what frames are. The definition is almost empty of meaning. To this point Goffman seems to be merely replacing one trope with another.

The next chapter introduces the idea of primary frameworks: "... a [primary] framework ... is seen by those who apply it as not depending on or harking back to some prior ... interpretation" (21). One use of this idea would be that physical reality is a primary framework. However, we still don't know what Goffman meant by a frame.

Chapter 3 deals with what Goffman calls "key," which he says is a central concept in frame analysis (43). By key, Goffman means "the set of conventions by which a given activity, one already meaningful in terms of some primary framework, is transformed by the participants to be something quite else" (43–44). Since this chapter begins with an extended discussion of animals playing at fighting, the meaning of key is clear: it is the set of signals that allow the animals to ascertain whether a fight is serious or only play.

However, the definition of key introduces an important new element. Before this point, framing is an individual activity. However, the definition of key concerns participants in the plural, so that keying is not just individual but unavoidably social. In order to fulfill its function, a key must then involve what Goffman elsewhere has called mutual focus of attention, or mutual awareness. This kind of mutuality has also been referred to by others as intersubjectivity, shared awareness, or attunement. I will return to this issue below.

I have proposed that although some of the definitions that form the early chapters of the book are clear, the basic one, frame, is not. The definition quoted above is casual and vague, and therefore the whole book is not clear.

There is also another problem with the early chapters of *Frame Analysis*. Goffman not only doesn't adequately explain what frames are, he also doesn't explain why we should care. What is the problem that frame analysis is intended to solve? There doesn't seem to be an answer to this question. Without understanding what frames are, and what good it will do to study them, the reader can get lost in the jumble of Goffman's complex prose.

I think that these two omissions explain most responses to the book: readers are highly critical, even dismissive; they simply paraphrase Goffman's treatment, or they misunderstand or ignore it. If Goffman had defined frames more clearly, and explained how they might be used, perhaps more readers would have responded in a constructive way.

Deciphering Frames

Goffman hinted at a direction that might be taken toward establishing a clear definition of frame, but in the middle of the book, and in passing, rather than highlighted in the introduction. In a later book he appears to have also explained the purpose of frame analysis. I will consider this issue first: the book's purpose.

This chapter began with my hunch that Goffman's book on frames might be about context. So I asked Gregory W.H. Smith, who knows as much about Goffman's work as anyone in the world, if Goffman had commented on the idea of context anywhere in his work. Smith directed me to an odd paragraph in *Forms of Talk* (1981, 67). It appears out of nowhere, like an apparition, unrelated to the text before and after. (Because of the length of the paragraph, I have numbered the last 3 sentences.)

> Commonly, critiques of orthodox linguistic analysis argue that although meaning depends on context, context itself is left as a residual category, something undifferentiated and global that is to be called in whenever, and only whenever, an account is needed for any noticeable deviation between what is said and what is meant. [2] This tack fails to allow that when no such discrepancy is found, the context is still crucial—but in

this case the context is one that is usually found when the utterance occurs. [3] (Indeed, to find an utterance with only one possible reading is to find an utterance that can occur in only one possible context.) [4] More important, traditionally no analysis was provided of what it is in contexts that makes them determinative of the significance of utterances, or any statement concerning the classes of contexts that would thus emerge—all of which if explicated, would allow us to say something other than merely that the context matters. (Goffman 1981, 67)

This paragraph occurs in Chapter 1 after 66 pages focused on low-level issues involved in discourse analysis. Out of the sea of mundane commentary, it suddenly breaches like a whale among minnows. It is followed by a paragraph stating that only Austin (1965) may have been moving toward addressing the issue of types of contexts, and then returns to the local issues in the structure of discourse.

The paragraph is extraordinary, especially the first and last sentences. The first sentence refers to one side of an issue that is so general as to apply to all social and behavioral science: his complaint about those who criticize studies that are acontextual, but without specifying what they mean by context. The last sentence goes on to imply that the idea of context could be developed beyond its status as a "residual (empty) category" by explaining the features that make it determinative of meaning, and by developing types of contexts.

The first and last sentences take aim at those who criticize acontextual studies. But sentences 2 and 3 imply that Goffman is also critical of acontextual studies, since he flatly states that *all* meaning is dependent on context. Studies that focus only on discourse, ignoring the larger context, may well misinterpret the meaning of the discourse.

Although the paragraph being discussed refers only to "orthodox linguistic" studies and their critics, it speaks to a issue that divides all social science: the gulf between quantitative methods, which sacrifice context in order to be systematic, and qualitative methods, sacrificing system in order to include as many details as possible, including those that make up the context.

Although Goffman doesn't refer to quantitative social science studies that use standardized scales, paper and pencil tests, or interview schedules, he could have included them alongside orthodox linguistic studies. All quantitative methods routinely omit most of the details that might be used to construct a context.

In upholding the crucial importance of context, Goffman also seems to be obliquely attacking Conversation Analysis (CA) and other forms of discourse analysis that focus on discourse alone, neglecting the larger setting in which it occurs. Criticism of CA and formal discourse analysis may be the subtext of the first chapter, and even the whole book.

Cicourel's Approach

There is nothing oblique about Aaron Cicourel's (1992, Chapter 11) attack on CA and discourse analysis, however. In his chapter concerning a strip of discourse between three physicians in a hospital, he shows how he constructed a context within which the discourse took place. The information he uncovered about the participants, their organizational roles, their previous exchanges, and their shared knowledge suggests how inaccurate an interpretation would be if it lacked this background, or even that it would be impossible to understand some discourse at all. The strip he highlights is phrased in technical medical terms, with most of the utterances syntactically fragmented and incomplete, as is true of most informal talk.

It is clear that this chapter is a response to acontextuality in formal studies of discourse and of conversation, since Cicourel cites specific studies of this kind (294). At least for informal talk in specialized language between equals who know each other, this study demonstrates that accurate interpretations are impossible without providing considerable contextual detail outside of the discourse itself.

In the same volume as Cicourel's chapter, Schegloff (1992) treats the issue of context by examining a strip of talk within the larger context of the whole verbal "story" of which the strip is a part. However, Schegloff doesn't take up the issue of the still larger context outside the text. The largest context for him seems to be limited to the text itself. In this way he ignores the challenge implied by Goffman, and stated openly by Cicourel.

Schegloff may be less concerned than Goffman, Cicourel, and others about context for several reasons. One would be the behaviorist tendency in the CA approach. CA doctrine is that they are interpreting only the externals, words and gestures, and not making inferences about events that occur within the speakers. Of course that is a misconception: any interpretation of human discourse involves swift and largely unconscious attributions to those involved in the discourse.

Another and more defendable source would be the nature of the discourse. It seems to me that the texts that CA tends to use are much closer to standard, formal English than Cicourel's excerpt. The speakers are often strangers, or at least equals, who are conversing about topics that are not highly specialized, with much of the necessary syntax and grammar. To the extent that the circumstances approach these conditions, to that extent less background information would be needed.

That being said, it is still true that background information is usually needed to avoid mistakes. Goffman makes this point by riffing on many variations of possible responses to the question "What time do you have?" (1981, 68–70. Some of his instances made me laugh.). His point seems to be that, at least in the case of this sentence, one can make it mean anything one wants it to mean by changing the context.

In the paragraph quoted above from *Forms of Talk* (1981), Goffman manages to be critical of both sides of the issue: he is critical both of acontextual studies, and also those who criticize these studies, because they don't explain what they mean by context. It is necessary, he says, to say something more about context than that it matters. Cicourel shows that it matters, but by providing a large amount of ethnographic detail, rather than engaging the issue of the structure of context.

Is there anyone who has gone further than J. L. Austin (1965) in defining what is meant by context? Perhaps the most extraordinary thing about the paragraph above is that Goffman doesn't refer to *Frame Analysis* (1974). It seems to me that Goffman had already developed an answer to his question himself, that the whole of the earlier book was a step toward defining the idea of context.

Before pursuing this issue, I want to note that some of Goffman's comments in the later book are puzzling. In the Introduction, in the middle of the first paragraph on the first page, referring to the chapters as papers, he states:

> All the papers (least so the first) are written around the same frame-analytic themes ... (1981, 1)

The parenthetical phrase "least so the first" is odd, since the first chapter contains the paragraph that seems to refer to what frame analysis is about, as well as other references pertinent to frame analysis. The first chapter was probably written in 1974, the same year that *Frame Analysis* was published. It is possible that Chapter 1 of the 1981 book was the first paper Goffman wrote after completing the text of the 1974 book. He had frame analysis and context on his mind at very nearly the same time. Could the left hand not know what the right hand was doing?[2]

I ask that question because the word *context* does not appear in the title of the 1974 book, nor in any of the titles of the fourteen chapters, nor in the extensive (ten-page) index. Yet it appears that the paragraph quoted above could have served as the core for the introduction to the book, and if it had, there would be much less confusion over what the book was about. Indeed, the book would have been better understood if it had the subtitle "Defining Context."

The idea that frame analysis is closely related to determinations of context comes up, in passing, in some of the responses to *Frame Analysis*. Indeed, Ronald Chenail (1995) treated context and frame as equivalent. Even so, as in the other responses, he doesn't spell out the equivalence, nor develop a detailed definition of frames. In order to find out if Goffman had defined context in terms of frames, I scanned the whole book. The word *context* is used 56 times, slightly less than once for each ten pages. All but one of his uses are casual and in passing.

On page 441 he gives an off-the-cuff definition of context in paren-thesis: "Indeed, context can be defined as immediately available events which are compatible with one frame understanding and incompatible with others." It is of interest to note that this page contains five more uses of the word *context*. Yet this definition, and his casual usage throughout the book, is exactly the kind that he ridicules as a residual category in the paragraph from *Forms of Talk* (1981, 67).

Mutual Awareness Models

Before describing the model of context that I think is implied by Goffman, it is first necessary to discuss the issue of mutual awareness. As already indicated, his discussion of keys and keying (1974, 40–82) requires mutual awareness of the participants. Both animals and humans recognize a strip as play or non-play because they are mutually aware of the key signals. Similarly, the idea of "footing," which seems to be just another word for frame (128 and passim), involves participants in mutual recognition of shifts in alignment of self and other.

The idea of mutual awareness can be identified in all of Goffman's work, though his language is evasive at times. He never states flatly, as Cooley did, that "we live in the minds of others." But most of his work seems to assume it. Certainly the most substantial chapter in *Presentation of Self in Everyday Life* (1959), on impression management, is concerned in its entirety with how we live in the minds of others (Scheff 2005; Chapter 3 in this book is based largely on the earlier article).

Furthermore, in his later work on language, the subtext implies that mutual awareness is crucial for actually understanding discourse. He chal-lenged the formal conversation and discourse analysis practice of restricting their attention to texts, without regard to the larger context. In the next to last sentence of one of his last articles, he stated:

> [In all social interaction] we find ourselves with one central obligation: to render our behavior understandably relevant to what the other can come to perceive is going on. Whatever else, our activity must be *ad-dressed to the other's mind,* that is, to the other's capacity to read our words and actions for evidence of our *feelings, thoughts, and intent.*[3] (1983a, 53, emphasis added)

The meaning of discourse is ultimately not in the text alone, but also in minds. This is a clear statement of the crucial importance of mutual awareness.

In one of my own earlier articles (Scheff 1967), I proposed a model of consensus that has a recursive quality like the one that runs through Goffman's frame analysis. The article suggested that consensus involves not only understanding the other, but also understanding that one is understood, and vice versa. Mutual awareness, I argued, involves not only a first-level agreement, but, when necessary, second and higher levels of understanding that there is agreement.[4]

As it happened, Goffman pursued a similar idea in some parts of his book (1969) on strategic interaction. Under certain conditions, as in spying operations, diplomatic and financial negotiations, and in my opinion, truly intimate relationships, it becomes necessary to be aware of higher levels of mutual awareness; that is, of mutual awareness of mutual awareness, etc. He implies that the winning spy or negotiator would be the one who is able to accurately understand a level higher than their competitor. And in my own work toward developing a concept of secure bonds or attunement that would include both true solidarity and genuine love, I propose that higher levels of mutual awareness are necessary, rather than optional components (see Chapter 7).

Finally, a similar treatment can be found in a book by the Russian mathematician Vladimir Lefebvre (1977), *The Structure of Awareness.* This book takes a step further than I or Goffman did by illustrating mutual-awareness structures graphically. Lefebvre uses both pictographs and mathematical notation. The former involves bracketing equations similar to those outlined below. As Anatol Rapoport mentions in the Preface (9), how this book, having nothing to do with Marxist doctrine, got published in the U.S.S.R. of the 1970s is a puzzle.

In addition, I wonder whether Lefebvre came up with the idea of reflexive mutual awareness independently of my model. He cites R.D. Laing et al. (1966), a brief work devoted to a recursive model of mutual awareness that preceded Lefebvre's book (1977). But he also cites his own earliest work on recursive awareness, an article (1965) that precedes the Laing et al. book.

It is possible that Lefebrve's work was based on my own (1967) model of recursive awareness. As Laing et al. (1966) indicate, their book developed from my presentation of the model in Laing's seminar in 1964. Since there were some 20 persons at my presentation, Lefebrve could have heard about the seminar from one of the persons present, or indirectly by way of others in contact with a seminar member.

Recursive Structures of Awareness

It is clear that the three treatments, by myself, Goffman, and Lefebrve, make mutual awareness recursive, since they involve repetitions of awareness of awareness. Of course actual consciousness is not always recursive. For example, there may be no recursion in the consciousness of survey respondents, who, unknown to one another, agree upon some issue. But there are also a wide variety of situations that seem to be recursive, perhaps extending to the second or even the third levels of repeating mutual awareness. Extended negotiations, spying/counterspying, and close, highly intimate relationships might extend a step or two still higher.

This idea was represented in a joking way in a popular song from the 1930s, with lyrics something like "I know, that you know, that I know, that you know ... etc., that we're in love." Although I haven't been able to find these lyrics, I am fairly sure that I didn't invent them, since I also remember the melody.

In another similar treatment, struggling to define what is meant by *perversion*, the philosopher Thomas Nagel (1979) came near to defining normal, or at least non-perverse sex in terms of recursive mutual awareness.[5] Although he does not use that term, or any of the others I have used, such as *intersubjectivity*, his definition of sexual love in terms of each knowing that the other knows one another's feelings certainly implies it:

> These [sexual] reactions are perceived, and the perception of them is perceived; at each step the domination of the person by his body is reinforced, and the sexual partner becomes more possessible by physical contact, penetration, and envelopment. (48)

The higher levels of mutual awareness in a recursive model of mutual awareness might clarify and extend Durkheim's idea (1915) of the "social facts" that individuals experience as external and constraining. He proposed that there are many areas of unspoken, taken-for-granted agreement in societies that constitute a *conscience collectif.* Although this phrase is usually translated into English as "collective conscience," it can equally as well be translated as collective consciousness, sometimes translated, albeit awkwardly, as *group mind.*

The complex cognitive structure of mutual awareness discussed here might help explain why members would experience social facts as "external." The recursive levels would insure their externality, since each individual understands them to be in the consciousness of others (Scheff 1967), and that his or her own participation in social facts or lack of it is also perceived by others.

Although Cooley, Mead, and Dewey don't engage this issue, the attribution of understandings to others can not always be pure projection, at least in the long run. As Garfinkel and writers in the CA tradition have made clear, one's understanding of the other person's utterance in one turn may be reaffirmed or challenged in subsequent turns. At least in discourse that has more than one turn, each speaker can observe signs that bear on the accuracy of his or her attributions to the other person.

This issue of the degree to which beliefs about the other(s) are pure projection turns out to be much more complicated than the CA approach has allowed. A wife who wants to believe her husband's claim that he loves her may ignore or misinterpret turns and behaviors that give the lie to his statement. The bestseller *Women Who Love Too Much* (Norwood 1985) is based on interviews with women in this situation. An example of this problem on a larger scale comes up in the politics of voter support for government. In the U.S. at this moment, it appears that a substantial proportion of voters still trust their government, even though it has proven itself not deserving of trust.

But in most cases, it would appear that the attributions that are components of social facts are not pure projections. That is, each individual's experience with others has given them external grounds for believing that their attributions are correct. To the extent that this is the case, the externality of the social fact to each individual is at least in part an objective fact, not just a projection.

At the time that my article (1967) was published, I had no way of explaining why social facts would be experienced as constraining. Subsequently, however, the sociology of emotions has suggested a possibility. If, as Lewis (1971) has proposed, the fundamental basis for genuine pride is attunement with others, and for shame, lack of attunement, then the incentive for participation in the awareness structures of social facts is not only cognitive, but also emotional.

The individual would feel powerfully constrained by social facts because he or she is rewarded by pride when participating in them, and punished by shame when not (Scheff 1988). Durkheim (1915) posited a social emotion that encourages social integration, but referred to it only as respect. In my formulation, respect is an emotional/relational correlate of the pride end of the pride/shame continuum. One is rewarded by pride to the extent that one participates, level by level, in the cognitive structure of mutual awareness, and punished by shame, level by level, to the extent that one does not. An iterative model of social facts in terms of levels of awareness would explain why social facts are experienced as external and constraining.

Personal, Organizational, and Institutional Components of Context

It would be helpful to be able to represent recursion of structures of mutual awareness in a compressed way even if, as is the usual case, there are only a few higher levels involved. But with the recursion of frames, if we are to accurately interpret informal and/or specialized discourse, and represent the micro-macro link, it becomes essential to the endeavor. Moving back and forth between the words and gestures of a strip of discourse and the personal histories, organizational settings, and social institutions they reflect and generate will require many recursive steps.

This idea can be illustrated by using the example of discourse that is at the center of Cicourel's article (1992), already mentioned above. He begins his analysis by showing only the strip of discourse that he recorded, without revealing the identity of the speakers or where they are located:

PA: Is this the one (we?) did yesterday?

IDA: No. This is the eye lady.

PA: (?)

IDA: Cellulitis

PA: Oh.

IDA: With group A strep. in shock.

PA: In shock. How about that.

IDA: I[t?] was gonna be more interesting / if she didn't

MR: / I'm (?)

IDA: have bacteremia but (laughing ...) now she's had / bacteremia so

MR: / There's a little problem / with that ... (295)

For brevity I have reported only the first 11 of the 41 lines that Cicourel presents. The question marks in parenthesis represent sounds that he had difficulty interpreting, and the slash marks (/) areas of overlap between speakers.

It is clear from this strip that there are three speakers, and that they are discussing a fourth person who is not present. Judging from the technical terms being used, one might guess that the three speakers are medical personnel, and that they might be discussing a patient. Judging from the informality, fragmentary, and incomplete nature of some of the utterances, we might also guess that the three persons are more or less equal in rank, and that they know each other well.

But beyond that, without knowing more the background, it seems impossible to understand most of the discourse even approximately, much less the fine points. For example, the strip seemingly opens with a question from PA that refers to a frame larger than the present discourse. Probably in response to a statement about a patient by IDA, PA asks: "Is this the one (we) did yesterday?"

IDA clarifies which patient he/she was referring to by saying "No. This is the eye lady." He further identifies the patient with a one-word utterance: "Cellulitis." So both speakers begin the strip assessing the other's frames, based on pre-strip occurrences, in order to identify the patient that is being referred to. This is Cicourel's point: the less we know about the larger context of discourse, the less able we are to understand it.

In establishing this idea, Cicourel goes on to indicate the identity of the four persons and their location. The three speakers are physicians, and their discussion involves a patient they have all seen in the teaching hospital where they work. Cicourel further shows that understanding this particular strip involves knowledge of earlier conversations they had about this and other patients, and about the location of the discussions in a teaching hospital, and knowledge of how teaching hospitals differ in some particulars from general hospitals. So correctly interpreting this strip involves at least five frames within what Goffman calls the "rim," the final frame the researcher uses for interpreting a strip of activity.

Interpreting Cicourel's strip of discourse requires frames that reach up to the institutional level, since the highest strip requires knowledge of a difference between teaching and other hospitals. But there are many much less complex utterances that require frames at a still higher institutional level.

The following example involves one of my own utterances. It is only two words, but understanding it requires a frame assembly, with the last frame at the level of international politics and economics. In this incident I was alone, driving my car at about 60 mph on a two-lane, undivided back road. The traffic both ways was moving very fast, most cars traveling at least 80 mph. I saw a very large SUV heading toward me at high speed, but weaving in and out of my lane. Although I couldn't be sure because of the distance and glare, it appeared that the driver might have had his head turned toward the passenger. I instantly ran my car off the road onto the shoulder, narrowly escaping being hit by the SUV as it went past me without slowing. My frames included his existence, but his didn't include mine, and he nearly ended it.

In the dust and flying rubble as my car slowed down on the shoulder, I cursed. My yell at the other driver as he passed was certainly not heard, since both of our windows were up; but I let fly without thought: "RIGHT-WING BASTARD!!!!"

To understand the meaning of my curse it is necessary to report some frames of mine in addition to the one I formed looking at the oncoming car (a car in my lane in which the driver doesn't see me). I make it a practice of driving no faster than the speed limit for several reasons. One frame is my own safety: I think fast driving is dangerous. Another frame concerns legality: I worry about getting a ticket for speeding. A third frame is that I know that fast driving is uneconomical in terms of gas consumption.

This latter frame is enclosed in turn by a fourth on a much larger scale. The incident took place after the war against Iraq began, which I presumed to be largely about oil. Like the first three frames, my political consciousness restrains my driving speed. It appears that I instantly assumed that the frames of the fast driver of the gas-guzzling SUV didn't include the national/international politics of oil, that he was as oblivious of it as he was of my car.

Note that the first two frames, safety and legality, need not be part of the frame assembly that embeds gas consumption in the large political/economic frame. These first two frames are only additive in the frame assembly.

Interpreting this brief utterance requires several orders of frames, and three points of view: mine and the other driver's at the time of the incident, and mine now, as I interpret the meaning of my utterance. To incorporate many orders of framing and several orders of mutual awareness in a way that will hold down vertigo, a compact way of representing frame/awareness structures will be needed.

Fractals

Fractal geometry represents a possible model. Andrew Abbott (2004) has defined fractals as: "... the property of recurring at finer and finer levels, always in the same form" (Abbott 2004, 250). The elegance of fractal geometry in the physical world arises because of the exact duplication of forms at different levels, with no difference except size. Snowflakes provide an example. Goethe, in his botanic studies, noted that in plants such as palms, the whorls of the trunk can be found repeated in smaller sub-units.

In his essay on disciplines (2001), Abbott applied this idea to the reproduction of conflict as represented in discourse at various levels between and within groups. But arguments over Marxism at various levels in the history of the socialist movement are similar in some ways and different in others. Certainly Proudhon's rebuff to Marx was never repeated, at least in so eloquent a form. The shape of snowflakes is elementary compared to the complexity of human discourse.

Both sides of the conflict between the Leninist and Trotskyite lines seem to have varied with each argument, depending upon context, emphasis, choice of words, overt and/or covert emotional content, etc. To use the fractal heuristic would require conceptual and operational definitions of each "line," so that the extent of variation could be noted. The same reasoning applies to Goffman's frame analysis.

Mathematical Notation

Chapter 8 of *Frame Analysis* concerns, in the main, informal bracketing that takes place in ordinary discourse. For example, to show that one is representing a person other than self, a speaker may bracket an utterance by using a flagrantly high or low voice. Men may speak falsetto to mime a woman's voice, and women *basso profundo* to mime a man's. A visual way of bracketing is by signaling quotation marks with strokes by two fingers of each hand. In the course of referring to this kind of everyday bracketing, Goffman briefly notes similar mathematical notation:

Mathematics, for example, employs the elegant and powerful device of simple typographic brackets ... [to] establish the boundaries of a strip of any length.... It is as though here all our human capacity to think and act in terms of frame were compressed and refined. ... (1974, 254–55)

In this passage, Goffman lapses from his usual detached, ironic tone, displaying what for him appears to be overwhelming enthusiasm: "elegant" and "refined." It is possible that with his eerie prescience, but without mathematical training, he sensed a possible use, but could not carry through. As indicated above, Einstein's first thoughts about relativity were completely intuitive.

Although Goffman didn't show how mathematical notation might be applied, Luiz Carlos Baptista follows up toward the end of his own essay on frame analysis (2003). Here I will follow and extend his notation. It is almost identical to Lefebvre's (1977) application to levels of mutual awareness, but slightly less complex. Baptista proposed (2003, 208) that any frame can be represented as composed of core frame, layers (laminations), and rim (the last and most complex frame):

$$F = l_{n+1} \, [l_n \cdots [l_2[l_1[l_0]]] \cdots]]$$

Where l_0 represents the core frame, F, the rim, and the other l's, zero to $n=$ represent all the layers between. It is my thesis that F, the rim, represents a model of the structure of the subjective context.

This notation will only accommodate the context inferred from a single point of view. It will need to be complicated by superscripts to represent another person or persons' point of view involved in the framing of a context.

So if I am now analyzing the frames involved in an earlier conversation I had with another person that I will call John, my present point of view could be represented by the superscript 3, my point of view at the time of the conversation by superscript 2, and John's point of view at that time by superscript 1:

$$F^3 = l^2_{n+1} \, [l_n \cdots [l_2[l_1[l_0]]] + l^1 \cdots]] + l^1_{n+1} \, [l_n \cdots [l_2[l_1[l_0]]] + l^2 \cdots]]$$

Where F^3 is the structure of the context that I will need to accurately interpret the strip of discourse.

It should be understood that all the layers within the brackets after l^2 except those with superscript 1 belong to my point of view at the time of the conversation, and those with superscript 1 represent my images of John's frames. Similarly, all of the layers within brackets after l^1, except those with superscript 2, belong to John.

If at any point during the strip the definition of the situation by either John or I changes, I must change the equation at this point. In the course of rapidly shifting frames in discourse between two persons, it may be necessary to use superscripts for each shift, rather than for the participants. With only two participants, each could be represented by some other notations, such as italics for one.

By enclosing the points of view of others within the brackets, as well as the frame layers, this notation represents structures of shared awareness, in addition to frame assemblies. In modeling more or less static awareness structures among large groups of people, as will be discussed below, the superscripts must be used for the perspective of each person. Lateral frames that don't fit into one of the assemblies can be included in each of them by mere addition.[6]

There is one more element needed if this notation is to be used to define frame structure in a way that can be taught and researched: a conceptual definition of frame. I can't find a definition in Goffman or in any of the commentary that is more than just a collection of metaphors. I have been searching the rubric "*schemas*" in the cognitive science literature, hoping to find at least an operational definition, if not a conceptual one.

B. Shanon (1990) recognizes that the term *context* is just a trope, but doesn't suggest a conceptual definition. Instead he states that contexts are mental representations that serve as premises or presuppositions. An earlier attempt was made by Ulrich Neisser (1976):

> A schema is that portion of the entire perceptual cycle which is internal to the perceiver, modifiable by experience, and somehow specific to what is being perceived. The schema accepts information as it becomes available at sensory surfaces and is changed by that information. It directs movements and exploratory activities that make more information available, by which it is further modified. (54)

Similar, if less wordy attempts can be found in Fredrick/Kenneth Bartlett (1932) and Craik (1943).[7]

It seems to me that these are the same kinds of loose definition as those used by Goffman and Gitlin. To carry my thesis forward, a frame can be defined tentatively as the statement(s) required to place and to understand a strip of activity: "on the beach," "play fighting," "an eighteenth-century drawing room," etc. Even if the actual frame is a nonverbal image, *it can be represented in verbal form as a name, phrase, or proposition*. Representing an image, like a drawing room, would be sufficiently complex to require an assembly of statements of its own.

Assembling a group of frames would require one more step, one that would indicate the relationship of each frame to the one below and above it. This could be done by use of simple verbal operators: *since, if, not, and, then,* etc.

In the example given above, some of the frames can be represented as simple propositions: to reduce risk of accident and avoid tickets for speeding, drive no faster than the speed limit; a similar proposition would represent the financial advantage of not speeding: save money on gas, wear and tear. The actual images in the interior theater of the mind may be propositions, phrases, names, or images, but may move so fast as to be outside of consciousness. The definition of frame assemblies as a series in the verbal mode is only an abstract representation, in order to slow it down so that it can be described.

The frame that involves my stereotype of a person driving an SUV too fast is complex. To represent it would require a statement with many elements: a person who is well-to-do enough not to care about the costs of an SUV, wear, tear, and fuel costs, and is either deluded, ignorant, or does not care about the political, environmental, and safety effects. The frame assembly (context) might be represented verbally in this way: *since* gasoline seems to be cause of the war, *and* is being wasted by this driver at high speed in a large SUV, *and* he is oblivious of my existence, *then* he must be a rich, oblivious, right-wing bastard.

Goffman's discussion implies that a subjective context usually involves more than a single frame. Rather it is likely to be an assembly of frames, one fitting within, or merely added to the other. The notation above, combined with the definitions of frame and operators just offered, can be taken to be a model of these assemblies.

The model suggested here spells out in detail what Goffman called "the organization of experience." Individuals and groups organize their experience of a situation by shuffling through their vocabulary of words, phrases, propositions, and images, acting as if they are joining the components with simple verbal operators, so that the situation becomes meaningful for them.

This model may enable us to build up a structure of context for any discourse, no matter how many persons, points of view, frames, and levels of awareness. In principle, we should also be able to represent the frame and awareness levels of a social fact by referring to the individual assemblies obtained from a large sample of individuals or texts.

At the moment, techniques for utilizing such a complex model do not exist since it requires that discourse be analyzed for recursive frames and levels of awareness. Perhaps such techniques could be developed most easily in an interview format, by patiently probing informants' responses about the structure of their beliefs and the beliefs of others. For example, one might try to determine to what extent the idea that the United States has a democratic form of government is a social fact. Such a study would require finding what the word *democracy* means to the informants, which will require understanding the frames they use, and the extent of mutual awareness they have of these meanings as they are held by others.

This kind of study could be a step toward resolving the key puzzle in social science, the way that actions of individuals reproduce or change society. Slang provides examples of both kinds. I learned recently that my students say "My bad" when they are acknowledging a mistake (rather than saying "Oops!" or "Sorry"). This usage doesn't reproduce language practices in the larger society, and it has not yet changed them either. But it may (or may not) someday.

Discussion

As indicated in an earlier chapter, there is a vast literature on alienation, but it has not provided a clear definition of the concept itself. Although there are many standardized alienation scales, there have been few attempts to decide, conceptually, what it is that these scales are supposed to be measuring.

Many key concepts in social science are ambiguous in a similar way. Self-esteem, perhaps the most studied topic in all of social science, seems to have a similar problem. A widely known study by Leary and Baumeister (2000) can be interpreted to mean that self-esteem scales confound both individual/relational and cognitive/emotional dimensions (Scheff and Fearon 2004).

Some key concepts, such as alienation and self-esteem, involve too many orthogonal meanings (such as individual, relational, cognitive, and emotional dimensions) to be measured by a single instrument. Others, such as irrationality, and, as already indicated, context, may be mere residual categories, conceptually empty boxes.

Conclusion

This chapter has argued that *Frame Analysis* (1974) can be read as an unpacking of the "global and undifferentiated" idea of context. A further step is taken to combine Goffman's recursive layers of frames with the recursive levels of mutual awareness proposed in earlier models of consensus, to model both subjective and intersubjective context. This approach could enable us to find the minimum amount of background information that would allow consensus as to accurate interpretations of strips of discourse, no matter how many persons, frames, and levels of awareness. It might also help us to construct a chain that links discourse, in the moment, with the highest institutional levels of society, the micro-macro pathway. This essay takes a further step toward representing a recursive model of frame and awareness structures with mathematical notation.

Many scholars of the human condition are likely to complain that this approach will lead to infinite regress. Indeed, among scholars in the humanities, it is often taken for granted that contexts involve infinite regress: "Everything is the context for everything else." This issue seems to be the main concern of many of the discussions of "mutual knowledge" (Clark and Marshall 1981; Sperber and Wilson 1995).

On the contrary, this chapter proposes that this is an empirical, not a conceptual problem. Context can be defined in an orderly way, enabling the representation of the least numbers of levels of frames and awareness that are needed to make valid interpretations of strips of discourse. This same method could lead the way to showing, in the moment, how the microscopic world of words and gestures is linked to the largest social structures. One of the social institutions in our society, mental health and illness, will be the subject of the next chapter.

Notes

1. My brief review of the responses is based in part on Koenig's (2004) lengthy one.

2. Manning (1980, 261) refers to the "almost systematic evasiveness" of Goffman's writing. It's possible, however, that Goffman was not evasive, but so alive with intuitive ideas that he was unable to explicate parts of his own work. Recall also the discussion of "reticence" in Chapter 1.

3. Once again, I am indebted to Greg Smith for calling my attention to this passage.

4. There is by now a considerable literature on this issue under the rubric "mutual knowledge" (Clark and Marshall 1981; Sperber and Wilson 1995).

5. Ronald de Souza called this essay to my attention.

6. Lefebrve's (1977) notation includes lateral frames.

7. The last three references were suggested to me by Keith Oatley.

Chapter 6

Building an Onion
Alternatives to Biopsychiatry

THIS CHAPTER CONCERNS THE RELATIONSHIP between psychiatry and its subject, the lives of persons named as patients. If psychiatry is to advance, it will need to consider not only the microworld of biology and individual psychology, but also many other worlds, notably, emotions, relationships, and social systems. Goffman and others have made contributions to this idea. Human beings are complex, involving a welter of interacting components; they have emotional and relational systems, and they are connected to social systems. One way that might help us understand these systems would be to examine inner and outer dialogue in great detail. Labeling theory, which concerns the social system, could be integrated with a theory of emotional/relational dynamics that occur within and between people. An analysis of verbatim dialogue from a single therapy session is used to illustrate this idea.

To simplify her task, when God created an onion, she may have started with the inner core working outward. However she could have also started with the outer skin, working inward. Even if you are not God, it doesn't seem to matter which way you start, as long as you realize an onion is not just the inner core, nor is it only the outer skin.

Biopsychiatry has so far sold the public on the idea that the inner core of mental disorder is all that matters. When the psychoactive drugs first appeared, they seemed to work miracles. But as with other miracle drugs in the past, it has become clear that most of their effect was placebo, and that there were damaging side effects for many.

In the last ten years there has been a strong trend in objective studies of the effects of psychoactive drugs. First let me clarify what is meant by "objective" studies. By now (2005) it has become clear that most of the published clinical trials had been financed by drug companies and that this circumstance compromised the findings. These studies departed from objectivity in many ways. For brevity, only two need be mentioned. First, it is now known that in most of studies, in order to get funding, the researchers had given control over publication to the funding companies. What happened was that companies did not allow negative or insignificant results to be published.

A second serious bias was testing only short-term effects, typically for a one month. Since drug companies did not favor testing effects over longer terms, few were carried out. But all the findings of these few show a rapid decrease in effectiveness over the longer term. By one year virtually all drug effectiveness has disappeared. These findings strongly suggest that most drug response is entirely placebo effect.

Over the years, there have been many objective (not funded and controlled by drug companies) studies suggesting that the effect of psychiatric drugs is largely placebo. For example, Irving Kirsch et al. (2002) analyzed an FDA (U.S. Food and Drug Administration) database of 47 placebo-controlled, short-term clinical trials involving the six most widely prescribed antidepressants approved between 1987 and 1999. Unlike published results, the database included "file drawer" studies, i.e., trials that failed but were never published.

What Kirsch and his colleagues found was that 80 percent of the medication response in the combined drug groups was duplicated in the placebo groups, and that the mean difference between the drug and placebo effects was "clinically insignificant." Other objective (non–drug-funded) studies have been published showing similar results for most of the psychoactive drug types. This study would seem to supply a much more accurate picture of drug effectiveness because it includes results that are rarely tapped in published results. Similarly, the studies of long-term effects (one year or more) also need to be included, since the picture they provide is quite different from studies of short-term (typically one month) effects.

Most psychological approaches also make a similar assumption: the cause and cure lie within the individual. The labeling theory of mental disorder (Scheff 1966; 1983; 1999) proposes the opposite metaphor, that the societal reaction, one of the outermost skins of the onion, is more important. But the truth of the matter is that most of onion, the great bulk, is neither core nor skin. We need to move beyond both tropes into the layers and layers that make up a complex phenomenon.

Goffman was the first contributor to what came to be known as the anti-psychiatry movement, along with T. S. Szasz and Ronald D. Laing, whose publications appeared independently in roughly the same time period. The psychiatrist Peter Breggin became the leader of the movement later with publication of his *Toxic Psychiatry* (1991) and many subsequent books. Their work challenged the assumption of individual causation that underlay most approaches in psychiatry and psychology. Goffman's (1957; 1958) description of the totalitarian form of mental hospitals implied social, rather than individual causation. Various strands of his critique were brought together in *Asylums* (1961a), one of Goffman's most widely read books, and continued more indirectly in the sizeable part of his work that deconstructed the individualistic idea of the self.

Szasz (1961) was the most widely read debunker of the idea that psychiatry should be based solely in the biology and psychology of the individual. Like Goffman and Laing, he is a rebel attacking the status quo. In this light, Szasz has taken what seems to be an absolutely necessary first step, directly challenging the trope of "mental illness." If he hadn't existed, we would have had to invent him.

Goffman's publication on total institutions (1958) is actually earlier than Szasz's. Like Szasz's work, it is a head-on challenge to the trope of mental illness. But Szasz's collision course with the idea of mental illness was clearer to the public at large than Goffman's because Szasz employed no concepts, only vernacular words. By comparison, Goffman's description of the characteristics of total institutions and the self is esoteric, if not arcane.

But writing in the vernacular, even after 44 years, and many books, has a significant drawback. Szasz has not offered any detailed alternative to the idea of mental illness. The same is true of Breggin; his work involves a complete rejection of the use of psychiatric drugs and electroshock, but offers no detailed alternative theory. Art and science, as Blake urged, need to deal with minute particulars. It might carry matters further if we are able to establish a model alternative to the myth of mental illness, one that encompasses the minute particulars of social, psychological, and biological reality. Most of this chapter will concern one such alternative, a theory of the emotional/relational world as it has been described in Retzinger (1991), Scheff and Retzinger (1991), and Scheff (1994; 1997c).

Szasz attacked a ruling metaphor in Western society. His target is the idea of mental illness, and its planetary system of concepts (symptoms, patients, hospitals, drugs as medicine, etc.). He was the first psychiatrist to forcefully and repeatedly propose that these concepts didn't fit reality. Since our society still accepts the myth of mental illness, Szasz's attack is ongoing.

Accompanying Szasz's challenge to the idea of mental illness was the work of others in the anti-psychiatry movement: Goffman, Laing, my own labeling studies, and many others. These studies, like Szasz's, were a step forward. But they were not sufficiently detailed, nor theoretically framed, nor broad enough to even start to solve the problem.

Although Goffman's approach is sociologically sophisticated, it does not contain a theory of mental illness. He defines his terms only conceptually, without attention to the problem of goodness of fit to actual instances. Laing's work is psychologically sophisticated, but involves even less conceptual development. Szasz, as indicated, uses no concepts; his approach is stated entirely in vernacular words. This approach makes it easy for anyone to understand, even laypersons. But it is much too narrow and simplified to use for analyzing and understanding real cases, each of which is apt to be quite complex, like most human conduct.

Szasz's reliance on vernacular words reduces his theory almost to caricature. For example, the terminology that Szasz suggests as an alternative to "psychiatric symptoms" is "problems in living." If adapted, this usage might help to de-stigmatize the sufferers. But the phrase is much too broad a tool for understanding, since it encompasses an impossibly vast realm of problems, like any residual category. Unrequited love, over-extension of one's credit, and the physical incapacities of old age are certainly all commonly encountered problems of living, but they are seldom seen as symptomatic of mental illness.

If Szasz had used the terminology "residual problems of living" (problems which don't have conventional names), he would have come close to my own approach to the problem. In any case, a social theory requires statements of explicit hypotheses, all of which are couched in terms of conceptual and operational definitions. Labeling theory was a step in this direction, but it was too narrow to grasp the intricacies of emotion and relationship that generate functional and dysfunctional behavior.

Another obvious limitation of labeling theory was that it dealt only with the societal reaction to residual deviance, but not with the origins of that deviance. It acknowledged bypassing the question of the biological, psychological, and other causes of symptoms. In some ways, this orientation was a strength. There are cases labeled as mental illness that do not involve symptoms. When I was observing mental hospitals in the 1960s in the U.S., England, and Italy, many of the patients were unhoused seniors who wintered in mental hospitals. In Stockton State Hospital in 1959, I found that there were many patients with no detectable symptoms who were being used as unpaid laborers. The vast laundry facility was run almost entirely by these patients, most of whom were Chinese immigrants to the U.S. who had never learned English. Perhaps symptoms had led to their original hospitalization. But, in any case, symptoms no longer played a role in their "mental illness."

But the single focus of labeling theory on societal reaction is also a weakness, a sin of omission. If human beings are going to live in peace, we need to better understand the origins of symptoms such as depression, delusion, compulsion, and obsession, for example. These symptoms can be found not only in mental patients, but scattered throughout whole societies, even among ruling elites. They are an important aspect of the human condition, and need to be further investigated.

Closer to the dialogue that is to be analyzed in this paper, labeling theory had a further weakness: it focused almost entirely on the formal, official societal reaction to residual deviance. As the dialogue excerpted from Rhoda's psychotherapy session below suggests, there is also an informal process of labeling that takes place within families, before there has been a formal reaction from officialdom. Informal labeling in the family, it would seem, is the next layer down of the onion, right beneath an outermost layer, the formal societal reaction. In his extraordinary paper on the growth of paranoid symptoms in individuals inside of organizations, Lemert (1962) provided an earlier description of the process of informal labeling and its effects. But labeling is only one of many processes that occur within interpersonal and intrapersonal worlds.

The Emotional/Relational World

This chapter points toward a dynamic model of the emotional/relational world (ERW), a world that is mostly disguised and ignored in Western societies. My approach requires integration between the social sciences in general, and between sociology and psychology in particular. It points toward a theory that could lead to the empirical study of actual social relationships, the core subject of all of the social sciences and a crucial subject for the mental health professions. With emotions and relationships routinely disguised and ignored in Western societies, social sciences that also ignore the ERW serve a conservative function, helping to preserve the status quo in the emotional/relational world.

But with the exception of one essay focused on embarrassment (1967), Goffman portrayed emotions mostly by implication. There is considerable embarrassment, shame, humiliation, and disgust implied in his representations, but it is seldom made explicit. In this respect, his methods of dealing with emotion are similar to the usual treatment of emotion in Western societies, disguising or misnaming.

Goffman was the poet and prophet of the emotional/relational world (see all of his books, but especially 1959; 1963a; 1963b; 1967). Yet his work is only a beginning since it doesn't involve an explicit theory, method, or systematic evidence. Another problem concerns his treatment of emotions. Compared to *most* social science descriptions, his are three-dimensional, dealing not only with thought and behavior, but also with feeling (see Chapters 2 and 3).

On the other hand, there are fruitful studies that go much deeper than Goffman into the minute particulars of human relationships, revealing whole new realms of filigree in human conduct. One such study is by Labov and Fanshel (1977), two linguists. They conducted an exhaustive micro-analysis of the first 15 minutes of a psychotherapy session. They analyzed not only what was said but also *how* it was said, interpreting both words and manner (the paralanguage). They based their interpretations upon microscopic details of paralanguage, such as pitch and loudness contours. Words and paralanguage are used to infer inner states: intentions, feelings, and meanings.

With such attention to detail, Labov and Fanshel were able to convey unstated *implications.* Their report is evocative; one forms vivid pictures of patient and therapist and of their relationship. One can also infer aspects of the relationship between Rhoda (the patient) and her family, since Rhoda reports family dialogues. Labov and Fanshel showed that the dispute style in Rhoda's family is indirect: conflict is generated by nonverbal means and by implication.

Indirect inferences, from a dialogue that is only reported, are made in order to construct a causal model. Obviously, in future research they will need to be validated by observations of actual family dialogue. It is reassuring, however, to find that many aspects of her own behavior that Rhoda reports as occurring in the dialogues with her family are directly observable in her dialogue with the therapist. For example, the absence of greeting occurs in both her report and in the dialogue with the therapist. Rhoda's covert aggression in the dialogue she reports with her aunt can be observed directly in the session itself (not included in this chapter but discussed in Scheff 1989).

The limitation of this and similar language-based studies is the opposite of that of the work of Szasz, Goffman, etc. Where their work was largely theoretical, the linguists, working inductively, had too little theory. In particular, they had no theory of emotion and relationship dynamics that would help them interpret the family conflict they reported. The following commentary on earlier study, and on the transcript of the session itself, is a beginning step in this direction.

The Feud between Rhoda and Her Family

Labov and Fanshel (1977) carefully examined an audiotaped dialogue between Rhoda, a nineteen-year-old college student with a diagnosis of anorexia, and her therapist. Rhoda had been hospitalized because of her rapid weight loss, from 140 to 70 pounds. When her therapy began, she weighed 90 pounds. At five feet, five inches in height, she was dangerously underweight.

Her therapy sessions took place in New York City in the 1960s. Rhoda lived with her mother and her aunt, Editha; her married sister also figures in the dialogue. The session that was analyzed by Labov and Fanshel was the twenty-fifth in a longer series which appeared to end successfully. The therapist reported improvement at termination. At a five-year follow-up, Rhoda was of normal weight, married, and raising her own children.

Labov and Fanshel focused on the web of conflict in Rhoda's life, mainly with her family and to a lesser extent with her therapist. The conflict was not open but hidden. The authors showed that Rhoda's statements (and those she attributed to the members of her family) were packed with innuendo. They inferred that the style of dispute in Rhoda's family was indirect: although the family members were aggressive toward each other and hurt by each other, both their aggression and their hurt were denied.

Labov and Fanshel's method was to state explicitly as verbal propositions what was only implied in the actual dialogue. This method proposed a cognitive structure for the conflict in Rhoda's family: it translated utterances, words, and paralanguage into purely verbal statements. The set of verbal statements served as a compact, clarifying blueprint for a dense tissue of complex maneuvers that were otherwise difficult to detect and understand.

In addition to this type of analysis, Labov and Fanshel also used another. Following the lead of the therapist, they pointed out cues that were indicative of unacknowledged anger. To reveal this emotion, they used verbal and nonverbal signs: words and paralanguage (such as pitch and loudness). Hidden challenges in Rhoda's family were made in anger and resulted in anger. Rhoda's therapist made explicit reference to this matter in the session: "So there's a lot of anger passing back and forth" (5.27[c] [The numbers refer to the Rhoda transcript, in Labov and Fanshel 1977, 363-71.]). There were also myriad indications of unacknowledged anger and other emotions in the session itself.

The Role of Anger and Shame in Protracted Conflict

Emotions were not central to Labov and Fanshel's study, but they are to mine. Building upon their assessment of cognitive conflict, and their (and the therapist's) analysis of anger, I show shame sequences in the session that were apparently unnoticed by both patient and therapist. Labov and Fanshel frequently noted the presence of embarrassment and of the affect they called "helpless anger," but they made little use of these observations. Nor did they comment on the labeling of Rhoda in her family.

My study leads me to conclude that labeling occurs at two different levels—the informal and the formal. At the informal level, labeling is quite symmetrical: Rhoda labeled and blamed Aunt Editha and her mother just as much as they labeled and blamed her. The family members casually insulted each other almost constantly. In some sentences, several different insults were implied at once. As Labov and Fanshel pointed out, conflict seemed to be endemic in this family.

At the surface level of labeling, however, there was no symmetry whatever. The mother and the aunt were just as violent with their insults, threats, and rejections as Rhoda, but it was only Rhoda who was physically violent: she tried to starve herself. In contrast to the constant verbal violence, Rhoda's overt violence was highly visible; her dangerously low body weight bore ostensible witness to her self-assault. Although the verbal violence seemed to be visible to the therapist and was documented by Labov and Fanshel, it was invisible to Rhoda and her family. If labeling theory is going to lead to further understanding of mental illness, it will need to take a new direction, to make visible what has hitherto been invisible: violence in the microworld of moment-to-moment social interaction.

I use two excerpts (Labov and Fanshel 1977, 364, 365) to illustrate this point. The first involves Rhoda's relationship with her mother; the second, with her Aunt Editha. The first excerpt occurred early in the session—it deals with a telephone conversation that Rhoda reported. The mother was temporarily staying at the house of Rhoda's sister, Phyllis. (Since pauses were significant in their analysis, Labov and Fanshel signified their length: each period equals .3 seconds.)

Excerpt 1

1.8 R.: An-nd so—when—I called her t'day, I said, "Well, when do you plan t'come *home*?"

1.9 R.: So she said, "Oh, why!"

1.10 R.: An-nd I said, "Well, things are getting just a little too *much*! [laugh] This is—i's jis' getting too hard, and ... ... I—"

1.11 R.: She s'd t'me, "Well, why don't you tell *Phyllis* that!"

1.12 R.: So I said, "Well, I haven't talked to her lately."

Rhoda, a full-time student, argues that she can't keep house without help. Her mother puts her off by referring her to Phyllis. The implication—that the mother is there at Phyllis's behest—is not explored by the therapist. Rather, she asks Rhoda about getting help from Aunt Editha. Rhoda's response:

Excerpt 2

2.6 R.: [a] I said t'her (breath) w-one time—I asked her—I said t'her.

[b] "Wellyouknow, wdy'mind takin' thedustrag an'justdust around?"

2.7 R.: Sh's's, "Oh-I-I—it looks *clean* to me," ...

2.8 R.: [a] An' then I went like *this*.

[b] an' I said to her, "*That* looks *clean* t'you?"

[It appears that at this point, Rhoda had drawn her finger across

a dusty surface and thrust the finger into Editha's face.]

2.9 R.: [a] And she sort of... *I* d'no-sh'sort of gave me a funny look as if I—hurt her in some way,

[b] and I mean I didn' *mean* to, I didn' *yell* and *scream*.

[c] All I did to her was that "*That* looks clean to you?"...

The therapist persists that Rhoda may be able to obtain help from Editha. In a later segment (not shown), Rhoda denies this possibility.

Rhoda's Helpless Anger toward Her Aunt

I will begin analysis with the least complex segment, the dialogue that Rhoda reports between herself and her aunt (2.6–2.9). Labov and Fanshel showed a thread of underlying anger, anger that is denied by both parties.

Rhoda has explained prior to this excerpt that dust "bothers" her—that is, makes her angry. The authors argue that the request that Editha "dust around" (2.6[b]) involves an angry challenge to Editha's authority, a challenge that neither side acknowledges. It assumes that the house is dusty, that Editha knows it, that she has ignored her obligation to do something about it, and that Rhoda has the right to remind her of it. Although Rhoda uses "mitigating" devices, speaking rapidly and casually, she ignores the etiquette that would have avoided challenge.

(Labov and Fanshel wrote, "The making of requests is a delicate business and requires a great deal of supporting ritual to avoid damaging personal relations surrounding it" [96].) To avoid challenge, Rhoda might have begun with an apology and explanation: *"You know, Aunt Editha, this is a busy time for me. I need your help so I can keep up with my schoolwork." (As customary in linguistics, an asterisk (*) is used to denote a counterfactual, a hypothetical statement not made in the actual dialogue.) Rhoda's actual request is abrupt.

Editha's response is also abrupt: "Oh-I-I—it looks clean to me ... " She has refused Rhoda's request, intimating inaccuracy in Rhoda's appraisal. The ritual necessary to refuse a request without challenge is at least as elaborate as that of making one. Editha could have shown Rhoda deference: *"I'm sorry Rhoda, but ... ," followed by an explanation of why she was not going to honor the request.

Rhoda's response to what she appears to have taken as an insult is brief and emphatic: She contemptuously dismisses Editha's contention. She wipes her finger across a dusty surface and thrusts it close to Editha's face: "*That* looks *clean* to you?" Labov and Fanshel noted the aggressive manner in Rhoda's rebuttal: she stresses the words *that* and *clean,* as if Editha were a child or hard of hearing. They identified the pattern of pitch and loudness as the "Yiddish rise-fall intonation": *"By *you* that's a *monkey* wrench?" implying repudiation of the other's point of view. "If you think this is clean, you're crazy" (202). Rhoda's response escalates the level of conflict: she has openly challenged Editha's competence.

Finally, Rhoda describes Editha's response, which is not verbal but gestural: she gives Rhoda a "funny look as if I—hurt her in some way." Rhoda denies any intention of hurting Editha, and that Editha has any grounds for being hurt: "I didn't *yell* and *scream*," implying that Editha is unreasonable.

Labov and Fanshel noted the presence of anger not only in the original interchange but also in Rhoda's retelling of it. The nonverbal signs, they said—choking, hesitation, glottalization, and whine—are indications of *helpless anger*: Rhoda "is so choked with emotion at the unreasonableness of Editha's behavior that she can not begin to describe it accurately" (191). Helpless anger, the authors wrote, characterizes Rhoda's statements *throughout the whole session*: "she finds herself unable to cope with behavior of others that injures her and seems to her unreasonable" (191).

Labov and Fanshel further noted that her expressions of helpless anger were "mitigated":

> All of these expressions of emotion are counterbalanced with mitigating expressions indicating that Rhoda's anger is not extreme and that she is actually taking a moderate, adult position on the question of cleanliness. Thus she is not angered by the situation, it only "bothers" her. Even this is too strong; Rhoda further mitigates the expression to "sort of bothers me."

Mitigation in this instance means denial: Rhoda denies her anger by disguising it with euphemisms.

What is the source of all the anger and denial? Let us start with Rhoda's helpless anger during her report of the dialogue. Helpless anger, according to Lewis (1971), is a variant of shame-anger: we are ashamed of our helplessness. In retelling the story, Rhoda is caught up in a shame-anger sequence: shame that she feels rejected by Editha, anger at Editha, shame at her anger, and so on.

Helpless anger has been noted by others besides Lewis. Nietzsche (1887) referred to a similar affect ("impotent rage") as the basis for resentment. Max Scheler (1912) used Nietzsche's idea in his study of *ressentiment*—pathological resentment and prejudice. Mardi Horowitz (1981), finally, dealt with a facet of helpless anger under the heading "self-righteous anger."

Rhoda and her family are caught in a web of *ressentiment*, to use Scheler's term. Each side attributes the entire blame to the other; neither side sees their own contribution. As Labov and Fanshel showed, one of Rhoda's premises is that *she* is reasonable, and the members of her family are unreasonable. The reported dialogues with her family imply that the family holds the opposite premise: that *they* are reasonable, but she is unreasonable.

The theory that will be developed here suggests that the dialogue between Rhoda and Editha is only a segment of a continuous quarrel. Since it is ongoing, it may not be possible to locate a particular beginning; any event recovered is only a link in a chain (Watzlawick et al. 1967, 58). Starting at an arbitrary point, suppose that Rhoda is "hurt" by Editha's failure to help. That is, she feels rejected, shamed by Editha's indifference, and angry at Editha for this reason. She is also ashamed of being angry, however. Her anger is bound by shame. For this reason it cannot be acknowledged, let alone discharged.

Editha may be in a similar trap. Rhoda is irritable and disrespectful, which could lead to shame and anger in Editha. She could experience Rhoda's hostility as rejecting, arousing her own feelings of helpless anger. Reciprocating chains of shame and anger on both sides cause symmetrical escalation.

The Impasse between Rhoda and Her Mother

Excerpt 1, as reported by Rhoda, may point to the core conflict. It is brief—only three complete exchanges—but as Labov and Fanshel showed, it is packed with innuendo. My analysis follows theirs, but expands it to include emotion dynamics.

Rhoda's first line, as she reports the conversation, is seemingly innocuous: "Well, when do you plan t'come home?" To reveal the unstated implications, Labov and Fanshel analyzed understandings about role obligations in Rhoda's family. Rhoda's statement is a demand for action, disguised as a question. They pointed out affective elements: it contains sarcasm (1977, 156), criticism (161), challenge (157, 159), and rudeness (157). The challenge and criticism are inherent in a demand from a child that implies that the mother is neglecting her obligations.

Implicit in their comments is the point I made about Rhoda's approach to her aunt. It would have been possible for Rhoda to request action without insult, by showing deference, reaffirming the mother's status, and providing an explanation and apology. Rhoda's request is rude because it contains none of these elements.

Rhoda's habitual rudeness is also indicated by the absence of two ceremonial forms from all her dialogues, not only with her family, but also with her therapist: any form of greeting, and the use of the other's name and title.

Does Rhoda merely forget these elements in her report of the dialogues? Not likely, since they are also missing in the session itself. Labov and Fanshel tell us that the transcript begins "with the very first words spoken in the session; there is no small talk or preliminary settling down.... Instead the patient herself immediately begins the discussion." Rhoda neglects to greet the therapist or call her by her name and title. Since Rhoda is junior to the therapist, her aunt, and her mother, the absence of greeting, name, and title is a mark of inadequate deference toward persons of higher status. Rhoda's casual manner is rude.

The mother's response is just as rude and just as indirect. According to Rhoda's report, her mother also neglects greetings and the use of names. Like Rhoda's aunt, she neither honors the request nor employs the forms necessary to avoid giving offense. Rather than answering Rhoda's question, she asks another question—a delay that is the first step in rejecting the request.

Labov and Fanshel stated that the intonation contour of the mother's response ("Oh, *why*") suggests "heavy implication." They inferred: *"I told you so; many, many, times I have told you so." (When Rhoda gives a second account of this dialogue [4.12–4.15], she reports that the mother actually said, "See, I told you so.") What is it that the mother, and presumably others, has told Rhoda many times? The answer to this question may be at the core of the quarrel between Rhoda and her family.

Whether it is only an implication or an actual statement, the mother's I-told-you-so escalates the conflict from the specific issue at hand—whether she is going to come home—to a more general level: Rhoda's status. Rhoda's offensiveness in her opening question involves her mother's status only at this moment. The mother's response involves a general issue. Is Rhoda a responsible and therefore a worthwhile person, or is she sick, mad, or irresponsible?

Labeling, Shame, and Insecure Bonds

At a superficial level, the mother's I-told-you-so statement involves only Rhoda's ability to function on her own. As can be seen from Rhoda's complaints at the end of the session, however, this implication is symbolic of a larger set of accusations that Rhoda sees her mother and sister as leveling at her: she is either willfully or crazily not taking care of herself, starving herself, and she doesn't care about the effect of her behavior on her family. Her family's basic accusation, Rhoda feels, is that she is upsetting them, but she doesn't care. Rhoda formulates this accusation at the end of the transcript.

Excerpt 3

T.: What are they feeling?

5.26 R.: ... that I'm doing it on purp—like, I w's- like they ...well-they s-came out an'tol' me in so many words that they worry and worry an' I seem to take this very lightly.

To Rhoda, the mother's I-told-you-so epitomizes a host of infuriating, shaming charges about her sanity, responsibility, and lack of consideration. Note particularly that the labeling process to which Rhoda refers here is not explicit; it occurs through innuendo.

The labeling of Rhoda by the other family members, and its emotional consequences, underlies the whole family conflict. Yet it can be detected only by a subtle process of inference, understanding the meaning of words and gestures *in context,* in actual discourse. Both the theory and the method of the original labeling theory were too abstract to detect this basic process.

Rhoda responds (in 1.10) not to the underlying implication of her mother's evasion but to the surface question, "Why do you want to know?" Because, she answers, " ... things are getting just a little too much ... " The key element in Rhoda's response is the *affect.* Labov and Fanshel stated that the paralanguage (choked laughter, hesitation, glottalization, and long silence [170]) is an indication of embarrassment (171). Rhoda responds to her mother's accusations by becoming *ashamed.* The shame sequence that is described is a marker for stigmatization that is otherwise hidden behind polite words.

Rhoda's shame may indicate that she feels that her family's charges have some basis, or that the implied rejection leads her to feel worthless, or both. Since no anger is visible at this instant, it is either absent or bypassed. The verbal text, however, suggests that Rhoda is feeling shame and guilt. She is acknowledging that she needs her mother—a need she has repeatedly denied in the past. She may feel that she is at fault for this reason.

Labov and Fanshel contrasted the force of the mother's response with the weakness of Rhoda's comment (at 1.10). The mother says, "Why don't you tell Phyllis that?" Labov and Fanshel stated that the hesitation and embarrassment that characterize 1.10 are absent from this response. It is a forceful rejection of Rhoda's claims and, by implication, a criticism of Rhoda for even making the request. The mother's emotional response to Rhoda's embarrassment is not simply unsympathetic; it is aggressively rejecting. From the emotional standpoint, Rhoda's back is to the wall. She is trapped in the helpless role of the blamed, with her mother as the aggressive blamer.

The analysis of shame in this dialogue points to an otherwise hidden issue. At this moment we can see that in her family, Rhoda has literally no one to whom she can turn. She is at odds with her aunt. We know from her reports of her sister's comments that Rhoda and she are also in a tangle. No father is mentioned. Rhoda and her family are in a perpetual war, a war hidden beneath the surface of conventional discourse. All of Rhoda's bonds are threatened, yet she has no way of understanding her complete alienation.

The stage is set for violent emotion and/or violent behavior: for mental illness (Rhoda appears to be delusional about her eating and body weight), murder, or suicide (in this case, self-starvation). That the potential for suicide arises when individuals have no one to whom they can turn was proposed by Sacks (1966) on the basis of his analysis of calls to a suicide prevention center. The repression of shame and the bondlessness that is its cause and effect can give rise to primary deviance in the form of mental illness, murder, or suicide.

In Rhoda's response (1.12), she continues in the role of the one at fault: "Well, I haven't talked to her lately." Her mother has defeated her on all counts. She has refused Rhoda's request without the ritual that would protect Rhoda's "face"; she has implied a victory over Rhoda ("I told you so") that undercuts Rhoda's status, and she has criticized her for making an inappropriate request to the wrong person.

Rhoda appears to feel too baffled, upset, and helpless for an angry counterattack. Her anger at her mother may feel too shameful to countenance. It is reserved for lesser targets: her aunt, her sister, and the therapist. Her mother's rejection, with the implied threat of abandonment, could be the basic source of Rhoda's shame.

Even to the casual reader, the mother's tactics are transparent. Why is Rhoda so baffled by them? Why didn't she use a response like the one suggested by the authors: *"Oh, come off it, Ma! You know it's really up to you when you come home, not Phyllis. Get off my case!"

Rhoda's ineptness may be due to her intense shame, evoked beginning with the first question, asking her mother for help. In this instance the massiveness of the unacknowledged shame is befuddling almost to the point of paralysis.

In the overt form of shame, one is so flustered that speech is disrupted, with inaudibility, repetition, stuttering, and fragmentation. Even though she is only reporting the dialogue, Rhoda's speech shows many of these markers. Bypassed shame, on the other hand, may disrupt one's ability to think clearly, forcing one into a holding pattern, repeating set responses not particularly appropriate to the moment (Scheff 1987). This dialogue suggests that Rhoda is overwhelmed with both kinds of shame.

At the heart of the quarrel is a series of threats between Rhoda and her mother. As in all interminable quarrels, it is not possible to identify the first link. I begin with Rhoda's basic threat, without signifying that it came first: *"If you don't stop shaming me, I will starve myself!" Her mother's basic threat: *"If you don't stop shaming me, I'll abandon you!"

The abandonment threat in this case is literal: the mother has left Rhoda to stay with her other daughter. Normally, the threat of abandonment would be largely symbolic; carrying out a threat of abandonment is probably rare. But whether it is real or symbolic, threats of abandonment may be the key link in the causal chain.

This chain has potentially lethal force because none of it is visible to both participants. There are four links: (1) Rhoda's shame in response to her mother's behavior toward her; (2) her threat to starve herself; (3) the mother's shame in response to Rhoda's behavior; and (4) her threat to abandon Rhoda. Rhoda is aware of none of these links. Nearest to her awareness is the mother's threat to abandon her, and next, the shaming by her mother. Rhoda is unaware that her mother is shamed by Rhoda's aggressive and self-destructive behavior, and she denies that she is starving herself. The mother is aware of only one link: Rhoda's threat to starve herself. Because of this awareness, she talks to and about Rhoda in code, not daring to mention Rhoda's threat. Her shame over Rhoda's behavior, her own shaming of Rhoda, and her threat to abandon Rhoda are apparently not experienced by her.

The driving force in the quarrel is not the anger that was interpreted by the therapist but the shame in the field between Rhoda and her family. The anger in this family is both generated and bound by shame. Rhoda experiences her mother's threat of abandonment and her mother's anger as shaming. The mother experiences Rhoda's threat of self-starvation and Rhoda's anger as shaming. The symmetry is complete: each side is threatened and shamed by the other, and each side can see only the other's threat.

The system of threats and hidden emotions is comparable to that preceding conflict between nations (Scheff 1994). Each side feels its credibility would be diminished by backing down in the face of threat. Each side therefore escalates the level of threat. The resulting emotions have no limit, unless outside mediation occurs or shame is dispelled. "War fever" may be code language for collective shame-rage spirals. Chapters 9 and 10 will also deal with spiraling emotions in warfare.

The theory advanced here attempts to explain the emotional sources of mental illness, and the excessive force of the societal reaction to mental illness, the roots of primary and secondary deviance. Rhoda and her family are caught in an interminable conflict that is driven by triple spirals of shame and anger within and between the disputants. For brevity, I have not included my (1989) analysis of the transaction between Rhoda and her therapist, but because of its relevance to the argument, I provide a brief summary.

Although Rhoda attacks the therapist surreptitiously, using the same tactics she uses against the authority figures in her family—her mother and her aunt—the therapist is too wily to become enmeshed in them. She gets angry, but she doesn't attack Rhoda back, as Rhoda's mother and aunt do. By avoiding enmeshment in the family conflict, the therapist is able to form a secure bond with Rhoda, leading ultimately to a successful course of therapy.

Research in the labeling tradition suggests that therapists like this one are probably rare. Therapists and other agents outside the family often become enmeshed in family conflicts, usually siding with the family against the patient. Murray Bowen's (1978) seminal analysis of family systems implies this course. Several earlier case studies illustrate the enmeshment of the outside agents on the side of the family (Retzinger 1989; Scheff 1966; 1987).

Conclusion

This chapter has proposed a dynamic model of estrangement within the emotional/relational world. I have analyzed dialogue from a therapy session that suggests how Rhoda, the patient of record, became estranged from her mother and other members of her family. The labeling of Rhoda as the problem was based, it seems, on unacknowledged shame. Rhoda and her family failed to acknowledge the cycle of rudeness and rejection that created shame for all sides. Rather than acknowledge shame, the mother and the aunt resorted to verbal violence against Rhoda. But Rhoda reciprocated not only with verbal violence against her family, but also with physical violence against herself, self-starvation.

Applying two unrelated theories (labeling and shame/anger theory) to a single case illustrates how some of the interior layers of the emotional/relational onion might be constructed. Biopsychiatry, on the one hand, and discourse analysis, on the other, can work from the bottom up to create further layers. Labeling theory, perhaps combined with other social/political/economic analyses, can work from the top down. We have a long way to go if we are to create a whole onion, but we must give it a try.

To illustrate one of the new directions advocated here, I will give one last example of concept development. The field of social work has been showing an interest in extending psychiatric diagnoses to include social dimensions in addition to individual ones. James Karls and his associates (1994) have been attempting to modify the *Diagnostic and Statistical Manual* (DSM), the bible of practicing psychiatrists, by adding social dimensions that have never been included in the DSM.

The PIE system proposed by Karls et al. implies two social systems in the DSM: the subject's system of social roles (family, work, and other interpersonal roles.) and any of six larger social systems (economic, educational, etc.) in which he or she is involved. This initiative seems to be a step in the right direction, toward overcoming the individualistic bias in the DSM. However, the Karls proposal still seems to focus on individuals rather than considering the new dimensions to be independent aspects of the situation in which diagnosis occurs.

A more radical break with the labeling aspects of the DSM would be to establish the role and social system dimensions as independent axes, so that what is being classified is not only the individual, but the social context. The new DSM might then have only two major axes, one individual, one social and situational:

1. Individual: Physical and psychological dimensions.
2. Social: family, neighborhood, community, and societal dimensions.

One outcome of such a system would be a move toward classifying functional and dysfunctional families, neighborhoods, communities, and nations. For example, a school environment in which the strong get away with bullying the weak could be rated as dysfunctional independently of the individual being diagnosed. Similarly, any or all of the social systems that foster racism, sexism, homophobia, blind nationalism, etc., could also be rated as dysfunctional.

Such a scheme would raise conceptual and research issues not usually addressed. For example, the whole problem of how individuals can be functional even though involved in dysfunctional interpersonal and/or social systems is only hinted at in current discussions of "resilience." The classification of solely individual dysfunction leads to the neglect of this kind of question. A whole new system of diagnosis is needed that integrates the DSM with interpersonal and social system diagnosis.

CHAPTER 7

What Is This Thing Called Love?

The Three A's: Attachment, Attunement, and Attraction

> Learning to love differently is hard,
> It hurts to thwart the reflexes
> of grab, of clutch; to love and let
> go again and again, as we make and unmake in passionate
> diastole and systole the rhythm
> of our unbound bonding, to have
> and not to hold, to love
> with minimized malice, hunger
> and anger moment by moment balanced...
> Marge Piercy (1980), "To Have without Holding"

AS ALREADY DISCUSSED IN CHAPTER 2, Goffman sought to deconstruct our vernacular language about self and society. Although he didn't articulate it clearly, as Gouldner did (see Ch. 2) , Goffman seemed to understand that ordinary language serves to maintain the status quo, and to thwart understanding of ourselves and the massive problems faced by individuals and groups in modern societies. Since Goffman didn't deal with love, in his manner this chapter will attempt to deconstruct conventional usage and offer a tentative definition of love as a concept. These two steps can serve to further our understanding of basic human relationships, and prepare the way for approaching problems of collective conflict in the later chapters.

It will be proposed here that the way love is used in ordinary language, especially in English, serves to hide and disguise the nature of human relationships, and the fundamentals of cooperation and conflict between individuals and between groups. In particular, if we are going to understand the meaning of social integration, that is, of solidarity and alienation, we will need to define both love and hate so that these concepts can be linked to other crucial social science ideas.

Both love and hate are emotions that seem to have escaped Goffman's notice. While this chapter will try to remedy that omission by providing a conceptual definition of love, the next chapter will propose a definition of hate. Attempting a clear definition of love might seem a fool's errand. Not only must one contend with a great mass of popular and scholarly writing, but, much more difficult, one must overturn vernacular, commonsense meanings. In terms of scholarship, I am just adding one more approach to the vast number of existing ones. But opposing the commonsense definition is bucking a mighty consensus. Most people, in their heart of hearts, believe in the vernacular meaning, no matter how contradictory, ambiguous, and confusing. Might as well stop the wind, or hold back the tide. Nevertheless, if we are to understand our relationships, it might be worth the effort.

Defining Genuine Love

I define *non-erotic love* as a combination of attachment and attunement (mutual and accurate identification, one with the other), the two A's. *Romantic love* also has these same two components, as well as a third, sexual attraction, which adds up to three A's. Like attraction, attachment is a physical bond. It is completely involuntary, beginning in infancy. But attunement, *shared identity/awareness,* is a psychological and emotional bond. These components can provide a definition of romantic love and non-erotic love much less ambiguous than the vernacular meaning, a *concept* of love.

Attachment gives a physical sense of a connection to the other. The most obvious cues to attachment are: (1.) Missing the other when they are away, and experiencing contentment when they return. (2.) Loss of the other invokes deep sadness and grief. Another less reliable cue is the sense of having always known a person whom we have just met. This feeling can be intense when it occurs, but it also may be completely absent.

Feelings of attachment or loss are not continuous, but they are much more stable than attunement, which varies from moment to moment. The attachment component accounts for an otherwise puzzling aspect of "love" in its vernacular sense: one can "love" someone that one doesn't even like. A popular song (1931) evokes this kind of "love":

> I don't know why I love you like I do,
> I don't know why, I just do.
> I don't know why you thrill me like you do.
> I don't know why, you just do.
> You never seem to want my romancing.
> The only time you hold me
> Is when we're dancing.
> I don't know why I love you like I do.
> I don't know why, I just do.

The lyrics of many songs suggest the same idea: "I don't like you but I love you. Seems that I'm always thinking of you" (Smokey Robinson 1963). One is attached despite one's self and regardless of the other's behavior, no matter how rejecting. Attachment, like hunger, thirst, and sexual desire, is at root a physical reaction.

Attachment gives the lover a sense of urgency, even desperation. Furthermore, attachment is like imprinting in non-human creatures; it occurs very early in infancy, and may last a lifetime. It is attachment that makes loss of a loved one profoundly and unavoidably painful. After such a loss, one may suffer grief for many months or years. Grief is the price that we pay for lost attachment.

When we lose a loved one, we may be in great pain, off and on, for a long period of time. This process is biologically based on genetic inheritance. It cannot be completely avoided. But it can be very long, months or years, or shorter, depending upon the intensity of the attachment and the completeness of *mourning*. If one completes what Freud called "the grief work," the work of mourning, the amount and duration of pain may be lessened considerably. On the other hand, the pain of loss can go on forever if mourning is absent or incomplete, giving rise to a syndrome known as "unresolved grief."

As Parkes ([1988] 1998) has indicated, modern societies do not recognize the necessity of mourning at any length, and therefore produce, to a large degree, unresolved grief. Our individualistic ethos maintains that we are all self-contained, not recognizing how dependent we are on others, especially those to whom we are attached. After a loss, a person who cries for any length of time, more than a month or so, is often discouraged from doing so by those around her or him. Such attitudes interfere with mourning, which is always necessary because attachment is genetically based. The common practice of immediately prescribing drugs is particularly insidious, since they usually numb the very emotions that need to be felt and resolved.

Mourning may involve working through other emotions in addition to grief, such as fear, anger, guilt, and shame. But grief is usually the most massive and central of the emotions. For that reason crying is always necessary to complete the mourning process. This idea turns out to be somewhat more complex than it might seem at first, since only a certain type of crying is cathartic (Scheff 1979). That is, cathartic crying requires distance from the grief, and is therefore not entirely painful. One has the sense of being both deeply connected to the pain, but also, at the same time, somewhat detached from it. By the same token, when one is entirely caught up in one's grief, the crying one does is extremely painful, and does little to help with the mourning process.

These niceties about crying, however, are lost on most people in our society, who think of any kind of crying as unseemly, and to a large extent, unnecessary for adults. This reaction is particularly strong for men. Most children are socialized to view crying as unmanly, rather than a natural and necessary response to loss. By the time a boy is seven or eight years old, he has suppressed tears to the extent that they are usually not available to him.

Both men and women in Western societies develop routines for automatically suppressing emotion, but these routines are more widespread and automatic in men. Most of these routines involve following the example of one's father, unthinkingly. But boys also quickly learn that indications of fear are apt to be seen as cowardly, embarrassment/shame and grief as signs of weakness. These emotions rapidly disappear from one's repertory of feeling. A boy who cries easily risks embarrassing his parents and being ostracized by other boys.

In modern societies, the whole attachment system is therefore disrupted, especially for men, but for women also, but to a lesser extent. By early or mid-adulthood, the majority of people in Western societies are suffering from unresolved grief to varying degrees.

Links between Attachment and Attunement

As already indicated, attachment is a physical system, and attunement, a psychological one. This is not to say that the two systems are completely unconnected. Attachment can find new objects based on clear or obscure similarities with an early attachment figure. This process has been described in psychoanalysis as "transference."

Transference may link attachment and attunement. For example, most people become deeply attached to their country of birth. Since smell or other physical characteristics of one's native land are probably not a primary source of patriotism, it could arise from transference of the feelings one has an infant and small child for one's parents. Most citizens more or less blindly admired and obeyed their parents as children, and as adults more or less blindly admire and obey their government.

Attunement

States of attunement, unlike attachment, vary from moment to moment. There is a dialectic of closeness and distance, reaffirming not only the union, but also the individuality of each member of the pair. The idea of the love bond as involving both continuous attachment and a balance between self and other solves a critical problem in the meaning of love. The bestseller *Women Who Love Too Much* (Norwood 1985) describes continuing relationships with husbands who are abusive of wife or children, or both.

The women profess that they can't leave these men because they love them too much. Since the word *love* is used so broadly in vernacular English, this usage is perfectly proper. But these kinds of relationships fail the test in terms of the way love is being defined here, because they lack balance between self and other. The husband is overvalued; the wife undervalues herself and/or the children. The wives are engulfed with their husbands. In these cases, the word *love* serves as denial of pathological dependency and/or passivity.

In terms of the idea presented here, these wives are at least attached to their husbands, and may also be sexually attracted to them. But it is clear that they are not attuned, in the sense of equally representing self and husband in their thinking and feeling. The husband counts too much, the wife too little. If, as proposed here, genuine romantic love involves a combination of attachment, sexual attraction, and attunement (equality of mutual awareness and identification), a relationship in which the wife is dependent on the husband in this way clearly fails the test. She overidentifies, valuing the husband's viewpoint much more than her own.

Attunement involves balancing the other's viewpoint with one's own, being both accurately aware of the other's viewpoint and one's own, and identifying with both viewpoints equally. Accurate awareness rules out infatuation as pseudo-love: one is attracted not to the real person, but to one's own inner fantasy, a mere projection onto the other person.

Balanced mutual identification means that each person thinks and feels as the other person does, valuing them as much as one's own thoughts and feelings, but no more and no less. One doesn't dismiss nor devalue the other's experience relative to one's own, nor does one dismiss or devalue one's own experience relative to the other's. The women who loved too much (Norwood 1985) gave up important parts of themselves in order to be loyal to their husbands. The men, on the other hand, devalued or dismissed the experiences of their wives and children relative to their own.

The idea of attunement can be applied to relationships at the macrolevel, as well as between individuals. For this reason it will play a central part in Chapter 11, on nationalism. Like the men whose wives loved them too much, nationalistic majorities overvalue their own viewpoints, and undervalue those of other nations, creating "us and them." Typically they also idealize their leaders and neutralize or vilify the viewpoints of leaders of other nations. The idea of attunement offers a precise idea of solidarity: neither idealizing one's own group and leaders, nor vilifying other nations, but considering both fairly and accurately.

Employing love as a concept rather than a vernacular word can help in the understanding of both interpersonal and societal relationships, since it can serve to differentiate genuine love and genuine solidarity from other forms of relationships. Combinations of attachment, attraction, and the three levels of attunement result in eight possible kinds of "love" (see Table 7.1, p.118). But only one kind represents Love as it is defined here. The other seven combinations represent affects that are often confused with love. This confusion, as mentioned above, may help to hide the alienation between individuals and between groups that is characteristic of modern societies.

New Directions

To the extent that the definition of love proposed here is an advance over other definitions, what practical application might it have? One implication concerns the possibility of change in each of the three underlying dimensions. The first two, attachment and attraction, are largely involuntary and constant. They are more or less given and fixed. But the third parameter, degree of shared identity and awareness, may be open to change through skillful communication.

Communication creates a bridge between persons. In a love relationship it can increase shared awareness and balance shared identity so that it is roughly equal on both sides, over the long run. That is, although one partner might be valuing the other's experience more (or less) than her own in a particular situation, momentary isolation or engulfment could be managed over the long term so that the experience of each partner, on the average, is equally valued in the relationships. This issue comes up continually, especially in marriage: the dialectic between being two independent persons and being a we: "I-ness" and "We-ness."

Partners seldom complain about too much "we-ness," although it is just as much of a problem as too little. It is customary to interpret engulfment with another person as closeness, or with a group as loyalty or patriotism. An eminent person I met at a party told me "I am a patriot; I do whatever my country tells me." But engulfment leads to problems down the road.

Unless both parties can contribute their own unique point of view, a kind of blindness ensues that inhibits cooperation and decision making.

On the other hand, too little "we-ness" is usually seen as a problem. A now divorced friend told me that the last straw was when her husband forgot he was supposed to meet her when her ocean liner docked. She said "I was never in his head." Isolation between partners is highly visible, at least to the one whose point of view is not being valued.

A second issue that is dependent on effective communication is shared awareness. Skillful communication and observation can lead to revealing the self to the other, and understanding the other. This issue is particularly crucial in the area of needs, desires, and emotions. By the time we are adults, most of us have learned to hide our needs, desires, and feelings from others, and to some extent, perhaps, even from ourselves. We develop automatic routines that obscure who we are. Long-term love relationships require that these practices be unlearned, so that we become *transparent* to our partner and to ourselves. Unlike attachment and attraction, frequent and skillful communication can improve the balance in shared identity, and increase shared awareness.

Especially in arguments and quarrels, it is crucial to use "I" messages, revealing one's own motives, thoughts, and feelings, rather than attributing them to the other person. This practice usually diminishes the intensity and length of conflict. On the other hand, the opposite practice, attributing negative motives, thoughts, and feelings to the other, usually increases it.

The practice of "leveling," being *direct* but *respectful* (Satir 1972), is a step toward effective communication. It is easy enough to be respectful without being direct, or direct without being respectful. But respectful assertiveness is a stretch for most of us. By using these and other communication practices, love, which is usually thought of as given, may be increased.

One final issue, the degree of attunement, needs further discussion. The definition of love offered to this point has not specified one issue that is quite important for practical reasons. How near to exact equality must the empathy and identification of each partner with the other be to qualify as love? All that has been said so far is that the amount should average out, over the long term, to near equality. But how near?

Exact equality of empathy between partners might exist in a few moments, but even there it would be rare. Usually one partner is more empathic than the other, in most of these moments, and therefore over the long haul as well. In terms of my definition, does this mean that the more empathic partner loves more? Yes, the definition requires that. But it doesn't eliminate the possibility of compensatory actions of other kinds in the relationship.

One such move could involve what might be called secondary attunement. If the less empathic partner becomes aware that he is understood better by his partner than he understands her, he can

Table 7.1 Love and Its Look-alikes: Non-erotic "Love"

Attunement (shared identity and awareness)	Self-focus	Balance	Other-focus
Attached	1. Isolated obsession	2. LOVE	3. Obsessive idealization
Not attached	4. Isolated interest	5. Affection	6. Idealization

compensate in other ways. For example, by listening longer to her than she does to him. Direct attunement is important in a relationship, but it is by no means the whole story, just as attachment and attraction are not the whole story either. Adult relationships are so complex that the three A's provide only a preliminary and tentative definition of love, to stimulate discussion.

Six Kinds of "Love"

Table 7.1 is a graphic representation to help visualize the kinds of non-erotic "love" not included in the new definition. It helps clarify two of the three basic dimensions and how they give rise to a definition of Love and its look-alikes.

Of the kinds of non-erotic "love" represented in this table, only one represents Love as it is defined here: #2. The other five cells represent affects that are often confused with love. This confusion, as already mentioned, may help to hide the painful separation that is characteristic of our society. Discussion of the seven types of pseudo-love can help to flesh out the idea embedded in the proposed definition.

Parental feeling toward an infant usually develops into non-erotic, one-way Love (cell 2). The parents will be strongly attached to the infant at the moment of birth, and the infant to the parents and other caretakers, but Love means not only attachment, but also attunement. Very early in the infant's life, however, the caretaker can learn to understand aspects of the infant's experience, by accurately interpreting body language and cries (Stern 1977). Perhaps during the first week, the caretaker is able to experience one-way, non-erotic love toward the infant.

Granting that strong attachment between infant and parent begins at birth, the infant cannot return the Love of the parent because it is unable to become cognitively and emotionally attuned to the parent. The parent and other caretakers must teach the infant how.

Some of this process has been described by Bruner (1983), as indicated in Chapter 3. The mother holds the doll in front of the baby's face, saying "See the pretty dolly." Her intention is only to teach the name of the object. But inadvertently, she is also teaching the child joint attention (attunement). After many repetitions, since the child sees that the mom is looking at the dolly and referring to it, the child senses that the doll is not only in its own mind, it's also in the mom's mind. Completing this process takes many years. Children vary considerably, but at some point between the third and eighth year, the child becomes able to take the role of the parent to the point that it becomes interdependent, rather than dependent.

But the beginnings of mutual attunement seem to occur long before the development of language. Tronick et al. (1982) have documented the exchange of smiles between infant and caretaker after only several months. Quite properly, according to the definition of love offered here, they refer to this process as "falling in love." From the moment of birth, the infant and the mother are intensely attached. Exchanging of mutual glances and smiles begins the other component of non-erotic mutual love, attunement. The infant and caretaker must learn to look, then look away, rather than stare. When both learn to smile in response to the look, they are taking the first step toward Love, because each senses the feeling of the other.

The cells in Table 7.1 can also represent romantic love if the component of sexual attraction is added. With this change, then cell #2 would represent one-way romantic LOVE. Perhaps the emotion of the Helen Hunt character toward the Jack Nicholson character in *As Good As It Gets* is of this type. She is evidently attracted and attached to him, and is able to share his point of view. But since he is unable to share hers, her Love for him is not returned. The affect he holds for her might represented by #1. With sexual desire added, this cell could be named isolated desire or infatuation. He is apparently attached and attracted to her, but is trapped within himself, to the point that he is not sufficiently aware of her thoughts and feelings.

Another variation on this kind of relationship is represented in *Remains of the Day*. The butler (played by Anthony Hopkins) is very competent in his job, but his emotions are completely suppressed. He is attracted to the house manager (played by Emma Thompson) and she to him. But they cannot connect because his emotional blankness rules out attunement. She cannot understand his feelings because he hides them.

Non-erotic affection (#5) is characteristic of most stages of effective psychotherapy. In the film *Good Will Hunting*, Will, the patient, doesn't understand or identify with Sean, the therapist (played by Robin Williams) until a session near the end of their meetings.

But Sean rapidly learns to understand Will. He shows his understanding in the crucial session. Sean knows from Will's dossier, and from his disclosures, that Will suffered brutal physical abuse as a child. Sean tells Will, "It's not your fault." This phrase, when repeated many times, breaks down Will's resistance to disclosing his emotions. Will has said nothing about feeling that the abuse was his own fault. Because of his experience as a therapist, Sean is able "to read Will's mind." That is, to be attuned with Will in the sense of identifying with him and understanding even those feelings which are hidden.

In most successful therapies, the patient becomes highly attached to the therapist, but without understanding the therapist, #4 (isolated interest) or #6 (idealization), depending on the patient's style of relating.

An instance of #5, non-erotic affection, but toward a group of persons, is represented in the climatic scene of the extraordinary French/Danish film *Babette's Feast*. The film takes place in 1869, after a wave of repression in France. Babette, a world-class French chef, is in political exile. Her husband and children have been killed, and she herself was in danger. A mutual friend has arranged for her to be taken in as a cook by two elderly sisters in a small village in Denmark. Her thoughts and feelings are completely unknown to the sisters and the villagers. Ordinarily, she prepares the simple food for the sisters that is customary in their village. But when she wins a lottery, she uses all of the money to prepare a feast, a last chance to be an artist, to bring to the village the wonder of art.

The villagers hugely enjoy the feast, but except for one outsider, they have no idea what they are being exposed to, nor for that matter, who Babette is and the great art she represents. Babette's understanding of the villagers, and their lack of awareness and understanding of her, gives the episode of the feast a poignancy that is both humorous and tragic.

It has been claimed (Goddard 1951; Evans 1960; Scheff 1979) that shared awareness (and its absence) among the characters within a play, and between the audience and the characters, is the key feature of all drama: it is what provides drama in the theatre. Evans (1960) calls misunderstandings "discrepant awareness." I (1979) have proposed that discrepant and shared awareness are the fundamental components of "distance" in drama: aesthetic distance, like the attunement in genuine love, involves a balance in the audience's perspective, being equally involved and detached from the drama.

Cell 1 characterizes most cases of intense jealousy, a pseudo-love. Jealousy, like infatuation (to be discussed below) often is mostly fantasy. In Shakespeare's play *The Winter's Tale,* King Leontes needed no Iago to spur his jealousy, nor even any indication that his queen (Hermione) desired another. It was entirely a fantasy. The king was not attuned with Hermione, although she was with him, a failure of mutual attunement.

The core emotions in jealousy derive from the response to real or imagined rejection (shame) by the loved one, and anger toward the rival. If there is attachment (in cell 1), jealous desire is obsessive. If there is little attachment (#1 or #3), there is still sexual desire but little or no obsession. The key to overcoming jealousy may lie in the way the shame component is managed. If it is acknowledged freely, both shame and anger will be diminished. But if the shame is not acknowledged, as is especially the case with most jealous men, the shame and anger may spiral out of control, as represented by Leontes in *The Winter's Tale,* and in "crimes of passion."

One-way desire without attachment or attunement is represented in #4 and #6. A man who desires a particular prostitute, but is not attached or attuned, would be an example. If she were not available, he might desire another equally. #1 and #3 represent the situation in which he becomes attached to her, adding obsession to his desire for her. In the film *Pretty Woman,* as in many others, at first the character played by Richard Gere is only attracted to the prostitute played by Julia Roberts, as in #4. As he gets to know her, he also realizes that he misses her when they are apart, as in #1. Finally he marries her, although the degree of his attunement with her is not clear. As in most commercial films and novels, little evidence is offered about the degree of attunement.

Infatuation

Most laypeople and many scholars think of infatuation as a rehearsal for love, or at least marriage, as suggested in most romantic films. However, as already indicated in Chapter 4, there are other possibilities. It seems to me that it is more likely that an infatuation will continue at that level, with the same or different persons. Infatuation, with or without attachment, seems to be much more common than genuine love.

Obsessive, non-erotic idealization is represented in #3 and #1. In families, a child may idealize one or both parents or a sibling, and be so attached that this person or persons occupies their attention. Idealization of kin is only one half of an important pattern in many families. The other half is vilification. Often there is a triangle in which two persons idealize or vilify another family member. A common pattern is a coalition between the child with one parent against the other. Vilification and idealization both create havoc in the family.

This pattern is represented in Shakespeare's *King Lear,* but it takes the form that the king mistakenly idealizes his two older daughters but vilifies his youngest. Since the two older daughters flatter him for their own ends, and the youngest refuses to because she is direct and honest, the play shows how he is made to suffer because of his obliviousness.

Number 3 represents non-attached idealization. In a group of friends, one may idealize one or more of the friends. With sexual attraction #3 represents light infatuation. Mutual infatuation seems to occur often among high school and college students, judging by their comments. Since both parties fear rejection, it may not lead to an actual contact.

It is important to emphasize the difference between romantic infatuation and Love, since the two are often confused, even by scholars of romance. Woody Allen's film *The Purple Rose of Cairo* has a scene that is emblematic of this kind of desire. The heroine, played by Mia Farrow, is a constant filmgoer. To escape from her husband's brutality, she has been spending her spare time in the movie house, viewing a romantic film over and over. She "falls in love" with one of the characters, played by Jeff Daniels. She is only mildly surprised when he jumps out of the screen to talk to her. She is telling her friend how wonderful he is: kind, gentle, attentive, etc. The friend says, "But Mary, he isn't real." The Mia Farrow character answers, "You can't have everything."

Infatuation can involve both attachment and attraction, but there is insufficient attunement. As is the case with Mia Farrow's character, the desire is less for a real person than for an imagined one. Attunement requires contact with the real person, so that one can understand their thoughts and feelings. Infatuation requires very little contact, or even none. Indeed, contact with the real person may reveal that she or he has thoughts and feelings that are unwelcome, and bring an end to desire.

Number 1 can represent mutual obsession where there is attachment. This arrangement usually leads to conflict if the two parties frequently interact and/or depend on each other. To the extent that each focuses on self rather than other, little learning takes place in the relationship; they bounce off each other like billiard balls. Number 4 represents a similar situation, but without obsessive attachment, the conflict may be at a lower level of frequency and intensity. How these relations are played out depends to a large extent on the style of response by the other party.

Number 5 represents a relationship that might be unusual: non-erotic, mutual attunement without attachment. Perhaps there are friendships like this. One is fond of another whom one also understands, but without urgency. Perhaps there are marriages or affairs in which the two parties understand and are attracted to each other, but with little attachment, as in #5. Again, how this relationship proceeds will be dependent on the response style of the other party.

Number 3 comes closest to representing the relationship between Cathy and Heathcliff in *Wuthering Heights*. Judging from the portrayal of them in the novel, they are obsessively and erotically engulfed with each other. This idea of requited "love" can also be found in many other novels and in the lyrics of popular songs. Similarly, one-way, obsessive, erotic infatuation is often called love in novels and popular songs.

Another similar combination is unrequited romantic love. Perhaps the love of the Helen Hunt character toward the Jack Nicholson character in *As Good As It Gets,* already mentioned above, is of this type. She is evidently attracted and attached to him, and is able to share his point of view. But since he is unable to do the latter, her love for him is not returned. Like an infant, he cannot partake of and value her point of view as much as his own. The affect he holds for her might be called obsessive desire. He is apparently attached and attracted to her, but tends toward self-focus, rather than balance between self and other. This cell also characterizes most cases of intense jealousy, which is also a pseudo-love.

The Effect of Hidden Emotions on Relationships

Most of the affects that I have referred to as pseudo-love may be generated by the denial of specific emotions, such as grief, anger, and especially shame. Chapter 3, on looking-glass selves, provided an explanation of why a certain kind of shame is an especially crucial impediment to genuine love.

What I call the pride/shame conjecture has three parts: (1.) All interaction with others, even imagined interaction, requires us to see ourselves from the point of view of the other. (2.) But seeing ourselves from the point of view of the other generates either pride or shame/embarrassment. (3.) For that reason, the issue of managing these emotions is present in most human experience.

If they are managed by shunting them aside, as they usually are in Western societies, they disrupt the experience of other emotions. *Unacknowledged shame/embarrassment often leads to either hostility or withdrawal* (Lewis 1971; Scheff 1990; 1994; 1997c; Retzinger 1991; Tangney and Dearing 2002), which in turn impedes or deflects the experience of love. This idea will be applied in Chapter 9 to the examination of hypermasculinity, both in its scholarly form and reflexively, in Goffman's life and work.

A scene in the film *Big* provides a humorous example of the way both love and shame/embarrassment may be masked with hostility. In the film Tom Hanks plays the part of a thirteen-year-old boy who is magically living in the body of a grown man. In one scene, a grown woman is trying to convey her attraction to him, but initially Hanks's character doesn't understand. When it finally dawns on him that it means that she likes him, Hanks laughs and gives the woman a playground shove.

The way that young boys are socialized to hide love, embarrassment, or shame behind hostility and aggression is captured in this harmless moment. But it is less funny in the actions of street gangs and presidents of nations. This issue is taken up more fully in Chapters 9 and 10. In modern societies, both men and women tend to routinely lose track of their emotions, creating a crisis of alienation.

Any kind of relationship that involves attachment, attunement, or attraction to any degree, no matter how much hostility or withdrawal are involved, is seen in an alienated society as preferable to no relationship at all. But this kind of vagueness obfuscates and confuses. As one step toward decreasing our confusion, a narrow definition of love may help.

Can the three dimensions of love be measured, or at least identified in discourse? The two physical variables, attachment and attraction, would not pose a problem. But identifying the degree of shared awareness and identity would. There is a large literature on what is called "Interpersonal Perception" that might be one place to start. The difficulty with these studies is that they are mostly static, and cannot be used to give dynamic assessments of the state of the bond. There are also by now some studies of "I-ness and We-ness" in relationships which might be more immediately helpful.[1]

Conclusion

This chapter has suggested that the mindlessly broad definition of love in modern societies is a defense against feeling the painful emotions generated in the emotional/relational world. The notion that love is sacred and/or indescribable can also function to defend ourselves against the pain of loss, separation, or alienation.

The narrow, explicit definition of genuine love proposed here might help uncover the emotions disguised by vernacular usage, and the kinds of dysfunctional relationships that are hidden under the many meanings of love. The next chapter takes up a parallel issue that Goffman didn't deal with. What is the meaning of hate and its cognates and near kin in current usage, and what should it be?

Note

1. S. Carrere et al. (2000) offer an empirical approach to mutual identity. K. D. Fergus and D. W. Reid (2001) supply a theoretical one.

CHAPTER 8

Hatred as Shame and Rage?

THIS ESSAY OUTLINES THE PRELIMINARIES to a theory of hatred, showing how it could be generated in individuals and groups. I propose that hatred is the vernacular name for hidden shame/rage sequences. One elemental source of hatred is the shame and rage of not belonging, forming groups that reject the group(s) rejecting them. The culture of such groups generates techniques of neutralization that encourage hatred and mayhem. One level is rage between individuals, generated by damaged bonds. There are also social and cultural conditions that give rise to collective hatred and rage. Finally, I review what is known about the opposite of hatred, seeking forgiveness through apology. In the last section, I discuss possible steps toward forgiveness and reconciliation.

Dictionary definitions of hatred focus on hostility as the key component.

> Hatred: 1. To feel hostility or animosity toward. To detest. 2. To feel dislike or distaste for: I hate washing dishes...
> Animosity: Bitter hostility or open enmity; active hatred. (*American Heritage Dictionary* 2000)

The inclusion of animosity in the definition is important because it emphasizes the intensity that is usually involved in hatred, counteracting the scaling down of the word in everyday, non-conflict situations, as in encounters with dirty dishes. The definition of animosity includes both bitter hostility, an attitude that may or may not be expressed, and open enmity.

The key to the intensity or bitterness of hatred could be an emotion that is a hidden component of rage and aggression: unacknowledged shame or humiliation. One way to deal with the feeling that one has been rejected as unworthy is to reject the rejector, rather than to blame one's self as unworthy. This is the process that will be discussed below as a technique of neutralization, but in the relatively new language of emotions, instead of being framed entirely in cognitive and behavioral terms.

Hidden, covert shame, in combination with either hidden or overt rage, may be the primary components of hatred. The first step is to discuss intense rage. An immediate problem in making this argument persuasive is the difficulty of describing in words the experience of rage and other compelling emotions. When readers are sitting in the comfort of their study, feeling more or less safe and secure, it will take some effort to help them visualize the intensity of "war fever," or of the feelings that lead to massacres on a vast scale. The intensity and primitiveness of fury beggars verbal description. How is one to convey intense feelings with mere words? Here I will resort to archaic literature, where this difficulty was dealt with by florid exaggeration, so that the words could point the reader toward the intensity of the actual feelings. These words, I take it, are not meant to describe outer reality, they are far too gross, but instead, to convey inner, experiential reality, the objective correlative, as T.S. Eliot called it, of a fit of rage.

There are indications in primitive epics of warfare that warriors worked themselves into paroxysms. It is known that in early times Irish warriors fought naked, with nothing but a sword, running and screaming at a high pitch, casting terror into the enemy. Here is an example from a twelfth-century Irish epic, "The Tain" (cited in Cahill 1995):

> [Cuchulainn then] went into the middle of them and beyond, and mowed down great ramparts of his enemies' corpses, circling completely around the armies three times, attacking them in hatred. They fell sole to sole and neck to headless neck, so dense was that destruction. He circled them three times more in the same way, and left a bed of them six deep in a great circuit, the soles of three to the necks of three in a circle round the camp.... Any count or estimate of the rabble who fell there is unknown, and unknowable. Only the names of the chiefs have been counted.... In this great Carnage on Murtheimne Plain Cuchulainn slew one hundred and thirty kings, as well as an uncountable horde of dogs and horses, women and boys and children and rabble of all kinds. Not one man in three escaped without his thighbone or his head or his eye being smashed, or without some blemish for the rest of his life. And when the battle was over Cuchulainn left without a scratch or a stain on himself, his helper or either of his horses.

This passage tries to convey intense fury by exaggeration, since it is unlikely that a single warrior, no matter how powerful, could have stamina enough to wage such wholesale destruction.

I propose that certain emotions in sequence, and the social and cultural settings that generate these emotions, are key causes of the kind of intense hatred that leads to rage and violence. Most social science writing on violent conflict assumes a "realist" or materialist perspective, that the real causes of human conduct always involve physical, rather than social and psychological reality. But eliminating emotional and relational elements as causes of violence may be a gross error. I am not arguing that material conditions are unimportant, only that violence is caused by a combination of physical and social/psychological elements. I will consider hatred first at the level of individuals, then at the collective level, showing how both hatred and violence are products of unacknowledged emotions, which are in turn generated by alienation and by cultural scripts for demonizing purported enemies.

This is another example from "The Tain" (Cahill 1995) describing the outward appearance of a warrior in a fit of rage:

> The first warp-spasm seized Cuchulainn, and made him into a monstrous thing, hideous and shapeless, unheard of. His shanks and his joints, every knuckle and angle and organ from head to foot, shook like a tree in the flood or a reed in the stream. His body made a furious twist inside his skin, so that his feet and shins and knees switched to the rear and his heels and calves switched to the front. The balled sinews of his calves switched to the front of his shins, each big knot the size of a warrior's bunched fist. On his head the temple-sinews stretched to the nape of his neck, each mighty, immense, measureless knob as big as the head of a month-old child. His face and features became a red bowl: he sucked one eye so deep into his head that a wild crane couldn't probe it onto his cheek out of the depths of his skull; the other eye fell out along his cheek. His mouth weirdly distorted: his cheek peeled back from his jaws until the gullet appeared, his lungs and liver flapped in his mouth and throat, his lower jaw struck the upper a lion-killing blow, and fiery flakes large as a ram's fleece reached his mouth from his throat. His heart boomed loud in his breast like the baying of a watchdog at its feed or the sound of a lion among bears. Malignant mists and spurts of fire ... flickered red in the vaporous clouds that rose boiling above his head, so fierce was his fury. The hair of his head twisted like the tangle of a red thornbush stuck in a gap; if a royal apple tree with all its kingly fruit were shaken above him, scarce an apple would reach the ground but each would be spiked on a bristle of his hair as it stood up on his scalp with rage. The hero-halo rose out of his brow, long and broad as a warrior's whetstone, long as a snout, and he went mad rattling his shields, urging on his charioteer and harassing the hosts. Then, tall and thick, steady and strong, high as the mast of a noble ship, rose up from the dead centre of his skull a straight spout of black blood darkly and magically smoking like the smoke from a royal hostel when a king is coming to be cared for at the close of a winter day.

The extraordinary intensity of enraged actions, as described in the first quotation, and of the experience of rage, as suggested in the second, leads to the belief that rage is a virtually irresistible force and that it is an elemental component of human nature. This essay will contradict both of these beliefs, first that it is elemental, and second, that it is irresistible.

The ability of primitive warriors to work themselves into a state of rage suggests that it is something that can be constructed, rather than an elemental. How did these warriors do it? We will probably never know the answer to that question. But studies of actual discourse suggest a sequence of events that seem always to occur prior to the outbreak of violent rage. At the group level, it may be that alienation and certain cultural beliefs militate toward states of hatred and rage, and violent behavior. I will begin with individuals.

As already indicated, rage may be a composite affect, a sequence of two elemental emotions, shame and anger. This idea has been advanced by other authors, notably Heinz Kohut (1971) and Helen Lewis (1971). Kohut proposed that violent anger of the kind he called "narcissistic rage" was a shame/anger compound. Lewis suggested that shame and anger have a deep affinity, and that it might be possible to find indications of unacknowledged shame occurring just prior to any intense hostility. This sequence has been demonstrated to occur in marital quarrels by Retzinger (1991), and in Hitler's writings and speeches (Scheff 1994), exactly as Lewis proposed. With all sixteen of the episodes of escalation of verbal violence in her data, Retzinger was able to demonstrate that prior to each episode, there had been first an insult by one party, indications of unacknowledged shame in the other party, and finally intense hostility in that party. This sequence can be seen as the motor of violence, since it connects the intense emotions of shame and anger to overt aggression.

Although there has been little research focused explicitly on pure, unalloyed anger, there are indications from the studies of discourse by Lewis (1971), Retzinger (1991), and my own work (such as Scheff 1990) that pure anger is rare and unlikely to lead to violence or even social disruption. On the contrary, anger by itself is usually brief and instructive. A person who is frustrated and unashamed of her anger is mobilized to tell what is going on, and to do what is needed, without making a huge scene. In my own personal case, I can testify that most of my experiences of anger have involved shame/anger, either in the form of humiliated fury, or in a more passive form, what Labov and Fanshel (1977) call "helpless anger." Both of these variants are long lasting and extremely unpleasant, especially for me. Shame-induced anger was unpleasant while happening, and even more unpleasant when it was over, since I inevitably felt foolish and out of control.

But in the very few episodes of what seems to have been, in retrospect, pure anger, the experience was entirely different. I did not raise my voice in any of them, nor did I put anyone down or engage in any other kind of excess. I simply told my view of what was going on directly, rapidly, and with no calculation or planning. I was overcome with what

I call "machine gun mouth." Everyone who was present for one of these communications suddenly became quite respectful. As for me, I did not feel out of control, even though my speech was completely spontaneous; on the contrary, I was wondering why I had not had my say before. It would seem that anger without shame has only a signal function, to alert self and others to one's frustration.

When anger has its source in feelings of rejection or inadequacy, and when the latter feelings are not acknowledged, a continuous spiral of shame/anger may result, which can be experienced as hatred and rage. Rather than expressing and discharging one's shame, it is masked by rage and aggression. One can be angry one is ashamed, and ashamed that one is angry, and so on, working up to a loop of unlimited duration and intensity. This loop may be the emotional basis of lengthy episodes or even lifelong hatred.

Social and Cultural Conditions for the Development of Intergroup Hatred

An earlier chapter (Scheff 1997a) described how *bimodal alienation* generates violence at the collective level. Bimodal alienation between groups occurs when there is "isolation" between them, but "engulfment" within them. That is, the members of group A are distant from the members of group B, and vice versa. But at the same time, the members of each group are suffocatingly close to each other, to the point that they give up important parts of themselves, in order to securely belong to the group.

The initial motor in this theory is the need to belong. It makes sense that the German language has the most beautiful word for home, in the sense of the place that you belong: *das Heimat*. It makes sense because, as both Elias (1996) and I (1994) have independently argued, historically the Germans seem to have long had an unsatisfied yearning for a place in which they belong, and have had great difficulty in managing the feeling of rejection, of not belonging and being accepted. Members of a group who feel not accepted both by foreigners and in their own group are in a position to surrender their individual identity in order to be accepted, giving rise in the German case to the principle of blind loyalty and obedience. But in any case, bimodal alienation (isolation between groups and engulfment within them) may be the fundamental condition for intergroup conflict.

Under the condition of bimodal alienation, a special culture seems to develop within each group that encourages hatred. There are various ways of characterizing this culture, but for my purposes here I will describe it in terms of "techniques of neutralization." This idea was originally formulated in criminology (Sykes and Matza 1957) to explain how and why teenagers engage in delinquent behavior, how a special culture develops among them that neutralizes the norms in their larger culture that oppose crime. But the idea has also been carefully applied by Alexander Alverez (1997) to the behavior of the German people in tolerating or actually engaging in genocide.

Alverez shows how each of Sykes and Matza's five techniques of neutralization can be used to explain the special culture that developed during the Nazi regime, a culture which neutralized the norms in the larger culture that forbid murder. The first technique is the Denial of Responsibility. Alverez shows that this technique in the German case usually took the form that the perpetrator was only carrying out orders from above. (2.) The Denial of Injury under the Nazi regime took the form of special language that hid or disguised what was actually being done, euphemisms in which killing became "special treatment," "cleansing" (also applied to the massacres in Bosnia) and many other similar examples. (3.) The Denial of Victim asserts that the victim actually brought on their own downfall. In the German case, Hitler and his followers believed that Jews were involved in a conspiracy to enslave the whole world, so that killing them was self-defense. Although a fiction, many Germans appeared to have believed it to be literally true.

(4.) Condemning the Condemners involved, in the German case, claims made by the German government and the media that the other countries that were condemning Germany were historically guilty of worse crimes, such as the treatment of Blacks and Native Americans in the United States and the treatment of native peoples in the French, British, and Spanish colonies. (5.) In the Appeal to Higher Loyalties, German perpetrators of genocide thought of themselves as patriots, nobly carrying out their duty. (6.) Finally, the Denial of Humanity is a category that Alverez himself added to those formulated by Sykes and Matza because of its special relevance to the Holocaust. Typical Nazi propaganda portrayed Jews and other non-Aryans as subhuman, filled with bestial impulses, such as the urge for destruction, primitive desires, and unparalleled evil. Although dehumanization often accompanies intergroup conflict, it seems in the German case that it was explicitly orchestrated by the government.

Any one of these six techniques can serve to encourage violence by neutralizing the norms against aggression and murder. To the extent that they are all implemented together, as they apparently were under the Nazi regime, to that extent a whole society can seemingly forget its moral values, in order to engage in wholesale slaughter. The idea of techniques of neutralization suggests the cultural foundation for collective violence. At the end of this chapter I will suggest ways of reducing violence by countering techniques of neutralization. In the remainder of this section, I will focus on the issue of reducing the emotional bases of violence by dealing with shame that has gone unacknowledged.

How can spirals of unacknowledged shame and anger, which are the emotional basis of hatred and rage, be avoided or terminated when they are occurring? One answer may lie in the direction of acknowledgment of shame.Acknowledgment, however, does not refer to merely verbal acknowledgment. Unfortunately, there have been very few discussions of this issue. Acknowledgment is one of those terms, like "working through" in psychoanalysis, which play a central role in professional discourse, but are seldom defined or even illustrated through concrete examples.

Since there is no literature focused directly on the acknowledgment of shame, I will resort to studies of apology, which deal with acknowledgment, if only indirectly. This literature is helpful since it places emotions and their acknowledgment within a social context. Seeking forgiveness through apology also helps to locate and conceptualize rage, because it is the opposite process: hatred and enraged behavior shatter the social bond, apology seeks to reinstate it.

Apologies

Reconciliation, repairing a disruption in a social relationship, can be seen as an acknowledgment of interdependence.[1] Viewed in this way, apologies as direct paths to repairing bonds expose many of the key elements in conflict and reconciliation. Describing the components of the ritual of apology may be a succinct way of unpacking the concept of acknowledgment.

The two leading theorists of apology and reconciliation are Goffman and Nicholas Tavuchis. Goffman (1971) considered apology in his treatment of remedial and reparative devices. Even though his discussion of apologies is brief, it bristles with ideas (1971, 113):

> ... apology has several elements: expression of embarrassment and chagrin; ... that one knows what conduct has been expected[;] ... disavowal of the wrong way of behaving and vilification of the self that so behaved; ... avowal henceforth to pursue that course; performance of penance and the volunteering of restitution.

Two aspects of this long sentence catch the eye. First, in a few lines, Goffman has loaded in not one or two, but seven necessary elements for a successful apology, a monument to concision. The other feature of this description that invites comment is that the first element of an apology that Goffman invokes is "expression of embarrassment and chagrin," which connects his argument to mine concerning shame. Moreover, placing this element at the head of the list possibly suggests that it should come first in time, or that it might be the most important condition, or both.

Goffman's discussion has proven fruitful in many directions, but it has also been criticized by Tavuchis (1991), whose discussion of apologies is much more comprehensive and detailed. Unlike Goffman, Tavuchis readily extends his analysis beyond interpersonal apology to individual-collective and collective remedial actions. He devotes chapter-length treatments to situations of apology of the one to the many, the many to the one, and the many to the many. In his treatment of interactions between individuals and groups, he covers some of the same ground as Braithwaite (1989), but in much more detail. The ceremonies of punishment and reintegration of offenders that Braithwaite describes involve the repair of bonds between the one and the many, which Tavuchis discusses in greater detail. Of particular relevance to group conflict is Tavuchis's discussion of apologies of the many to many: the path to reconciliation between groups.

Tavuchis's two central complaints about Goffman's treatment are that in the main it concerns individuals, rather than relationships, and that to these individuals an apology may be a game in which the actor is not emotionally involved (1991, 138):

> ... apologies (for Goffman) are conceptualized as a "set of moves" or interpersonal management ploys used by social disembodied actors trying to maximize their (questionable) moral credibility ... Goffman argues that an apology entails the "splitting" of the self, whereas I underscore the necessity of "attachment" to the offense ... there is no mention of what I take to be central to apology: sorrow and regret ... an actor could follow all the steps described by Goffman without producing a speech act that is socially recognizable as an apology, or, its moral reciprocal, forgiveness.

Both of Tavuchis's criticisms cut close to the bone. Although Goffman uses many relational terms, his basic frame of analysis is individualistic rather than relational; it concerns a harried, anxious individual seeking to maintain her/his sense of self and status in a jungle of trying situations. The language of rules and norms, which Tavuchis also uses, is itself not quite relational, since it emphasizes the individual as much as the social bond. Perhaps a new language of relationships is needed. In the physics of light, mathematical language provided the link between particle and wave formulations. We have no such language for linking individuals and relationships.

Tavuchis's second criticism is also just. Goffman's analysis is largely behavioral; it concerns the surface of interaction, with very little access to the interior, the meaning of events to the actors. Even Goffman's mention of embarrassment and chagrin as necessary parts of apology involves an ambiguity. He does not say that the actor should *feel* these emotions, but only that they should be expressed. In Goffman's world, a gesture indicating embarrassment (covering the face with a hand, for example) might be adequate, even if it were merely enacted in the absence of any feeling. (In *The Odyssey,* when addressing an audience, Ulysses would wipe his eyes with the hem of his robe to indicate grief. The wily Ulysses would fit exactly into Goffman's scripts.)

In Tavuchis's (31) description of apology, there are two essential parts, both equally important and equally necessary. One must say one is sorry, and one must also feel sorry. Without these two components, the ritual is incomplete. Tavuchis's critique of individualistic and behavioral bias locates two important flaws in Goffman's approach. To test the adequacy of some particular apology, one can invoke what I will call Tavuchis's rule: an apology will be genuine to the extent that one both says one is sorry and actually feels sorry. His rule concerns congruence between outer and inner, as already mentioned above. An actual instance of a defective apology will provide an example.

Albert Speer, one of Hitler's chief lieutenants, was tried and convicted of crimes against humanity at Nuremberg. Unlike any of the other defendants, however, his life was spared. Instead of being executed, he spent twenty-one years in solitary confinement at Spandau prison, outside of Berlin. During this period, he wrote his memoirs (Speer 1970). One recurring theme is the regret he expresses about the role he played in Hitler's Germany. In some ways, the whole book can be read as an apology for his actions.

If the book is an apology, however, it doesn't seem to be an adequate one; it is frequently off-pitch in some essential way. It is true that some of the apologetic statements sound genuine. But even one false note in a text can call into question the validity of an entire apology: perhaps most of the words sound right, but does the one apologizing actually feel sorry? There are many lapses in Speer's memoirs.

In an insightful review, George Steiner (1971) describes Speer's attempts at apology as "motions, presumably sincere in their own hollow, cerebral way, of retrospective horror." Although Steiner did not provide examples to show how hollow and cerebral Speer's attempts were, they can be easily found in the text. One (Speer 1970, 24) begins with a statement that almost strikes the right note:

> By entering Hitler's party I had already, in essence, assumed a responsibility that led directly to the brutalities of forced labor, to the destruction of war, and to the deaths of those millions of so-called undesirable stock, to the crushing of justice and the elevation of every evil.

Even in this passage there is inappropriate phrasing. But it hints at some feeling of responsibility and remorse. One touch is that he heads his list of crimes with "the brutalities of forced labor," a crime in which he was directly implicated as the overseer of the armament industry.

But in the rest of the paragraph, the tone falters: "In 1931 [when he joined the Nazi party] I had no idea that fourteen years later I would have to answer for a host of crimes to which I subscribed beforehand by entering the party." Although somewhat indirect, this sentence seems to be more of an excuse ("I didn't know") than an apology. It denies his own responsibility for his actions by implying that once having joined the party, a youthful folly, blind loyalty was inescapable.

The paragraph ends with a whimper: "I did not yet know that I would atone with twenty-one years of my life for frivolity and thoughtlessness and breaking with tradition." There is a thread of self-justification and self-pity running through the entire paragraph, faint at first, but in the last sentence, dominant. Instead of expressing gratitude that his life alone was spared, of all the Nuremberg defendants, he seems to complain about the length of the prison sentence. The most shocking element however, is the terms used to describe the causes of his adherence to the Nazi Party: "frivolity and thoughtlessness and breaking with tradition."[2] These terms would be appropriate if he had participated in a panty raid, but not in crimes whose scope and vileness beggar the imagination.

Speer's apology fails the second part of the Tavuchis rule. Although Speer says many times that he is sorry, the way he says it suggests that he does not feel sorry. His failure occurs with both cognitive and emotional aspects. In terms of the cognitive content, self-justification is exactly the opposite of what is required in an apology, taking responsibility for one's own actions with no excuses.

Speer's apology also fails to pass at the emotional level. The connotations of many of his words and phrases work against the expression of remorse. One example is the phrase "undesirable stock." Although Speer qualifies this phrase with "so-called," it still strikes the wrong note. He is referring to the victims of Nazi atrocities, such as the Jews and Slavs who were murdered or worked to death. To use a term from his Nazi past rather than from the present day is an appalling blunder, since it suggests that in some ways his point of view, and therefore his feelings, still have not changed. Sustaining the right tone in an apology seems to require actually feeling remorse, the second part of the Tavuchis test.

My discussion of the Speer case suggests that Tavuchis's analysis is helpful in understanding the nature of apology, and therefore of acknowledgment of feelings. However, I would like to extend the description of the core ritual of apology further than Tavuchis takes it, in order to resolve an issue that he leaves unresolved. In many different passages, Tavuchis puzzles over a mystery: how can mere words resolve conflict? He notes that an apology, however fastidious, does not undo the harmful act. Tavuchis repeatedly indicates that successful apologies are like magic: using only words, one can obtain genuine forgiveness for an injurious act (1991, 122):

> ... although I have referred frequently to forgiveness as a crucial element in the apologetic equation, this mysterious and unpremeditated faculty has not been adequately addressed or formulated. If, as I have argued, sorrow is the energizing force of apology, then what moves the offended party to forgive? ... [the] social and psychodynamic sources [of forgiveness] have been relatively neglected.

Shame dynamics, which Tavuchis does not invoke, may speak to the issue which Tavuchis raises: what are the social and psychodynamic sources of apology and forgiveness? I will deal first with psychodynamic sources, the vicissitudes of emotions and feelings, then with social ones.

I agree with the first part of Tavuchis's rule: in the English language at least, one must say one is sorry, or words to that effect. But in order to understand the "magic" of apology, it may be necessary to unpack the second part of the formula, that one must also feel sorry. What are the emotional components of feeling sorry? In the passage just quoted, Tavuchis states that sorrow, that is, grief, is the energizing force of apology. I disagree. Although feeling and displaying grief might be helpful, it may not be the main emotion required for an apology to accomplish its purpose.

I propose that an effective apology requires that the predominant emotion of the party making the apology be one of embarrassment or shame. This is difficult for the participants to see, or even for observers, because in our civilization, embarrassment and shame are so frequently and deeply disguised and denied as to be rendered almost invisible (Lynd 1958; Lewis 1971; Scheff 1990; Retzinger 1991). Although Tavuchis (1991) discusses shame at several points (as in note 4, p. 151), it does not figure prominently in his discussion. It does figure prominently in Miller's (1993) discussion of apologies; he proposes, as I do, that shame or embarrassment is the predominate emotion in a genuine apology.

Suppose, for purpose of argument, that after one party has been injured by another, both parties are in a state of embarrassment or shame. Depending on the gravity of the injury, the intensity of shame may range from slight embarrassment through severe, lengthy states of humiliation. The injured party may feel helpless, rejected, powerless, or inadequate, because of the treatment received; the injuring party may feel unworthy because he/she has injured the other. All of these terms have been rated as encoded references to shame (Gottschalk et al. 1969; Lewis 1971; Retzinger 1991). The shared mood of the two parties is bleak: they are in a state of shared embarrassment or shame.

The function of apology under these conditions is to allow both parties to acknowledge and discharge the burden of shame they are carrying with respect to the injurious act, rather than deny it. This function is difficult for the parties to be aware of in Western societies, because shame is routinely denied. Perhaps if social psychology brought unacknowledged shame to light, we might be able to understand and increase the magic of apology.

An effective apology is also difficult because it depends on a veritable symphony of verbal and nonverbal activities jointly enacted and felt by both parties. Each must coordinate their words, gestures, thoughts, and feelings with those of the other. It is a dance, a *pas de deux,* requiring not only the right words, the lyrics, but also the right music. That is, the timing (rhythm) of the moves of each party, relative to the moves of the other, is crucial, as are the emotions displayed (melody) and felt (harmony).

This formulation in terms of emotion dynamics may remove some of the mystery from apology and forgiveness. If the lyrics and the melody of the party apologizing are right, and the attitude of the party apologized to accepting, then a dramatic mood change can occur: the parties can go from a state of shared shame to one of shared pride in a matter of minutes, from fluster, awkwardness, and emotional pain to rapport and pleasure.

My explanation of the apology/forgiveness process to this point is incomplete, however, because it has concerned only the emotional sources, not the social ones. To move toward these sources requires discussion of the nature of social relationships and social bonds at an abstract and general level.

Social relationships are difficult to describe in Western societies because human interdependency, like shame, is routinely denied. Our public discourse is in the language of individuals, rather than relationships. A social bond may be defined in terms of the mix of solidarity and alienation (Scheff 1990; Retzinger 1991). A secure bond is a relationship in which solidarity prevails: accurate understanding of both parties of the other's thoughts and feelings, their short and long-term intentions, and their character prevails over misunderstanding or lack of understanding. In an insecure or threatened bond, alienation dominates: there is lack of understanding or misunderstanding in these matters on one or both sides. Most social bonds are a mix, but either solidarity or alienation predominates.

As already indicated, alienation occurs at both of the two poles of interdependence. Using Elias's (1989) "I-we" language: a secure bond requires balance between the importance of the individuals and importance of the relationship. Too much emphasis on the individual means isolation; each cannot know the other and reveal the self because they are too distant. Too much emphasis on the relationship means engulfment: each cannot know the other and reveal the self because loyalty and conformity demand that important parts of the self, basic desires, thoughts, and feelings may be hidden, even from one's self. Secrecy, deception, and self-deception go hand in hand. Modern societies tend toward individuation and isolation, traditional ones toward conformity and engulfment. Both formats are equally alienated.

The apology/forgiveness transaction signifies the removal of a threat to the social bond. In relational language, in every moment of every encounter, the bond is either being maintained, strengthened, repaired, or damaged. This is one of Goffman's (1967) central themes: every action (or inaction) by each party has an effect on the relative status and sense of self of the parties, without exception.

By verbal and nonverbal means, an effective apology is a master stroke in this scenario, a repair of a threatened or insecure bond. When one party has injured another, the bond is threatened, the parties are disconnected emotionally and/or cognitively, i.e., they are in a state of shame. A successful apology allows both parties to acknowledge and discharge the shame evoked by the injury. The apology "makes things right" between the parties; both emotionally and cognitively, it repairs the breach in the bond. The success of the action of repair is felt and signaled by both parties: they both feel and display the emotion of pride.

Bond language is needed if we are to understand and describe the process of denial and acknowledgment: acknowledgment of the state of a relationship (the degree of attunement and its accompanying emotions) leads to building or repair of bonds; denial, to damage to bonds.

Tavuchis's analysis of apology and my commentary on it suggest the complexity of the concept of acknowledgment and of its practice in real life, even at the interpersonal level. At the level of relations between nations, the issues are further complicated by the large number of participants, the vastly increased volume of discourse, and particularly by the lack of consensus that characterizes modern societies. In the theory proposed here, acknowledgment of interdependency and emotion, the state of the bond, is crucial not only for individuals, but for whole societies.

Conclusion

This discussion points toward several paths for conciliation between belligerent groups. My theory of protracted conflict suggests that the foremost cause is mass alienation within and between the groups. Any steps that would decrease mass alienation would automatically lessen the potential for conflict. In an earlier essay on alienation (Scheff 1977, Ch. 4), I proposed that teachers need to be retrained to be aware of the way in which they reject working-class and minority students. I also suggest classes on family relations that would help young people form stable families. Also in that essay I recommend reform for welfare programs to lessen rejection and shame. Young men form the bulk of combatants for intergroup and international conflict. If they could be better integrated into work or welfare, school, and family, they would be less vulnerable to pressure to fight an external and, often, what amounts to, an imagined enemy.

At the level of culture, to undermine the sources of intergroup conflict, we need to counter the techniques of neutralization (Sykes and Matza 1957; Alverez 1997) that are used to foment hatred and violence toward purported enemies. Although there are attempts to control hatred in the mass media, they still have not been comprehensive enough to help reduce the pressure toward violence. An obvious example is the continuing sexism and violence toward women in commercial films, not to mention fringe films. An expensive film like *Revenge,* with major stars (Kevin Costner, Madeleine Stowe, and Anthony Quinn), degrades women and encourages violence toward them, yet is being widely distributed and shown both in theaters and on TV and video. Although racism and xenophobia have been toned down somewhat, they still form an undercurrent in many current films. They seem particularly flagrant in "action" films (such as those starring Sylvester Stallone). Needless to say, both sexism and racism are rife in most of the old films that are constantly being rerun on TV.

Learning to identify and acknowledge shame and rage in self and others is also a fundamental step toward decreasing conflict. I have proposed in this chapter that alienation and unacknowledged shame are basic causes of destructive conflict, as important as material causes. Obviously material interests matter in human affairs. They are topics of quarrels. But these interests can always be negotiated, if there is no unacknowledged emotion, in a way that allows parties maximum benefit or perhaps least destructive outcomes. Unacknowledged shame figures large because it makes rational negotiation of interest difficult or even impossible, given the non-rational, that is, the elements of insult and rejection when shame is not acknowledged by both parties.

The manipulation of fear, shame, and rage in the U.S. public seems to be the key element in the Bush regime strategy. Finding plausible outside enemies serves to distract the public from criticizing its reckless political and economic maneuvers. The framing of aggression against Iraq for the past decade by the U.S. government has made ample use of techniques of neutralization. Denial of Victim has been especially important in that our government makes the claim, with no evidence, that Iraq poses a threat to the United States and to the world. The war against Iraq has made frequent use of the Denial of Injury. One example is the use of the phrase "collateral damage" to disguise the killing of civilian men, women, and children. Another example is the idea that the purpose of the war is to "liberate," rather than control, Iraq. The idea that the United States is liberating Iraq is also an Appeal to Higher Loyalties.

This chapter concerns the emotional/relational components of hatred and aggression, how they are generated, and how they might be overcome. I have proposed that there is always an irrational component in protracted hatred and violence that is the product of unacknowledged shame. Can anything be done to lessen the influence of this component?

Changing individuals might require long-term projects. One approach would be to introduce courses on emotional/relational issues in early schooling. A course on mediation and conflict resolution could be introduced in junior high schools, and at the high school level, a course on dating and family communications. I have been teaching a course on communication for many years to university students in their first year. Most of the students have been very receptive. A large majority in every class seems to understand that their own communication practices can be improved, as well as those of the people in their lives.

Even if all schools introduced such courses, which is unlikely, major changes in the management of the emotional/relational world would still be a long time coming. In the meanwhile, it might be worth the effort to try to make changes at the collective level. One impressive institution that might work is the kind of Truth and Reconciliation Commission that proved to be effective in the transformation of relationships in South Africa.

Perhaps in the future it will be necessary to institute this project to clarify the emotional, political, and economic origins and consequences of the war on Iraq. A first step might be to form committees on the Gulf War, since there are many questions that need to be raised. One would be the origins of that war. Ramsey Clark (1994)—the Attorney General during Jimmy Carter's presidency—has claimed that the United States instigated this war through Kuwait, and by deceiving Iraq. Another issue would be the treatment of the U.S. veterans of that war, especially the claims that many were sickened by the war, but have been unable to get treatment. Each of these initiatives is only a small step, but many undertaken together might make a difference.

Note

1. Some of this section is based on one part of Chapter 6 in Scheff (1994).

CHAPTER 9

Human Bonds

Love, Pride, and Shame

> Love is not all: it is not meat nor drink
> Nor slumber nor a roof against the rain;
> Nor yet a floating spar to men that sink
> And rise and sink and rise and sink again;
> Love can not fill the thickened lung with breath,
> Nor clean the blood, nor set the fractured bone;
> Yet many a man is making friends with death
> Even as I speak, for lack of love alone...
> Edna St. Vincent Millay, "Sonnet"

GOFFMAN'S WORK, FOR THE MOST PART, concerned what I would call threatened or insecure bonds. As already indicated, he didn't see much love and solidarity in the world around him. His actors and actresses scurry about insecurely in an insecure landscape, managing the impressions they make catch-as-catch-can.

His portrayal of the tone and style of the social world in modern, urban/industrial societies may be quite just for the majority of occasions and inhabitants of this world. The family interactions that will be described below certainly seem to fit Goffman's portrayal. Even so, his analysis is hardly the last word. For one thing, there is probably a minority of persons in our society, even a sizeable minority, whose bonds are in large part secure, or at least, have significant moments of security.

But my interest in this book is not primarily about the accuracy of Goffman's analysis. What I want to do is to use his work as a stepping-off place into significant issues that Goffman didn't address. The idea of the social bond is one such issue; it could become a crucial part of theories of interpersonal and societal relationships. This chapter will illustrate my conception of the social bond by applying it to some ordinary, everyday family dialogues. My purpose is to illustrate bond work on a small, intimate scale, before jumping into large-scale collective cooperation and conflict in the later chapters. Because of this purpose, the language of this chapter will be closer to everyday usage than other more technical chapters.

Origins of Relationship Troubles

For many of us, close relationships are problematic. Not just marriages, but also parent/child, teacher/student, office or workplace, even friendships. Why can't we get along better with the people in our lives? What do we need to understand to be better partners, parents, or colleagues? How can we avoid or at least limit conflict? Is it possible to have more pleasure and less pain in our contacts with others?

Attempting to answer these questions is a challenge. There is tension between being faithful to the complexity of human beings, on the one hand, and accessibility for the reader, on the other. For this reason there is a gulf between technical and self-help books on relationships. Most of the former sacrifice accessibility to complexity. They are written by experts for other experts in the specialized language of their profession. Even the best of them can hardly be understood by the general reader. There is a special language and style of discourse that is familiar only to the writer's psychotherapy or social science discipline, but off-putting to everyone else.

On the other hand, self-help psychology sacrifices complexity for accessibility. These books use ordinary language, often claiming a few easy steps to good relationships. Although some of these volumes may be helpful to their readers, they function within a severe limitation. The vernacular language they use reflects and helps to maintain hidden ideas and patterns about human nature, emotions, and relationships that are *taken for granted* in our society. Vernacular language is part of the problem, in that it helps keep our thinking and talking entrapped in underlying assumptions of modern societies. As indicated in Chapter 1, this is the basic problem that Goffman set out to resolve with his own new language. Conventional language is a crucial part of the *routines* to be described here, routines that keep people disconnected, rather than connected.

This book uses several crucial concepts that are clearly defined, rather than being part of ordinary language. Three emotion terms—"love," "pride," and "shame"—will be defined in a way that is different than current usage. A fourth term, the "social bond," at least in the way it is used, finds no ready similar phrase in the vernacular. "Deep mutual understanding and identification" comes closest. In respect to these four concepts, this book is like other books written by experts. The difference is that these concepts will be explained so that the reader can use them, and locate their meaning with respect to the vernacular terms that would ordinarily be used. In this way novel ideas—ideas that serve to break down conventional assumptions—can be introduced.

Current usage defines shame narrowly as only *disgrace shame,* and love very broadly, including many kinds of dysfunctional patterns. In ordinary language, the meaning of pride is tainted by the idea of arrogance or self-satisfaction. Finally, attunement, the sharing of consciousness, is called "mind reading," and is thought to be rare and peculiar. These usages are not only crude and imprecise, they are also misleading. They camouflage and hide the emotional/relational world from our view and our understanding, and thereby reaffirm the status quo in our society.

This book represents recent thinking on the microworld of emotions and relationships, the emotional/relational world (ERW). It is a world that we all live in every day of our lives, but have been trained not to notice.

Our obliviousness to the emotional/relational world seems to be a creation of the modern urban/industrial society. In traditional societies, the ERW was virtually the only world. But in modern societies there is an infinity of duties, distractions, and diversions from feelings and relationships. Leaning to ignore the ERW takes place, for the most part, in early childhood. Our parents model for us the routines that help suppress our own emotions and ignore those of others. The same thing can be said for relationships: in modern societies we learn very early to pay attention to individuals and to ignore relationships. This focus is so taken for granted that it is virtually automatic; it is part of everyone's routine.

How can one overcome one's whole upbringing, and the conventions of our society, in order to notice and respond to a world that we have been taught to ignore? Later in this chapter, discussions of student family dialogues in my undergraduate classes on family relationships are reported. In some classes, I had students discuss the relationships in their own families of origin, particularly their relationships to their parents. There were no lectures; most of the class time was spent with students role-playing dialogue from their own lives.

A majority of the students in these classes start on the long road to noticing the ERW. Sometimes the group that does so is only a bare majority, sometimes much larger. But there is always a minority, occasionally a substantial one, that doesn't seem to learn. They are puzzled that they cannot take notes, since there are no lectures. They also appear to be baffled by the intense reactions of their classmates. What could all this fuss be about? This minority appears to be unable to grasp what is being taught.

The majority of students, however, seem to wake up from a long sleep. All of these students experience surprise, if not shock, when they begin to notice cues to the ERW. A typical reaction in the student evaluations suggests both appreciation and surprise: "This course suddenly made me aware of a whole new world. At first I could hardly believe what I was learning. It was always there, I just hadn't noticed it."

Initially most students attribute their relationship difficulties to the other person. They seem chagrined at first to find that they are also contributing. But most are also relieved when they realize that there may be something they themselves can do to deal with the problem.

Emotions and Attunement

This book seeks entry into the ERW, a forbidden world, through a consideration of three emotions—love, pride, and shame—and a relationship concept, the social bond. The argument draws from across the social sciences, psychiatry, and psychoanalysis. The emotion of love is distinguished from the broad way this word is used in the vernacular. Shame is described in terms of its significance for interpersonal and group connectedness, how it serves as a warning signal of threat to the bond.

The state of social bonds is defined in terms of degree of *attunement,* how much mutual identification and moment-by-moment emotional/cognitive understanding there is between persons or groups. The conception of shame used here assumes that pride, genuine pride, is its opposite. Just as shame signals threat to the bond, authentic pride signals attunement, the momentary joining of consciousness and identity between two or more persons, a secure bond. Authentic pride signals connecting, and shame/embarrassment signals disconnection, or the anticipation of it.

The idea of attunement plays a key role in conceptualizing love as a particular kind of bond. Non-erotic love is defined in terms of attunement, like the social bond, but it also contains another component, equally important: attachment. Attunement is cognitive/emotional but attachment is physical. Although completely physical and involuntary, attachment gives rise to powerful feelings, especially grief or sadness in the absence of the person to whom one is attached. The shared awareness and identity of attunement, together with attachment, are the basic components of non-erotic love. In addition to these two components, romantic love contains a third component, sexual attraction. This definition leads to a concept of love much more specific than the ones used in popular and scholarly usage.

The central thesis of the book concerns the role of hidden emotions and lack of attunement in disrupting relationships, particularly love and other types of solidarity relationships. The main culprits among the emotions seem to be grief, fear, and shame—the vulnerable emotions—and anger. Acknowledging these emotions plays an important part in maintaining close relationships. Allowing another person to enter one's private world of feelings cements the bond in a fundamental way. By the same token, when the vulnerable emotions are hidden or ignored, the bond is weakened.

An equally significant threat to the bond is disowning or hiding one's vulnerable emotions from one's self. In this latter case, not only does the person not know others, but also fails to know him- or herself. *This book proposes that failure to acknowledge vulnerable emotions damages most relationships between persons and between groups in Western societies.* In these societies, hiding emotions under behavior and thought, and ignoring relationships in favor of individuals, appears to be not only a personal defense, but also a cultural one. Most of the chapters in this book elaborate on and explore these ideas.

Some of the chapters focus on what might at first seem to be a narrow issue: the role of one particular emotion, unacknowledged shame, in disrupting relationships. The basic thesis is that individuals and groups are basically cooperative, unless there is a sizeable backlog of unacknowledged emotion, especially shame. When that is the case, there is a strong tendency toward either conflict or withdrawal. *The central thesis of these chapters is that cooperation, both between persons and between groups, breaks down when most shame experiences go unacknowledged.* Unacknowledged shame is seen as playing a central, and usually unnoticed role in blocking genuine love.

The opposite proposition is that acknowledging shame is a powerful step toward cooperation, intimacy, and sustained relationships. This idea is usually seen as surprising in modern societies, since shame is usually ignored or disguised. One exception can be found in the practices of Alcoholics Anonymous (AA) and its spin-off groups. The verbal expression of shame in these groups is thought to be a necessary condition for recovery. From my point of view, this idea is a step in the right direction, but its application is somewhat limited because it is based on the vernacular meaning of the word *shame,* and on practices which are largely verbal. The more complex idea of shame presented here could lead to new directions in AA practices, and in professional practice as well, in the various forms of psychotherapy, counseling, and mediation. It is also relevant to improving communication in families and in schools.

Perhaps the largest hurdle the reader will have to overcome will be the process of "coming out" on the emotion of shame. As Chapter 4 indicates, shame is a deep secret in Western societies. The other major component of this book, relationship, is at least speakable. Although women tend to be much more interested in speaking about it then men, the word *relationship* is not usually a conversation stopper, as shame is apt to be.

Most men and women alike have trouble dealing with shame. Only when used in a throwaway line (What a shame!) is it speakable in ordinary talk. Even pride, a much more positive emotion, has similar, if lesser, limitations. In Western languages, at least, one must qualify the word with adjectives such as "authentic," "justified," or "genuine" in order to talk about it. Otherwise one must be cautious, because the word, when not qualified, implies arrogance or hubris. One device is to resort to code words, such as "high self-esteem." Another is to avoid using both words, "pride" and "shame," altogether.

In conceptualizing pride and shame as largely social, and in broadening shame to include positive variants, such as modesty, shyness, and "a sense of shame," this book attempts to remove the taboo from shame, and make it available to our understanding and everyday experience. Assuming that authentic pride is a crucial part of close relationships rejects current usage that inflects arrogance into pride.

The core of this book concerns the dynamic interaction between the state of the social bond (degree of attunement and mutual identification) and love, pride, and shame. To the extent that there is mutual understanding and identification, then genuine love is possible. To the extent that there is lack of attunement and too little or too much mutual identification, then love is alloyed with other kinds of relationships, or replaced entirely.

Discovering the Emotional/Relational World

In my university classes, students role-play brief exchanges with parents or others important in their life. On the first day, students are told the class will involve role-playing and discussion rather than lectures (some students usually leave the class at this point). Through discussing short passages in their own remembered *dialogues,* students begin to notice their own contributions to relationship troubles. Initially most students are unaware of their part in these problems. With only rare exceptions, they see only the part played by the other person or persons. Although other kinds of exchanges are also touched upon, a useful place to start seems to be quarrels, on the one hand, or impasses, on the other. Dialogues centered on invitations or requests are also student favorites.

At first sight it might seem misleading to try to understand a whole relationship, much less a whole family, on the basis of excerpts from conversations. It is possible however, that because of the complexity of human communication, every exchange is a microcosm, representing many of the elements of the larger relationship of which it is a part. Each exchange is like the smallest functioning unit of the relationship, standing to the whole as a cell does to the living organism. One cannot understand everything about the host organism from the cell. But, on the other hand, knowledge of the cell is of considerable help in understanding the larger system of which it is a part, and vice versa.

Human communication is so complex and ambiguous that in order to understand it, participants must constantly be shuttling back and forth between the smallest parts, the words and gestures, and the largest wholes: not only the whole conversation of which the exchange is a part, but the whole relationship, family, society, and civilization out of which each utterance has grown. If the excerpt is the smallest cell, the society is the host organism. Human communication is an open system, incredibly charged with both meaning and ambiguity. Correctly deciphering it requires skill, agility, and perseverance in the participants. In particular, there is a skill at improvisation that seems necessary in order to understand dialogue. There is a lot of guesswork involved in understanding self and others.

In this chapter, I employ the same kind of part/whole analysis of utterances that participants seem to use.[1] I apply this technique to a set of verbatim texts. My interpretation of some of the dialogue also uses my own eyewitness observation, as in the case of the role-plays of the student dialogues in this chapter, and conversations with students in my office. These extra-dialogue components provide further observations and context for the dialogues.

Direct observation allows one access not only to the words but also to the paralanguage, the *manner* of talk, as well as its verbal content. Like the thicket of gestures in which dialogue is enclosed, these facts provide a backdrop for a part/whole analysis in order to ground verbal texts in their larger matrix of meaning. Specifically, I note recurring communication *routines,* which are directly observable, and hidden emotions, which can only be inferred from verbal and nonverbal cues.

This approach has two advantages not usually available to the participants. First, I can make explicit my assumptions and observations, describing in great detail how I have come to make my interpretation, and the facts upon which it is based. Actual participants are usually too immersed in their activity to have the luxury of such explicitness. The second advantage is closely related to the first. Unlike the participant, the researcher is able to replay an event as many times as necessary before making a decision. These two advantages suggest a resolution to the problem of meaning in human relationships, the problem that Geertz (1973) has described as "thick description" (Scheff 1986).

One way to make one's assumptions explicit is to use a formal theory. My theory concerns relationship patterns, the emotions of love and shame, and the relationship between the two. Personal relationships are based on communication, on dialogue. I propose that both interminable conflict and impasse are generated by dysfunctional communication patterns, unacknowledged shame, and lack of attunement. I will first discuss communication patterns.

Cooperative relationships involve more than a little *leveling* (Satir 1972). That is, it is possible to voice one's immediate thoughts, feelings, and needs to others without injuring or insulting them, so long as one's *manner* is respectful. Leveling means being direct but in a respectful way. Most utterances in disputes are not leveling. They either are direct but not respectful, or respectful but not direct.

Leveling is an important idea, since we often assume that in our relationship to a particular person, some topics are automatically dangerous, others completely safe. As it turns out, this is not the case; we can get into trouble with safe topics, and escape trouble with dangerous ones, depending not only on *what* we say, but *how* we say it. In close relationships, nonverbal elements like tempo, loudness, facial expression, and other bodily gestures are often as important as words. Offense, insult, and humiliation, i.e., shame, usually arise out of manner; if one is respectful, any topic can be discussed and any criticism can be made with little risk of trouble. In interminable conflicts, the *manner* of the disputants is always disrespectful, which evokes shame.

Continued escalation may be caused not only by conflicts of interests, but by disrespectful words and manner, and by shame that is not acknowledged. In the absence of shame, or if shame is acknowledged, disputing parties can usually find a compromise which provides maximum reward or at least minimum punishment to the parties. In other words, it is hidden shame and disconnection, leading to insult and retaliation, that interferes with cooperation or compromise. Hidden shame/disconnection also interferes with the ability of participants to love each other.

Communication tactics involve not only manner, but also a wide variety of styles that are seldom noticed. Most of these styles are ways of avoiding leveling, and do not result in the growth of a relationship, and may actually damage it. Satir (1972) called attention to several of these styles: *blaming, placating, distracting*, and *computing* are some of her categories.

Another maneuver for avoiding leveling has been called "*triangling*" (Bowen 1978). Instead of revealing their own immediate thoughts, feelings, and needs, one or both parties can resort to talking about a third party, not present. This device not only excludes the absent party, but also interferes with the relationship between the speakers, since it substitutes gossip about another person for revealing self and learning about other.

Given these concepts, it is possible to discern a type of alienation that usually goes unnoticed, what Bowen (1978) called fusion or *engulfment*. The style of alienation that Bowen calls *isolation* is obvious enough; one or both parties place the self over and above the relationship, resulting in distance and separation. Computing, blaming, and open conflict usually occur in this mode.

Engulfment is the opposite mode of alienation, in which one or both parties place the relationship over and above self. One or both give up significant parts of the self in order to be loyal. Placating and distracting are usually in this mode. Since the participants in engulfed relationships usually think of themselves as close and supportive, considerable self-deception is also involved. Engulfment is a pervasive mode in normal families, since it provides a surface appearance of closeness.

As already indicated, a secure bond—balance between self and other—is a key component of genuine love, as already discussed in Chapter 7.

Family Discourse

This remainder of this chapter concerns family relationships. The dialogues reported here are taken from a total of forty-one students that were available to me from a single class conducted in 1991, as well as fourteen role-plays in either the classroom or my office. I report here on several typical situations. These examples show similar patterns of routinization between the parents and between each parent and their child. None of the names used are real.

Becky's Family

The student in the first set of excerpts, Becky, sees her mother as her enemy in two different ways—one direct, one indirect. She believes that her mother is hostile and critical toward her, and that she also interferes with her (Becky's) relationship with her father by nagging him about her. Becky's dialogue concerning her car illustrates both ideas.

1. Father-daughter dialogue

Father: Your mom's really bugging me to do something about your car, so if you don't deal with it, I'm selling it. And I mean it this time.

Becky: Okay, Dad. I'll do something. I want my car.

2. Mother-daughter dialogue

Mother: It's the same thing with your car. You don't want to deal with it. What's it gonna take?

Becky: Why is my car always brought up? It happened a year ago. I'm sorry. It wasn't on purpose.

It may be that Becky's understanding of these dialogues with her parents is faulty, as is her understanding of her relationships with her parents as a whole. The texts of the dialogues suggest that she is *idealizing* her father and *vilifying* her mother. Furthermore, they show that all three relationships in the triangle are alienated, and that none of the participants are aware of the depth of the alienation.

Becky's comments about her mother suggest a third dialogue that could be imagined between the father and mother.

3. Father-mother dialogue* (The asterisk is the conventional symbol for a counterfactual text, imagined dialogue.)

Mother: Why are you so lenient with Becky about the car? She is being completely irresponsible. You have got to come down on her.

Father: Yes, dear, you're right. I'll take care of it.

Although I imagined this third dialogue, Becky confirmed that it was similar
to an exchange she had overheard, but about a different topic.

Family systems theory points to dysfunctional communication patterns
in all three of these dialogues. One of the faulty tactics, triangling (Bowen
1978), appears in two of the conversations. In each case, one of the participants refers to an absent person, rather than revealing their own position.

In dialogue 1, Dad makes a threat: if Becky doesn't take care of her
car, he'll sell it. However, he doesn't take responsibility for the threat
himself; he blames it on his wife instead. This tactic illustrates triangling:
instead of revealing something about himself (in this case, his desire about
Becky's car) he invokes an absent third party.

The daughter is also implicated in Dad's maneuver, since she doesn't
complain: *"Never mind what Mom wants, Dad, what do you want?" Since
the daughter does not complain, she is colluding with Dad in blaming Mom.
She allows Dad to maintain the fiction that he is good and that Mom is bad.
In this respect, he is probably not only deceiving Becky, but also himself.
He is ensnared in his own communication tactics.

I will refer to this type of alienation as engulfment, a type of false solidarity. Both parties are withholding thoughts and feelings, which gives each
a false sense of security. However, both parties are giving up parts of self
to maintain this pretense. Dad might be angry at Becky, but denies it, or at
least he doesn't acknowledge it explicitly. The threat and the abruptness of
his language imply anger that is being denied. Just as he may not have been
aware of his desire in the case of Becky's car, he is probably also unaware
that he is angry at Becky, and, as will be suggested below, at Mom also.

Becky's evasiveness is more subtle than Dad's. First, in allowing him
to blame Mom for the threat he is making, she is giving up the opportunity
to come to know Dad better. What does he actually want her to do, and
more indirectly, how does he feel about Mom's nagging? Second, by colluding in blaming Mom, she is setting up obstacles to resolving her own
differences with her mother.

Dialogue 2, Becky and Mom, also indicates alienation, but a different
type than with Dad. If Becky and her father are engulfed, then she and her
mother are isolated. In this case, Mom is openly critical and disrespectful
toward Becky, and there are signs of anger on both sides. Mom implies that
not only is Becky irresponsible, but she is also grossly unresponsive to her,
the mother ("What's it gonna take *[to get you to respond to my request,
an earthquake]?" the language of insult).

Becky responds in kind, with a counter-insult. "Why is my car always
brought up? It happened a year ago." Just as Mom implies that Becky is

unresponsive, Becky, in turn, implies that Mom is unreasonable, that she is a nag. Immediately after insulting Mom, however, Becky retreats by apologizing in a half-hearted way, and then, again half-heartedly, attempts to justify herself ("It wasn't on purpose"). Just as the style of interaction between Becky and Dad is one of false (exaggerated) solidarity, the style between Becky and Mom is one of isolation and conflict.

Exchange 3, the counterfactual between Mom and Dad, shows many of the same characteristics as the other two exchanges. As in the first dialogue, the two participants are triangling against a third who is not present: Mom is complaining about Becky; Dad does not object. Mom is also critical of Dad, but in a somewhat indirect way. Rather than stating her criticism of him directly (*"You are too lenient with Becky"), she asks a question, "Why are you so lenient ... ?," which implies a criticism of Dad. However, she is direct about criticizing Becky, who is not present, in the second sentence. In the third sentence, she issues a command, "You have to come down on her."

Although Dad has indicated to Becky in exchange 1 that it is not he but Mom that is critical of Becky, he does an about-face in his exchange with Mom. That is, he makes no effort to defend Becky, siding instead with Mom's criticism of her with a blanket agreement ("Yes, dear, you're right ... "). Mom and Dad collude in vilifying Becky.

There is evidence in this dialogue that Mom is angry at Dad, but is not expressing it directly. She is indirectly critical of Dad, demanding, and uses a word in describing Becky ("completely") that indicates not only that she may be angry at Becky, but in a state of anger at the time of this dialogue. Words like "completely," "never," "always," etc. are called "extenders" in the analysis of emotions in discourse. Since they are exaggerations, they imply hidden anger. Mom is in an angry, blaming mode.

Since Mom is critical and demanding toward Dad, we might expect that he might be angry in return. However, the words show no evidence of anger; they are placating. However, some of his comments in exchange 1 suggest that he may be angry at Mom. He tells Becky that Mom is "really bugging me" in regard to Becky's car. This phrase may have a double meaning—that Mom is pressing him, but also that she is making him angry.

The three dialogues can be used to derive a style of communication tactics and emotion management for each of the family members. There is no leveling in any of the dialogues; no one is direct in a respectful way. All three are indirect both about their desires and their feelings. Mom is an angry blamer and critic with Becky, and critical and blaming in an indirect way with Dad. Dad is completely placating with Mom, but threatening and indirectly blaming with Becky. Becky, finally, is placating with Dad, and first blaming, then placating with Mom. The three exchanges illustrate a system of dysfunctional communication in this family; instead of leveling, all three dialogues are in the blame-blame or blame-placate modes.

The exchanges shown above supply only verbal information, no nonverbal information was included. In the role-playing exercises with Becky, however, she provided nonverbal gestures as well, her own, and, in mime, she portrayed those of Dad and Mom. Based on both the verbal and nonverbal information, a classification of the styles of emotion management can be made, with emphasis on the management of shame and anger.

Mom is the most overt with anger; she shows anger in her words and gestures directed at Becky, and in a less overt way, toward Dad. Becky is next-most overt; she shows some overt anger toward Mom, but quickly takes it back. She shows none at all toward Dad. Dad is the least overt; he shows no anger at all toward Mom in her presence, and only covert signs of anger toward her in her absence. In Becky's presence his words and gestures imply covert anger.

The indications of shame in this family are much more subtle than those of anger. One indication of shame is how indirect all three members are with each other, at least when the other is present. The indirection of anger is particularly indicative that each person is ashamed of their anger. Another indication is that all three dialogues are entirely oriented toward a *topic,* the car; no one comments on *relationship* issues. For example, no one complains directly about the other's manner toward them, although respect is clearly an issue in the dialogue between Becky and Mom, and indirectly, between Mom and Dad. To understand the shame dynamics in this family, it will help to discuss relationship dynamics, how each of the three relationships might affect each other over time.

I have argued that Becky and Dad idealize themselves and each other, and collude in vilifying Mom. Becky and Mom engage in overt, angry conflict. Mom shows covert anger toward Dad, but he placates in return. One place to start with the interactions between each of the subsystems is to visualize what would happen if Dad tried to level with Mom.

Suppose that in the dialogue with Mom, instead of his blanket endorsement of her criticism of him, her criticism of Becky, and her demand that he take action against her, the conversation had gone like this:

*Father: I'd prefer that together you and I talk about this issue directly with Becky, rather than behind her back.

Although Mom might experience this line as an attack, she might also feel relieved that the issue is finally out in the open: how does Dad himself feel on this (and other) issues? Mom might experience the placation in his actual response as somewhat false; there is a monotony and flatness to his four affirmations of her position inside of two short sentences. She also might have a sense that Becky's defiance of her wishes could mean that Dad is covertly backing Becky, and defying Mom. The combination of Dad's bland compliance toward her (Mom), and the sense of a secret alliance between Dad and Becky, could generate feelings of confusion, powerlessness, rejection, and anger in Mom, a situational paranoia.

This counterfactual was used to illustrate the idea of the routines that dominate the three relationships. To start arbitrarily with one of the relationships, without implying that it is the cause more than any other: to the extent that Becky and Dad idealize themselves and each other and vilify Mom because she is so critical (angry), to that extent Mom will feel excluded, rejected, and angry (critical) toward both of them. To the extent that Mom is critical and angry toward Dad, to that extent he will placate and withhold his own feelings. To the extent that he placates and withholds toward Mom and Becky, the anger between Mom and Becky will be increased, a feedback loop around the three-way system. Impression management in this family is a disaster. Goffman would certainly have understood this kind of alienation.

Janie's Family: A Mother-Daughter Alliance

Another student's family system shows much the same patterns as Becky's, except that in this case the daughter and mother are allied against the father. Janie's dialogues started with her father's TV viewing:

1. Father-daughter

Father: Sssh!!! I'M WATCHING THE NEWS!!!

Janie: THAT'S ALL YOU EVER DO, WATCH TV. TV IS MORE IMPORTANT TO YOU THAN YOUR OWN DAUGHTER!!!

2. Mother-daughter

Mother: Oh! I just don't understand your father. I just don't understand why he won't help with the housework.

Janie: I don't know, Mom. I just don't know.

3. Father-mother* (Counterfactual)

Father: The roast is overcooked again.

Mother: Sorry. I didn't watch it because I was so busy cleaning the house.

Although this last dialogue is hypothetical, Janie confirmed that she had heard many such exchanges between her father and mother on various topics. The communication patterns in this family are similar to those already reported in Becky's family, but this time the mother and daughter are aligned, the dad is out in the cold. I will begin with the father-daughter exchange.

Janie has walked into the living room where her father is watching TV. Rather than go all the way around him to get his attention, she speaks to him from behind, as she is walking toward him: "Dad, I have a question.... "As indicated in the exchange above, he interrupts her by shushing her before she can finish her sentence. This exchange takes the form of an overt quarrel, with both father and daughter raising their voice angrily, and with no eye contact during the whole dialogue. The consequences are predictable: Janie leaves the room hurt and offended. Characteristically, instead of confronting the problem, she withdraws.

The father's response to Janie's request to talk is disrespectful; he commands her to keep quiet in a loud voice, and he continues watching the TV rather than turning away from it to face her. Without the courtesy necessary to turn down her request without offense, his words and manner are harsh, abrupt, and rejecting.

Although Janie was unaware of it at the time, her approach to her father was also disrespectful. She didn't raise her voice in requesting his attention, but she also was discourteous. A more respectful beginning would have been to avoid talking to the back of his head. Janie could have walked up to him from the side, seeking eye contact, but waiting to speak until he turned toward her. This approach would have been a tacit admission that she was interrupting him. She might even have apologized for the interruption: *"Dad, I know you're busy, but I need to talk to you." If she had begun this way, perhaps the dialogue would have taken a different direction:

*Father: Can you wait ten minutes till the news is over?

Janie: Yes.

Like Becky, Janie was unaware of her own part in the ongoing quarrel with her dad. She became aware only in reenacting it in class.

Students often had strong emotional reactions when they became aware of some new feature of their family relationships, but not always. Becky's emotional reactions were mild; she shed a few tears when she realized her role in excluding her mother. Janie's reactions were much stronger. At first, when she became aware of her part in excluding her father, she seemed stunned. She also seemed excited to have discovered something new about herself and her family. Her emotional response to new knowledge about her relation with her mother was still stronger.

The exchange between Janie and her mother, like the one between Becky and her father, is an example of triangling. Instead of thrashing the issue of housekeeping duties out with the father, the mother complains about the father to Janie. Although the mother's statement is in the form of a question, it is not a real question, but a complaint. (Janie indicated that her mother had asked her the same question many times.) Like Becky, Janie also colludes with one parent against the other since she doesn't object. Instead of suggesting to her mother that she complain directly to the father, Janie evades answering by stating that she doesn't know.

In the role-playing that took place during class, Janie became aware of the part she was playing in the ongoing quarrel with her father, but did not become aware of her role in the impasse with her mother. Awareness in this instance occurred later, in my office, when Janie and I were discussing her dialogue with her mother.

I questioned her about what she was feeling when her mother complained about her father to her. First she said that she felt proud that her mother was confiding in her. In response to my question about any other feelings, at first she said there were none. When I repeated the question, however, she began to cry, and became red in the face. When I asked her what she was feeling, she said that she felt anger at her mother for coming between her and her father. She cried deeply and for a considerable length of time. At the end of our talk, however, she was glowing with enthusiasm. She said she was hopeful, because now she saw that there was something that she herself could do to improve her relationships with both her parents.

I will present one exchange from the family system of a third student, Lyn, because it contains an element different from the two already discussed. Both Becky and Janie were involved in an overt quarrel with one of their parents: Becky with her mother, Janie with her father. Lyn's relationship with one of her parents (her mother) was one of idealization and pseudo-solidarity, much like the relationship between Becky and her father, and Janie and her mother. However, Lyn's relationship with her father involved little or no quarreling. It involved instead a *silent impasse*: tension, distance, and the slow withdrawal of affection. Lyn's exchange with her father illustrates this kind of conflict:

Father: Do you have something in mind that you want to do tonight?

Daughter: No, nothing in particular.

The impasse in this situation is carefully disguised. Each participant seems to have been hiding their thoughts and feelings not only from each other, but even from themselves. The father's question came at the end of dinner. When he asked it, Lyn was expecting her father to suggest an activity that the two of them could do together, a game, perhaps, or watching a particular TV program. She was disappointed and stunned when instead he rose to go, saying "Well then, I have some work to do in my room."

Apparently Lyn and her father had played out similar exchanges many times before. Both seem hesitant to make the first step. Each does not want to intrude on the other's privacy, or is apprehensive about closeness. This kind of hesitancy and mutual misunderstanding is reminiscent of Harrington's (1989) study of romantic propositions: although both participants may want to date, each waits for the other to be the initiator. Apparently this kind of dance is not limited to romantic invitation, but can obtain in any kind of relationship, as in the case of the father-daughter situation in Lyn's exchange.

Lyn was surprised when she realized during role-play in my office that she was as responsible for the impasse as her father; she had been assigning all the responsibility to him. Lyn had a strong emotional reaction to her realization; she wept intensely. However, when she later role-played the exchange in class, she showed little emotion. She told me afterwards that she felt she needed to swallow her feelings in front of such a large group.

Richard's family system seemed to be quite different from any of the others. The exchanges he described involved his mother and his stepfather. Unlike the other students, he was combative and seemingly alienated from both parents. His exchange with his stepfather was particularly intense, each forcefully criticizing the other's actions. However, I gathered from the way he role-played the exchanges that his bonds were probably more secure than most of the other students, since the conflict in his family was largely out in the open. Conflict does not necessarily lead to alienation; the crucial issue is the manner that the participants show in disputes. If one's manner is respectful, than disputes can have beneficial effects. Open conflict can lead to needed adjustments in relationships, as Simmel (1955) and others have argued. I think it indicative that out of this class, there was only one family in which leveling was frequent.

My experience with the students in this class caused me to change my mind about gender issues in middle-class families. Like most of the students, I had assumed that the traditional role of the father, the hard-driving, somewhat distant breadwinner, was one of the fundamental causes of the high levels of alienation in modern families. In the students' families, the father was more often cast in the role of the distant or vilified parent, by a ratio of almost two to one. However, after seeing the same faulty communication patterns repeated by all three participants, it seems to me that gender is not a central component in the problem: in all of the family systems we examined, all three family members—father, mother, and offspring—seemed equally implicated in causing and maintaining the status quo. When the father is the odd man out, his exclusion is more noticeable than the mother's; his isolation is more visible than the mother-child engulfment. In our society, the male role is correlated with the isolated style of alienation, and the female role with engulfed style. Judging from the students' family systems, however, these differences are only superficial; the emotional and communication patterns are equally dysfunctional and disruptive, no matter whether a relationship is isolated or engulfed. Janie's and Lyn's relationships with their mothers were as alienated as their relationships with their fathers, since they maintained them by ignoring key parts of their selves, such as their anger.

Awareness and Emotion

In the class as a whole (forty-one students) there were variable reactions to the family system exercises. The students divided into three roughly equal groups. About a third did not seem to gain any new awareness of their own family system. (Even though virtually all students claimed that they understood family systems better in the course evaluations.) Another third obviously gained awareness, but had little or no emotional reaction, like Becky. The last third, finally, reacted like Janie and Lyn: they seemed to grow in awareness, and had strong emotional reactions.

Judging from their later comments, I would guess few of the students in the first group will undergo change as a result of the class. In the second group, perhaps half or less might change. In the last group, virtually all will probably change. This is to say that I believe that new awareness is less likely to result in personal growth unless it is accompanied by strong emotional responses.

One reason for students' resistance to awareness, emotion, and change was that they were all enmeshed, in varying degrees, with their own family systems. How can such a self-perpetuating system change? Perhaps by changes in the communication tactics and acknowledgment of emotions by one or more of the participants. If Dad levels with Mom, instead of withholding, or levels with Becky instead of colluding with her against Mom, the whole system must change.

There are three key dimensions of the system under consideration: solidarity-alienation, communication tactics, and emotion management. Solidarity involves attunement: each party understands self and other both cognitively and emotionally. Alienation involves misunderstanding or lack of understanding. Solidarity promotes trust and effective cooperation; alienation promotes suspicion and conflict.

Solidarity reflects and generates effective communication tactics, some form of respectful leveling. These tactics involve both truthfulness toward others and self-knowledge. Dad is not intentionally deceptive with Mom and Becky; his deceptiveness, and the deceptiveness of the other two family members as well, arises out of self-deception. He is not aware of many of his own desires and emotions.

Alienation from self and others reflects and generates dysfunctional communication tactics. Blaming flows from idealization of self and one's allies, and vilification of one's opponents. Blaming the other party may generate placating, distraction, or computing, but it can also generate counter-blaming, as in the exchange between Becky and Mom. This analysis shows that because of the interactions between the relationships in a system, a blaming-placation relationship (peace) in one part or phase of a system can generate an interminable blaming-counter-blaming relationship (war) in another part of the system.

At the interpersonal level at least, triangling seems to be a crucial tactic leading to interminable conflicts. Two or more parties in the system communicate secretly concerning a third party. These two parties usually become engulfed in a mutual admiration society, which conspires against the third party. This engulfment may be quite ineffective in the long run, however, if the parties become zealots, yes-persons because they over-conform, idealizing themselves and each other, and undervaluing the opponent.

Bowen (1978) defines triangling strictly in terms of two parties communicating about a third party, rather than revealing themselves. However, there is another type of faulty communication tactic that involves a triangle, but with objects or topics, rather than another party. In dysfunctional family systems, communication is usually locked into topics (tasks in the home, money, sex, education, ideas, etc.) in a way that relationship issues are avoided (Watzlawick et al. 1967).

In such systems, parties do not reveal or reflect on their own feelings, or the feelings of the other; instead they triangle onto other parties or topics. For this reason, there is considerable misunderstanding or ignorance of one's position and that of the other members, a state of alienation. As students in my classes sometimes remarked, their parents were strangers to each other, even though they had lived together for most of their adult lives. The routine of topic talk, and the other routines mentioned earlier, can take over a relationship, to the point that these routines *are* the relationship.

It is of interest and concern that in the large class from which this case was taken, transfer of knowledge to the student's own family system from another student's seemed to take place only very slowly. That is, students watched case after case of role-playing that revealed the alienation underlying the appearance of solidarity and/or conflict to the student involved, and to the class as a whole. Students could correctly apply concepts such as engulfment and isolation to other's dialogues, but most seemed to find it difficult to see the same patterns in their own.

When students role-played their own family system they could become aware of its dynamics. It appeared that their awareness was blocked by intense emotions that they were unable to countenance on their own. In the safety of the class setting, or my office, they seemed able to deal with these emotions; then they could apply what they had learned abstractly in the class to their own case.

Since I did not role-play dialogue with all forty-one of the students, it is possible that there are exceptions, students who correctly understood their own family system on their own. Even so, it seems to me that for the majority, abstract, dispassionate knowledge is not enough. Contact with their own painful emotions is a precondition for increased self-awareness.

Summary

The family systems of my students, the three described here, as well as almost all of the others in the class that I have not included here, share several patterns in common. In the great majority of cases (all but one) communication among family members seemed to be indirect. The evasiveness and indirectness of communication suggest that shame is a pervasive presence in these families, even though it is usually denied. Family members seem ashamed of the thoughts and feelings, especially shame and anger, that are inevitable in close relationships.

Shame is both cause and effect of protracted conflict. It is a signal of the alienation in these families, i.e., the lack of understanding and the misunderstanding between the members, and yet a signal that is uniformly ignored and denied. It is not shame that causes interminable conflict, but its denial. Continuing shame is also a consequence of unending conflict: family members cycle through disrespectful words and gestures, shame and anger, which leads to further disrespectful gestures, and so on around the loop. Disrespect all around brings feelings of rejection (shame) that are usually denied.

Whether openly conflictful or bypassed, family members in most of the dialogues did not seem to understand each other, or misunderstood each other, or, in most cases, a mixture of both. Denial of shame is both cause and effect of a continuing cycle of deception and self-deception about thoughts and feelings. Judging from some of the students' comments, the system of relationships in each family was static, having existed for as long as the student could remember, and showed virtually no change or variation over time.

In most of the students' families, the relationships among the members were almost entirely based on routine. Of course in close relationships, some routine is inevitable and even desirable, in that it saves time, effort, and emotion. But in these families the relationships seem to be *all* routine. Nothing new happened between the members.

There were two kinds of routines in these families. The most immediate routines concerned the style of interaction between the members: blame-blame, blame-placate, distract-distract, and so on. But there were two routines that were the key to all of the relationships: automatically withholding or ignoring emotions, and triangling or attending to *topics* rather than to the immediate relationship. All of the dialogue reported above concerns topics, rather than what is going on between the parties to the dialogue. No one reports on their current feelings, or asks about the feelings of the other. There were not even questions or statements that might avoid misunderstanding, such as "What do you mean?" or "I don't understand what you are saying." As long as feelings are not revealed and relationships are not discussed, they stay the same, frozen in time.

Most students seemed unaware of the routines or other basic features of their family systems. Typically students idealized both parents, or idealized one and vilified or misunderstood the other. In every case students seemed unaware of their own contributions to maintaining the system. They saw their family conflicts as exterior and constraining, to use Durkheim's (1915) phrase. That is, by denying their own part in producing unresolved quarrels and impasses, they experienced them as coming from others (exterior), and controlling and limiting their own behavior (constraining).

As already indicated, students were always surprised and often stunned or shocked when they discovered their own role in maintaining their family system. This effect stood out particularly in the students who first showed understanding only of others' family systems. Even though they had gained abstract understanding of alienation and faulty communication tactics, they had been unable to apply these ideas to their own families. When they were able to apply them, they reacted with surprise and even shock.

Students seem to pass through two gates before acquiring personal knowledge: intellectual understanding and emotional understanding. Some parts of this book may also have the same two gates. Entering either gate marks an advance, but it would be best to pass through both of them. Unlike many social science books, this one suggests that the reader try to apply the ideas offered here to his or her own life. Actual rather than merely cognitive understanding seems to require that step.

The next chapter will consider how another set of routines—hypermasculinity, what Goffman called "the male mystique" (1967, 209-70)—contributes to conflict at both the interpersonal and group levels.

Note

1. The idea of part/whole analysis is based on Spinoza's dictum that human beings are so complex that we need to link the "least parts" and "greatest wholes" (Scheff 1997a). Although Spinoza didn't specify what he meant by the least parts, for my purposes I will take them to be the words and gestures of dialogue. The greatest wholes would be the larger systems in which any dialogue is embedded, starting with the entire history of the particular relationship, and ending with the civilization in which the dialogue has occurred.

CHAPTER 10

Masculinity and Emotions

The Silence/Violence Pattern

THIS CHAPTER PROPOSES THAT GOFFMAN made a powerful but somewhat indirect contribution to the understanding of hypermasculinity in his long essay "Where the Action Is" (in Goffman 1967). In my interpretation, the particular emotional/relational configuration that his essay implies may be one of the primary causes of gratuitous hostility and violence. Four emotions seem central: "the vulnerable emotions" (grief, fear, and shame), on the one hand, and anger, on the other. The relational component is the virtual absence of close bonds to others. It is possible that suppression of vulnerable emotions, acting out anger, and isolation gives rise to *the silence/violence pattern*: meeting what are perceived as threats to self with either silence or violence. This pattern seems to occur much more frequently in men than in women.

Two instances of massive violence illustrate these ideas: the massacre of civilians at My Lai, Vietnam, ordered and assisted by William Calley, and the monstrous violence orchestrated by the Germans under Hitler. The biographical material for Calley is fairly thin, but clearly suggests no close bonds, and that frequent and intense failure and shame went unacknowledged. Hitler's biographies, much more plentiful, provide many examples that can be seen as linking his extreme violence to suppression of vulnerable emotions, anger tantrums, and absence of bonds. The silence/violence pattern may result in violence directly through leaders like Hitler and Calley, and also indirectly, when this pattern is the basis of public support for violent leaders.

161

One of Goffman's most important contributions to the analysis of hypermasculinity occurs in "Where the Action Is," the last and by far the longest chapter in one of his early books (1967). As is the case with many of his other contributions, this one has to be interpreted by the reader, since Goffman does not articulate its meaning clearly.

The title of the chapter refers to a colloquial usage, "action" as opportunities for gambling: "Do you want a piece of the action?" means, "do you want to place a bet?" Most of the chapter, the first three quarters, is descriptive of gambling itself. However, there is an abrupt change of density in the last quarter of the chapter. The discussion of gambling is almost entirely descriptive, the remainder of the chapter, conceptual and abstract.

The turning point comes after sixty pages of text when Goffman acknowledges that his discussion of "action" is about male, or better yet, masculine behavior (209), what he calls "the cult of masculinity." At the same time that he makes this admission, the purview of "action" begins to broaden out far beyond gambling to all kinds of risky challenges. He notes, for example, that dueling is and has always been almost entirely a male domain.

Goffman appears to have used the long descriptive passages about gambling merely to lead into what seems to be his central concern, "character contests." He proposes that scenes of "action" are occasions that allow the display of "character," in the sense of establishing one's degree of "courage, gameness, integrity, and composure" (229). Of the four components, Goffman gives most attention to the last. By composure, he means poise, calmness, and above all, control over one's emotions. Character contests are competitions in which risks are taken to determine which actor has the most character, and particularly, control over their emotions.

It is possible that the cult of masculinity is a subtext of much of Goffman's work, even though it is not always made explicit. An explicit reference to masculinity occurs in Goffman's first article:[1]

> The mark's readiness to participate in a sure thing is based on more than avarice; it is based on a feeling that he will now be able to prove to himself that he is the sort of person who can "turn a fast buck." For many, this capacity for high finance comes near to being a sign of masculinity and a test of fulfilling the male role. ("On Cooling the Mark Out," 1952)

My sense is that much of Goffman's work until the publication of *Gender Advertisements* was more concerned with the masculine and hypermasculine than with feminine behavior. Note, however, that in this early publication, Goffman's attention was focused only on the mark. His later analysis of "character contests" suggests that the con's art of deception emphasizes hypermasculine competitiveness much more than the much weaker involvement with masculinity of the mark.

This chapter concerns the relationship of hypermasculine control of emotions to violence. Goffman's whole discussion implies that it is men, masculine men, that have "character." For example, a man with character who is under stress is not going to cry and blubber like a woman or child might. Although Goffman didn't use the current phrase, his chapter is about "pissing contests." Social occasions are seen as opportunities for one to test one's own character as compared to that of the other person or persons. The hypermasculine pattern promotes *competition*, rather than *connection* between persons.

Goffman sees hypermasculine control of emotions as a virtue, akin to courage and integrity. The purpose of this chapter is to suggest the opposite, that it is a fatal flaw in character that can lead to violence or at least the taken-for-granted acceptance of violence. Here is an account of the killing fields of World War I (Koenigsberg 2005).

> In the following report, British General Rees describes the massacre of his own brigade as they moved toward German lines.
>
> "They advanced in line after line, dressed as if on parade and not a man shirked going through the extremely heavy barrage, or facing the machine gun and rifle fire that finally wiped them out. I saw the lines, which advanced in such admirable order melting away under fire. Yet not a man wavered, broke the ranks, or attempted to come back. I have never seen, indeed could never have imagined such a magnificent display of *gallantry, discipline and determination.* The reports from the very few survivors of this marvelous advance bear out what I saw with my own eyes: that hardly a man of ours got to the German Front line." (emphasis added)

General Rees apparently didn't explain how he managed to survive when his whole brigade was wiped out. Like Goffman, he sees the men's self-control as virtuous, but it might be better seen as a vice, both by the leaders of the men and the men themselves, a lethal addiction to the cult of masculinity.

It seems to me that Goffman's theory of character contests is of great general interest in understanding masculine behavior (whether men or women: the behavior of women like Margaret Thatcher can be just as masculine as men). It also may be of specific interest if applied to Goffman himself. Perhaps it can be used as a key to understanding Goffman's testing, hazing, and other hostile behaviors, as described in Chapter 1.

I will mention another of several possible causes of Goffman's hazing behavior toward me in particular—although it is impossible to document —his slight stature. According to Yves Winkin, he was referred to by the islanders where he did his doctoral research as "perrie" (small) Goffman. He was perhaps five feet and three inches, a whole foot shorter than I am. That might have given him another reason for hazing me, in addition to what I consider to be the major cause, my obliviousness, already mentioned in Chapter 1.

When Goffman felt demeaned, slighted, or rejected, as I think he did with me and many others, he didn't reveal those feelings; he showed composure, poise, and control of emotions instead, as suggested by his model of masculine "character." He struck out, instead, with what might be called verbal assault, or in some cases, as in the incident on the plane, verbal aggression. There was also a widely quoted incident of shoving that might have been physical aggression.

The incident reported to me by many persons concerned what they called a fight between Goffman and Greg Stone in which Goffman knocked Stone down with one punch. However, the one person I spoke to who was an eyewitness, Howard Becker, didn't report it as a fight. The incident occurred at a party held by a publisher during an annual meeting of the American Sociological Association (ASA). According to Becker, Stone, who was sitting in a chair at the time, was very drunk. Goffman pushed Stone, who fell off the chair. Why did he push him? According to Becker, he may have been irritated by something that Stone said. Harvey Farberman told me essentially the same story, as reported to him by Stone.

Neither Becker nor Farberman knew what Stone said that may have irritated Goffman. However, many persons who knew Stone have reported outrageous things that they saw him do or say. I had such an experience myself with Stone at another ASA meeting. Having just met Stone for the first time, he told me that he would like to talk at length about ideas he got from reading the manuscript of *Being Mentally Ill* (1966) prior to publication. I was doubtful, since Stone was obviously drunk.

However, I agreed to go to his hotel room to talk. When we got in the elevator, there were three priests, one small and old, the other two young and very large. Stone stuck his face right into the face of the largest priest, saying, "You don't believe in Jesus Christ and all that shit, do you?" The priest said "Why not?" Stone said, "Why?" and the priest repeated his same response. At this point the elevator stopped at our floor. I stepped between them, saying, "I apologize for my friend."

When the elevator door closed, I said to Stone, "The next time you do something like that to me, I swear I'll never talk to you again." Stone nodded dimly, and we went on to his hotel room. Even though I was going through my hypermasculine phase myself at the time, I threatened him verbally, but felt no inclination to hit or shove him, as Goffman apparently did. The incident with Stone is the only one that I know of that involved physical assault. However, as already indicated, Goffman was famous for his verbal assaults, or to put it another way, as John Irwin did, he was a master of the putdown. Why?

It might seem unfair to even speak of Goffman, an extraordinarily gifted scholar, in the same breath with mass murderers like Calley and

Hitler. This chapter calls attention to one of the few characteristics they had in common, hypermasculinity. Otherwise, they might be from different planets entirely.

Perhaps the most obvious difference between them is that Goffman was an extraordinarily complex individual, but Calley and Hitler were not. The personalities of the latter two men were simple in the sense that from their youth, they seemed programmed to go in a single, unerring direction, toward catastrophe. Goffman, on the other hand, was many things in different situations and times of his life. He seems to have undergone considerable change, for example, after his move from Berkeley to Pennsylvania.

Another huge difference is in the goodness of fit of the model of violent hypermasculinity outlined here. Calley and Hitler seem to illustrate all three aspects exactly: they suppressed all signs of the vulnerable emotions, acted out anger, and from childhood had not a single secure bond. Goffman fit the model only with respect to emotional repression and acting out anger. It seems to me, however, that he was never without secure bonds to others.

There is little evidence concerning Goffman's childhood, but published materials and my interviews suggest that he maintained many close bonds even during his most feisty period, at Berkeley, and made many new close bonds during his life in Pennsylvania. Winkin's discussion of his time as a researcher on one of the Shetland Islands suggests that even in that difficult role, he made and kept at least one close bond.

It appears that unlike Calley and Hitler, Goffman's personality was nowhere near being a closed system. He seemed to be learning and growing for most of his lifetime. Many people have remarked on his graciousness near the end of his life in his role as president of the American Sociological Association. The association made here between Goffman, Calley, and Hitler is limited to a single facet, their hypermasculinity. In this respect, Goffman's personality was much closer to that of the average male in modern societies than it was to Calley's or Hitler's. He was hypermasculine, but like the average male, this trait didn't completely dominate his personality.

The absence of any secure bond with another person seems crucial in creating violence. For example, most of the males who "go postal," killing their colleagues or schoolmates and teachers, have been loners. The great majority of men have sealed over their vulnerable emotions, and a large minority act out anger. Yet only a small percentage of men are violent. I propose that complete isolation triggers violence when it occurs in those who have repressed their vulnerable emotions and act out anger.

Silence/Violence and Hypermasculinity

Boys learn early that showing vulnerable feelings (grief, fear, and shame) is seen as a sign of weakness. First at home, then at school, they find that acting out anger, even if faked, is seen as strength. Expressing anger verbally, rather than storming, may be seen as weakness. At first merely to protect themselves, boys begin suppressing feelings that may be interpreted as signs of weakness.

In Western cultures most boys learn, as first option, to hide their vulnerable feelings in emotionless talk, withdrawal, or silence. I will call these three responses (emotional) Silence. In situations where these options seem unavailable, males may cover their vulnerable feelings behind a display of hostility. That is, young boys learn in their families, and later, from their peers, to suppress emotions they actually feel by acting out one emotion, anger, whether they feel it or not.

I call this pattern "silence/violence." Vulnerable feelings are first hidden from others, and after many repetitions, even from self. In this latter stage, behavior becomes compulsive. When men face what they construe to be threatening situations, they may be compelled to *silence* or to rage and aggression.[2]

Even without threat, men seem to be more likely to engage in *silence* or violence than women. With their partners, most men are less likely to talk freely than women about feelings of resentment, humiliation, embarrassment, rejection, joy, genuine pride, loss, and anxiety. This may be the reason they are more likely to show anger: they seem to be backed up on a wide variety of intense feelings, but sense that only anger is allowed them. (The phrase "backed up" was first used by Tomkins; see selections from his work in the volume edited by Virginia Demos [1995], pp. 57, 92-94, 275-76.)

Why did Tomkins use such an awkward phrase, rather than the more obvious choice: "repressed"? To understand his choice requires a brief digression into the history of psychology during the period that he was writing, in the sixties and seventies. There was little hard evidence for or against the concepts of repression and the unconscious at this time, and there is not much more today. By and large, most psychotherapists assumed it to be true, and academic psychologists assumed that it was not true. Indeed, academic psychologists ridiculed these ideas, especially the idea that emotions exerted "hydraulic" pressure on everyday life.

In this context, Tomkins didn't use terms like *repression* and *unconscious,* perhaps in an attempt to avoid open conflict with the vast majority of his colleagues. But his system assumes the repression of painful emotions to the point that they become unconscious in everyday life. Although he was an academic psychologist himself, he found it necessary to invent terms that would allow his theory of emotions to involve repression and the unconscious emotions that result.

My own view of emotions is based largely on my experiences as a teacher, as a marriage counselor (1971-1976), and in my own personal life. For the last thirty-five years of teaching, my classes came close to being forms of group psychotherapy, even the large classes. Although I never called attention to the similarity, students often did. Usually the comments they made in this regard were approving; most of them thought it added to the value of the class. The format of my classes, whatever their official names, basically involved having the students examine their own experiences to help them understand their emotional/relational worlds.

During the period of student activism against the Vietnam War, these classes became intensely emotional. In a large course titled "Interpersonal Relations," taught many times over a period of three years, students underwent mass weeping and laughing, both in the large meetings, small discussion groups, and in office visits by groups of students. In 1979 I received the Distinguished Teaching Award from the University of California, Santa Barbara (UCSB), Academic Senate largely on the basis of these classes. Most of my views on emotional/relational issues were formed by my close contacts with thousands of students.

My personal life has also been dense with emotional/relational issues. Between the ages of fourteen and forty I certainly fit the pattern of male repression of vulnerable emotions. I had learned to be a strong and silent male like my father, and that expressions of fear, grief, and shame at school made me prey to bullies. Although I have no memory of my dad equating fear with cowardice, it was implied in his comments and actions. Over the course of childhood, I seem to have gradually numbed out feelings of fear. In my late thirties, during the Vietnam protest, I took many risks that seem shockingly unacceptable to me now. Some of my colleagues complimented me on my courage, but looking back it seems to me I was merely reckless.

Numbing out fear, particularly, makes men dangerous to themselves and others. Fear is an innate signal of danger that helps us survive. When we see a car heading toward us on a collision course, we have an immediate, automatic fear response: WAKE UP SLEEPYHEAD, YOUR LIFE IS IN DANGER! Much faster than thought, this reaction increases our chance of survival, and repressing it is dangerous. If the sense of fear has been repressed, it is necessary to find ways of uncovering it.

Although the idea is only hinted at by Tomkins, it now seems likely that repression of emotions leads to a vicious circle. One represses emotions in order to avoid painful feelings. At first the painful feelings have their origins in the reactions of others, especially our parents and schoolmates. Certainly as a child I sensed that expressions of grief or fear were seen by my father as indicating weakness. He often used a Yiddish expression in these circumstances: "Zai ayne mensch." At the time I took it to mean "Be a man" (instead of acting like a baby). What was painful to me was less the words (which actually mean "Be a real person") than his signs of impatience and even disgust at my emotionality.

In order to avoid pain inflicted by others, we learn to repress the expressions of feeling that lead to negative reactions from others. After thousands of curtailments, repression becomes habitual and out of consciousness. But as we become more backed up with avoided emotions, we have the sense that experiencing them would be unbearably painful. In this way, avoidance leads to avoidance in an ever-increasing, self-perpetuating loop.

For a lengthy period as a teenager and young man, it never occurred to me to try to identify and talk about the various feelings I might have had. I was angry much of the time, and sometimes enraged. As my son later told me, my anger was unpredictable. It was a problem in all of my relationships.

However, at age forty, both by accident and through various forms of therapy, I began to learn how to cry and feel fear, rather than numb it out. My first experience of intense crying at this age led to a solid year of crying every day, without exception. It was as if I had a backlog of tears to deal with.

My experiences of fear were different, however. There were only two of them, but they were profound, about six months apart. The first occurred as a result of therapy, after intense episodes of crying and laughing. The second was triggered by a death threat on the phone from an irate citizen. During this time I was both chair of an academic department and an anti-war activist. This combination increased my visibility, and it irritated a lot of people, both in and outside of the university.

Both fear episodes were quite similar in content and in duration. They each lasted about twenty minutes, and involved what would have looked like epileptic seizures from the outside. As I lay on the floor, my body went through convulsive shaking with an earthquake-like intensity, and sweating that soaked my clothes as if I had been swimming in them. Unlike my crying episodes, there was no mental content associated with the two fits of fear. Also, unlike the crying, which occurred so easily as to become commonplace, I felt utterly transformed after each fear episode.

These fear experiences also had an immediately visible effect. After the second one, I begin to actually experience fear when I was in danger. Since I was still deeply involved in the Vietnam protest, I became less reckless. Isla Vista, the student community where most of my activity took place, was a dangerous place at this time. Student protesters and the police were in open warfare. My change with respect to fear probably helped protect me and other protesters from injury.

Surprisingly, neither the crying nor the fear episodes were painful. Indeed, they were more pleasurable than painful. In the fear response, particularly, I felt somewhat like a child on a delicious roller-coaster ride. Apparently all of these changes occurred at what I have called optimal distance (in my theory of catharsis, 1979). That is, I was both in a state of grief or fear, but also outside of it, looking on like a member of an audience in a theater.

Making the acquaintance of my own shame came later, with more difficulty. At any rate, episodes of anger and rage became less frequent, briefer, and less intense as I learned to identify and feel vulnerable emotions. Another decisive step in this direction occurred as a result of marriage to my present wife, Suzanne Retzinger. After we began living together, she would usually come home from her job as a mediator in a child custody court, laden with talk. She would go on for what often seemed to me an interminable time, reviewing events of her day at work. Sometimes she would recount the same event several times. Listening to this daily drama, I was rapidly becoming exasperated.

However, after several months of suffering in silence, I noticed that she usually seemed to feel much better after her marathon of talk. A new thought occurred to me: if it works for her, maybe it will work for me! So we took turns reviewing the events of our day. At first I could hardly fill five minutes, much less the forty-five that Suzanne usually took. But with some patient probing and questions on her part, I learned how to go over the events of my day, finding and trying to finish unfinished emotion-laden events. As I learned to do that, I began to feel better. On the basis of my own experiences and as a teacher, I have come to believe that everyone needs to experience the *full range of their emotions* if they are to thrive.

Gender Differences in Emotion Management

In my experience, most women express vulnerable emotions more fully than most men. Certainly they express fear and grief more. The difference between men and women with respect to shame is probably smaller, but with women still more expressive of this emotion, if only obliquely. That is, women seem more likely to review the events of their day, either to themselves or with another person, than men. In doing so, they are likely to encounter one or more of the vulnerable emotions.

On the other hand, more women are inhibited about expressing anger, whether verbally or acting it out. Each year of teaching hundreds of students about emotions, I would come across at least one female student who claimed never to have felt anger. This student usually wore a continuous smile that was difficult for her to remove, even on request. When such a student did hit upon the experience of anger during the course exercises, she appeared both alarmed and delighted.

There also seems to be a huge difference between most men and women in feeling and expressing love. Men learn early on from fathers and schoolmates that love, like fear, grief, and shame, is likely to be interpreted as a sign of weakness. It, too, is seen as a vulnerable emotion. As already mentioned in Chapter 7, there is a humorous illustration of this tendency in the film *Big,* when the Tom Hanks character expresses his liking for another person with a shove. A similar gesture is found in the way young men will hit each other on the shoulder, at times with force, to show closeness.

My impression is that the gender difference in these four emotions is slowly decreasing as women are being prepared at home and school for careers. This change is clearest with respect to anger; more women are expressing anger either verbally or by acting out. The change toward the masculine pattern of vulnerable emotions is less clear, and may be quite slow. It seems that even career women still cry much more freely than men and are quicker to acknowledge fear.

Studies of unresolved grief and of alexithymia (Krystal 1988) indirectly support the different management of emotions by men and women. Alexithymia, meaning absence of feeling and emotion, is a recent addition to diagnostic categories. Unresolved grief is an older diagnosis. Unlike most psychiatric diagnoses, there is almost unanimous agreement that this syndrome is one whose "cause is known, whose features are distinctive, and whose course is predictable" (Parkes 1998).

At any rate, although these studies do not comment on gender differences, in the case studies reported, men outnumber women by a ratio of about four to one. A patient who shows up in a psychiatrist's office with symptoms of alexithymia or unresolved grief is much more likely to be a man than a woman.

K. Doka and T. Martin (1998) have argued that men's grieving is not recognized as such, because it is largely cognitive and behavioral, rather than affective. In this and other publications, Doka has sought to back up his idea with empirical data. But it seems to me that his data, based on paper and pencil inventories, hardly touches the realities of grieving. However, his idea that grieving has cognitive and behavioral, as well as emotional components, is probably valid. And not just for grief, but also for fear and shame: talking about feeling has a role in reframing trauma that is partially independent of feeling.

Kathryn Newman (2004) collected information about all episodes of mass killing at schools between 1974, when they were unusual, and 2002, when they had become more frequent. All told she found 27 shootings involving 29 boys (in two of the episodes, there were two shooters). No episode with a girl shooter was found. Women can be as verbally abusive as men, and commit single homicides, but not mass killings. That seems to be a male preserve. Clearly, it's not that women's marksmanship is better.

As far as I can tell, none of the boys seemed to have a single secure bond. They were isolated from schoolmates, teachers, and family members as well. One might think at first glance that at least in two of the episodes, the boys did have a secure bond. What was the nature of the bond between the two boys in the two cases that involved a pair of shooters, rather than just one? There is very little direct evidence, but several comments suggest that the collaborating boys had an engulfed bond, shutting out the world of other possible relationships.

At this writing, the most recent school shooting occurred at Red Lake Senior High School in Minnesota. This particular case is somewhat unusual in that the shooter, Jeff Weise, left a long record of writing on the

Internet. On March 21, 2005, he killed seven people and himself. He was a very obese (6 feet, 250 lbs.) sixteen year-old, whose father had committed suicide ten years earlier. His mother, who had been driving drunk, was brain damaged in an accident in 1999. According to Weise's online postings, since her accident, she had been beating him mercilessly, and he never stood up to her.

In another posting, he stated, "I have friends, but I'm basically a loner in a group of loners. Most of my friends don't know the real me, I've never shared my past with anyone, and I've never talked about it with anyone. I'm excluded from anything and everything they do, I'm never invited, I don't even know why they consider me a friend or I them ..." (*Santa Barbara News-Press,* March 25, 2005).

This boy was obviously without a single secure bond, rejected continually and relentlessly by everyone around him, including his mother and his so-called friends. It is little wonder that he seemed to be drowning in shame, as indicated in another of his postings: "I really must be fucking worthless ..." He had attempted to slit his wrists a year earlier, was seeing a therapist, and was on antidepressants. The news reports provide no information about the number of sessions with the therapist or what transpired in them.

However, the fact that he was on antidepressants suggests yet another rejection, this time by the medical profession. This boy's main problem was that his immediate social life was a living hell, which needed immediate intervention, change, and personal attention. Whoever put him on antidepressants is guilty of gross negligence and malpractice. Yet providing psychotropic drugs only is overwhelmingly practiced in the United States, regardless of the social surrounding. In this way lack of secure bonds is not only interpersonal, but also embedded in the social structure. Men, especially, because of the isolation caused by their training for achievement, suffer more than women from lack of secure bonds.

The difference between men's and women's attitudes toward violence can be seen in the various polls that are relevant to the support of the Iraq war. No matter which poll or the framing of the question, women always express less support for the war. Women are much less keen on violence in its collective form than men. At the level of families, women are also much less likely to commit violence than men, especially physical violence.

A recent literature review of responses to stress (Taylor et al. 2000) finds that women, much more than men, are likely to "tend-and-befriend" rather than "fight-or-flight." The attachment/networking response seems to be more alive in women than in men. The *tend-befriend* pattern can be viewed as the default variant for females, an important modification of Cannon's idea of fight-or-flight.

This chapter proposes that the silence/violence pattern is the corresponding variant for males. The violence part obviously corresponds to fight. But the silence part is equivalent to flight, if withdrawal includes not just physical flight, but also withdrawal in its psychological sense. The

Taylor et al. *tend-befriend* pattern for women, when combined with the silence/violence pattern for men, suggests that the fight/flight response is crucially modified by culture-driven gender differences.

It seems to me that my analysis of what I call "the silence/violence pattern" (2005) can be applied to the masculine mystique in general, and to Goffman's hostile behavior in particular. Hypermasculine men are silent about their feelings to the point of repressing them altogether, except for anger and hostility. Repressing the vulnerable emotions (grief, fear, and shame, the latter as in feelings of rejection or disconnection) leads to either silence or withdrawal, on the one hand, or acting out anger (flagrant hostility), on the other. Composure and poise of the kind that Goffman recommended, according to my theory, are recipes for silence, withdrawal, or aggression.

The way in which the U.S. military continues its policy of discrimination against gays, in defiance of court rulings, and not giving service women combat duty equally with men suggests the crucial role that hypermasculinity plays in collective violence. But the evidence is indirect. The role of hypermasculine emotions in actual events is difficult to evaluate directly because of inadequate reporting of the emotional/relational world.

Conventional reporting involves the behavioral/cognitive world, at best. But the nature of the emotions involved, and relationships, can be inferred from these materials if they are interpreted within the larger context. This method is first applied to the case of William Calley, the army officer convicted of ordering and helping carry out the massacre at My Lai, and then to the much fuller accounts of Hitler's life. But there is one dramatic difference between the two that makes Calley's behavior seem almost as disturbing as Hitler's: even though he organized the murder of millions, Hitler is not known to have ever killed even one of those that he led others to kill. Calley not only ordered murder, but killed many of his victims himself.

William Calley and the My Lai Massacre

This account is based on several sources. The first is the online record of a PBS broadcast: *The American Experience: Vietnam* (PBS, undated). The second is based on a recent review of Calley's conviction for murder, within the larger perspective of the U.S. military involvement in the Vietnam War (Belknap 2002). Other biographies are also cited: Hersh 1970; Calley 1971; Everett 1971; Greenshaw 1971; Hammer 1971.

Charley Company reached My Lai village on March 16, 1968, led by Lt. William Calley. Like some of the men serving under him, Calley's background was unheroic. (The following account is an abbreviated version of the PBS text.)

[His] utter lack of respect for the indigenous population was apparent to all in the company. According to one soldier, "if they wanted to do something wrong, it was all right with Calley." Seymour Hersh (1970) wrote that by March of 1968 "many in the company had given in to an easy pattern of violence." Soldiers systematically beat unarmed civilians. Some civilians were murdered. Whole villages were burned. Wells were poisoned. Rapes were common.

On March 14, a small squad from "C" Company ran into a booby trap, killing a popular sergeant, blinding one GI and wounding several others. The following evening, when a funeral service was held for the killed sergeant, soldiers had revenge on their mind. After the service, Captain Medina rose to give the soldiers a pep talk and discuss the next morning's mission. Medina told them that the VC were in the vicinity of a hamlet known as My Lai 4, which would be the target of a large-scale assault by the company.

The soldiers' mission would be to engage the enemy and to destroy the village of My Lai. By 7 a.m., Medina said, the women and children would be out of the hamlet and all they could expect to encounter would be the enemy. The soldiers were to explode brick homes, set fire to thatch homes, shoot livestock, poison wells, and destroy the enemy. The seventy-five or so American soldiers would be supported in their assault by gunship pilots.

Medina later said that his objective that night was to "fire them up and get them ready to go in there; I did not give any instructions as to what to do with women and children in the village." Although some soldiers agreed with that recollection of Medina's, others clearly thought that he had ordered them to kill every person in My Lai 4. Perhaps his orders were intentionally vague. What seems likely is that Medina intentionally gave the impression that everyone in My Lai would be their enemy.

At 7:22 a.m. on March 16, nine helicopters lifted off for the flight to My Lai 4. By the time the helicopters carrying members of Charlie Company landed in a rice paddy about 140 yards south of My Lai, the area had been peppered with small arms fire from assault helicopters. Whatever VC might have been in the vicinity of My Lai had most likely left by the time the first soldiers climbed out of their helicopters. The assault plan called for Lt. Calley's first platoon and Lt. Stephen Brooks' second platoon to sweep into the village, while a third platoon, Medina, and the headquarters unit would be held in reserve and follow the first two platoons in after the area was more-or-less secured.

My Lai village had about 700 residents. They lived in either red-brick homes or thatch-covered huts. A deep drainage ditch marked the eastern boundary of the village. Directly south of the residential area was an open plaza area used for holding village meetings. To the north and west of the village was dense foliage.

By 8 a.m., Calley's platoon had crossed the plaza on the town's southern edge and entered the village. They encountered families cooking rice in front of their homes. The men began their usual search-and-destroy task of pulling people from homes, interrogating them, and searching for VC. Soon the killing began. The first victim was a man stabbed in the back with a bayonet. Then a middle-aged man was picked up, thrown down a well, and a grenade lobbed in after him. A group of fifteen to twenty mostly older women were gathered around a temple, kneeling and praying. They were all executed with shots to the back of their heads.

Eighty or so villagers were taken from their homes and herded to the plaza area. As many cried "No VC! No VC!" Calley told soldier Paul Meadlo, "You know what I want you to do with them." When Calley returned ten minutes later and found the Vietnamese still gathered in the plaza he reportedly said to Meadlo, "Haven't you got rid of them yet? I want them dead. Waste them." Meadlo and Calley began firing into the group from a distance of ten to fifteen feet. The few that survived did so because they were covered by the bodies of those less fortunate.

What Captain Medina knew of these war crimes is not certain. It was a chaotic operation. Gary Garfolo said, "I could hear shooting all the time. Medina was running back and forth everywhere. This wasn't no organized deal." Medina would later testify that he didn't enter the village until 10 a.m., after most of the shooting had stopped, and did not personally witness a single civilian being killed. Others put Medina in the village closer to 9 a.m., and close to the scene of many of the murders as they were happening.

As the third platoon moved into My Lai, it was followed by army photographer Ronald Haeberle, there to document what was supposed to be a significant encounter with a crack enemy battalion. Haeberle took many pictures. He said he saw about thirty different GIs kill about 100 civilians. Once Haeberle focused his camera on a young child about five feet away, but before he could get his picture the kid was blown away. He angered some GIs as he tried to photograph them as they fondled the breasts of a fifteen-year-old Vietnamese girl.

Meanwhile, the rampage below continued. Calley was at the drainage ditch on the eastern edge of the village, where about seventy to eighty old men, women, and children not killed on the spot had been brought. Calley ordered the dozen or so platoon members there to push the people into the ditch, and three or four GIs did. Calley ordered his men to shoot into the ditch. Some refused, others obeyed. One who followed Calley's order was Paul Meadlo, who estimated that he killed about twenty-five civilians. (Later Meadlo was seen, head in hands, crying.) Calley joined in the massacre. At one point, a two-year-old child who somehow survived the gunfire began running towards the hamlet. Calley grabbed the child, threw him back in the ditch, then shot him.

In prior studies (Collins, 1990) of massacres like the one in My Lai, the most prominent hypothesis concerns what has been called "a forward panic." This idea proposes that any group in a highly emotional state, especially a state of fear, is capable of massacre.

The parallel upon which this idea is based is the behavior of audiences in theater fires. In a panic to get out of the theater, members of the audience may trample on each other. A panic state of this kind leads to unintentional, indeed compulsive behavior. A telling detail from these accounts is that many audience members seem to have no memory of the panic. In their desperation to flee the theater, they may have experienced an *absence,* which is French for temporarily losing your mind.

The idea of panic seems to explain collective behavior in theater fires very well. A panic suggests flight behavior driven entirely by a single emotion, fear, and that it has no basis in the previous history of the members of the crowd. Forward panic adds a new idea, that instead of flight, panic can also lead to fight. In the case of massacres, fight would take the form of slaughter.

There are several studies of massacres by soldiers that strongly suggest forward panics (Collins 1990). Military units that had no history of earlier violence, under conditions of great danger, have committed mayhem against either captive enemy soldiers or helpless civilians. In Collins's forthcoming study of collective violence, he suggests that the slaughter at My Lai may have been caused, at least in part, by forward panic.

While there are some indications of forward panic in the massacre at My Lai, there are many indications that suggest other causes as well. The prior history of the behavior of the soldiers in Company C is rife with episodes of earlier violence against civilians, suggesting a habitual pattern of behavior as one of the causes of the My Lai massacre.

There are also many suggestions that point toward intentionality by Calley and by his superior officers, including his immediate superior, Capt. Medina. Both the orders from above and Calley's actions themselves can be seen as intentional. Although Medina's orders are not completely unambiguous, certainly Calley's comments and actions suggest intention, rather than compulsive actions during a panic.

Another, more obvious limitation of the forward panic hypothesis is that there seem to have been other emotions involved, in addition to fear. It seems obvious that fear was a part of the pattern. In the events leading up to My Lai, Company C had been exposed to grave and constant danger. They were fighting an enemy that was virtually invisible, attacking under thick forest cover, and in silence. The lives of these soldiers had been on the line 24/7 for many days. Surely they were living in fear of their lives.

But the account above suggests other emotions as well. The U.S. soldiers found the skillful tactics of their enemy frustrating, which is one of many vernacular ways of implicating the emotion of anger. Anger is also implied in regard to the death of one of their sergeants and the wounding of several of their fellows, only two days before the arrival at My Lai: "[The] soldiers had revenge on their mind." The idea of revenge involves not only anger, since revenge implies a shame-anger sequence. The inability of the men to even find, much less defeat the enemy appears to have given rise not only to fear and anger, but also to the feeling of defeat and its consequence, humiliation.

Neither Calley's autobiographical statement (1973) nor his biographies are sufficiently detailed to allow a clear analysis of his emotional life. With the exception of a temporary bond with his older sister, he appeared to have formed no close bonds with anyone. Even though lacking in details, his biographies do uniformly suggest conditions for one emotion, the emotion of shame. Judging from his history, beginning as a high school student and extending into his life after leaving school, he had encountered a long and virtually uninterrupted series of scornful treatments from others and unremitting failures.

Calley failed many courses in high school and college, and failed at many jobs after leaving school. By some monstrous error, when he enlisted in the Army, he was chosen for Officers' Candidate School (OCS). But his record both in OCS and in his regular service was one of failure and scorn. The officer who was his immediate superior in Vietnam, Capt. Medina, is recorded as never referring to him by his name, but instead used only scornful epithets. For example, in front of his platoon, Medina referred to Calley as "Lt. Shithead."

Given this record of unremitting scorn and failure, it is instructive to read Calley's version of his life (as told to John Sack, 1973). Calley was utterly silent about his long history of failure and scorn. The difference between the biographies and Calley's version of his life would seem to support the idea that violent men suppress their emotional lives.

Calley's behavior during the massacre itself provides a vivid image of the silence/violence pattern. While ordering and participating in the murder of women and children, he was emotionally silent. Note the details in the final paragraph on page 174, repeated here (PBS, undated):

> Calley was at the drainage ditch on the eastern edge of the village, where about seventy to eighty old men, women, and children not killed on the spot had been brought. Calley ordered the dozen or so platoon members there to push the people into the ditch, and three or four GIs did. Calley ordered his men to shoot into the ditch. Some refused, others obeyed. One who followed Calley's order was Paul Meadlo, who estimated that he killed about twenty-five civilians. (Later Meadlo was seen, head in hands, crying.) Calley joined in the massacre. At one point, a two-year-old child who somehow survived the gunfire began running towards the hamlet. Calley grabbed the child, threw him back in the ditch, then shot him.

It should be noted that some of his troops refused to obey Calley's murderous commands, and that one who did obey (Meadlo) was seen crying afterward. Calley's behavior stands out not only because of its violence, but also because it was so unemotional. There were undoubtedly many other massacres in Vietnam similar to the one at My Lai, some of them unreported. But even the reported ones received little attention compared to My Lai. Perhaps Calley's combination of emotional silence and flagrant violence made it so inhuman and repugnant that there was no way of avoiding it.

Many studies of battlefield behavior have shown that to kill effectively, soldiers' greatest struggle is with their own conscience. Their personal morality dictates it is wrong to kill other human beings, even enemy soldiers. But Calley came to battle with the conscience problem long overcome: he had numbed out not only fear and grief, but also feelings of shame, the basic ingredient of conscience.

The Silence/Violence Pattern in Hitler's Biographies

The evidence for unresolved grief is indirect: there is not a single mention of Hitler crying, not even as a child. There are a host of indications, however, that he prized manliness, strength, and fortitude in the face of adversity. All of these indications run counter to placing any value on crying or other expressions of grief.

Hitler's ideal of iron strength was not merely ideological, since he had distinguished himself as a good soldier in World War I (see below). His courage under fire may also suggest the numbing out of fear, since it is difficult to distinguish between courage and the mere absence of fear.

The Swiss psychoanalyst Alice Miller (1983) has suggested a family origin of Hitler's psychopathology, the conjunction of his father's physical/emotional violence and his mother's complicity in it. Miller argues that the rage and shame caused by his father's treatment might have been completely repressed because of his mother's complicity. Although she pampered Hitler and professed to love him, she didn't protect him from his father's wrath, or allow Adolf to express his feelings about it.

Hitler's mother, Klara, as much as Adolf, was tyrannized by her husband, but offered only obedience and respect in return. Because of his mother's "love" for him, as a young child, Adolf was required not only to suffer humiliation by his father in silence, but also to respect him for it, a basic context for repression.

In later years Hitler (1927) was to gloss over his treatment by his parents, which is congruent with repression. He described his father, Alois, as stern but respected, his childhood as that of a "mother's darling living in a soft downy bed" (Bromberg and Small 1983, 40). However, Alois's son,

Alois, Jr., left home at fourteen because of his father's harshness. Alois, Jr.'s son, William Patrick, reported that Alois, Sr., beat Alois, Jr., with a whip. Alois, Jr.'s first wife, Brigid, reported that Alois, Sr., frequently beat the children, and on occasion, his wife Klara (Bromberg and Small 1983, 32–33).

It would appear that Hitler's early childhood constituted an external feeling trap from which there was no escape. This external trap is the analogue to the internal trap proposed by Helen Lewis (1971): when shame is evoked but goes unacknowledged, it generates intense symptoms of mental illness and/or violence toward self or others. Under the conditions of complete repression that seem to have obtained, Hitler's personality was grossly distorted. His biographies suggest that he was constantly in a state of anger bound by shame.

One indication of Hitler's continual shame/rage was his temper tantrums. Although in later life some of them may have been staged, there is no question that in most of his tantrums he was actually out of control. His older stepbrother reported that even before he was seven:

> Hitler was imperious and quick to anger ... If he didn't get his way he got very angry. He would fly into a rage over any triviality. (Gilbert 1950, 18)

In his teens, Hitler's rages were frequent and intense, evoking such expressions as "red with rage," "exceedingly violent and high-strung," and "like a volcano erupting" (Kubizek 1955).

Hitler's compulsive anger is suggested by the slightness of provocation that triggered rage. A. Kubizek's memoir provides two examples: one occasion on learning that he had failed to win a lottery, another when he saw "Stephanie" with other men. Stephanie was a girl who Hitler longed to meet, but never did so. He was infatuated with her, but never introduced himself (Bromberg and Small 1983, 55–56).

The most obvious manifestations of Hitler's shame occurred after he became Chancellor. Although easily the most powerful and admired man in Germany, he was constantly apprehensive (183):

> His anxieties lest he appear ridiculous, weak, vulnerable, incompetent, or in any way inferior are indications of his endless battle with shame.

Further manifestations of chronic shame states occurred in his relationships with women. In attempting to interest a woman in himself (183):

> even the presence of other persons would not prevent him from repulsive groveling. [He would] tell a lady that he was unworthy to sit near her or kiss her hand but hoped she would look on him with favor ... one woman reported that after all kinds of self-accusations he said that he was unworthy of being in the same room with her.

These latter descriptions of Hitler's shame states suggest overt, undifferentiated shame, emotionally painful states involving feelings of inadequacy and inferiority. How then is one to understand the other side of Hitler's personality, his arrogance, boldness, and extreme self-confidence? How could a man so shame-prone also be so shameless?

Lewis's (1971) conception of the bimodal nature of unacknowledged shame provides an answer. In addition to the overt shame states discussed above, Hitler also had a long history of bypassed shame. Many aspects of his behavior suggest bypassed shame, but I will review only three: his temper tantrums, his "piercing stare" (Bromberg and Small 1983, 309), and his obsessiveness.

As already indicated, shame theory suggests that protracted and destructive anger is generated by unacknowledged shame. Normal anger, when not intermixed with shame, is usually brief, moderate, and at times even constructive, serving to call notice to adjustments needed in a relationship (Retzinger 1991). Long chains of shame and anger alternating are experienced as blind rage, hatred, or resentment if the shame component is completely repressed. In this case, the expression of anger serves as a disguise for the hidden shame, projecting onto the outside world the feelings that go unacknowledged within. According to Lewis (1971), persons in whom shame is deeply repressed "would rather turn the world upside down than turn themselves inside out." This idea exactly captures the psychology of Hitler's lifelong history of intense rage states, and his projection of his inner conflict onto scapegoats in the external world.

The second indicator of bypassed shame is Hitler's demeanor, especially the nature of his gaze. As early as sixteen, it was described as "blank" or "cruel" (Bromberg and Small 1983, 51). On the other hand, there are descriptions at a later time (21) of him having "an evasive manner," being "shy," and "never looking a person in the eye," except when he was talking politics (70). These descriptions suggest that Hitler may have been in a virtually permanent state of shame, manifested as either bypassed shame (the stare) or overt shame (avoiding eye contact). As his power increased, the bypassed mode was more and more in evidence, in the form of arrogance, extreme self-confidence, isolation, and obsession.

The prison psychiatrist James Gilligan (1997) studied the emotions of male prisoners convicted of violence. He found evidence that each of them harbored a kind of shame similar to Hitler's. Gilligan's term for it is not unacknowledged or bypassed, but "secret." He proposed that secret shame was a fundamental basis for the violence of these men.

Isolation from Others

The biographies and psychological studies emphasize Hitler's isolation as a child and adult (Bromberg and Small 1983; Bullock 1964; Davidson 1977;

Miller 1983; Stierlin 1976). As an infant and youth, he was pampered by his mother. But even as young as three, his relationship with his father was charged with violence, ridicule, and contempt. By the age of six, he apparently was walled off from everyone, including his mother (Bromberg and Small 1983; Miller 1983; Stierlin 1976).

The three most likely candidates for a close relationship after the age of six are August Kubizek, Albert Speer, and Eva Braun. Hitler and Kubizek were companions for three years, beginning when they were both sixteen. Kubizek's memoir of Hitler (1955) shows that his relationship to Hitler was not that of friend, but adoring admirer. Kubizek describes Hitler as a compulsive talker, brooking no interruptions, let alone any disagreement. Lacking any other listeners at this age, Hitler used Kubizek as a sounding board.

Speer, an architect-engineer, was closest to Hitler among his officials during the last years of World War II. In an interview after the war, Speer revealed that although he spent countless hours with Hitler, there was no personal relationship between them (Bromberg and Small 1983, 112): "If Hitler had friends, I would have been his friend."

Her diary (Bromberg and Small 1983, 107–108) shows that Eva Braun, Hitler's mistress, came no closer than Kubizek or Speer. For most of their fifteen-year relationship, he attempted to keep it hidden, confining her to her rooms during meetings with others. A few entries suggest the tone of the whole diary. In 1935, when she was twenty-three and Hitler forty-six, she complained that she felt imprisoned, that she got nothing from their sexual relationship, and that she felt desperately insecure: "He is only using me for definite purposes" (March 11). Most of the women with whom Hitler had sexual relations either attempted or committed suicide. (Small and Bromberg count seven such relationships, with three of them attempting, and three completing suicide [1983, 125].) Eva Braun made two such attempts.

In 1942, Hitler inadvertently suggested his isolation from Eva. Hearing of the death of one of his officials, Fritz Todt, chief of armaments, he said that he was now deprived of "the only two human beings among all those around me to whom I have been truly and inwardly attached: Dr. Todt is dead and Hess has flown away from me!" (Toland 1976, 666). As Bromberg and Small (1983) note, this statement leaves Eva out entirely, mentioning instead "a remote man who could rarely be induced to sit at Hitler's table and a man he could not bear to converse with, denounced as crazy, and wished dead" (150).

Neither as a soldier nor as a politician did Hitler have close attachments. His experience as an enlisted man in the army during WWI is illustrative. Although he was a dedicated soldier who demonstrated fearlessness in battle, he was a "loner" who had no intimates. This may be one of the reasons that although he was decorated for bravery, he was little promoted after four years. He left the army at the rank of lance corporal, the equivalent of a private first class. In his evaluations, he was described as lacking in leadership.

After becoming the leader of the Nazi Party, he moved no closer to human relationships. A description of his campaign the year before gaining power is representative (Small and Bromberg 1983, 108):

> [In the campaign, Hitler] had almost no real contact with people, not even with his associates, who felt they were touring with a performer ... He remained a lone wolf, now ... more distant from his senior associates, and contemptuous of them.

Although the adored leader of millions of people, Hitler apparently had no secure bond with anyone after the age of six.

Application

If it proves to be the case that the silence/violence pattern arises out of anger, repression of vulnerable emotions, and lack of bonds, and that this pattern is much more prevalent in men than in women, what would be the practical implications?

Obviously one direction would be for men to unlearn their suppression of the vulnerable emotions, express anger rather than act it out, and to bond to at least one other person. Reviewing events of one's day, as indicated above, can be a particularly simple and effective way of moving toward all three of these goals. However, even if most men agreed with this direction, which they don't, it would still take a long time to see effective change. By adulthood, the silence/violence pattern is compulsive, as is the repression of the vulnerable emotions, compulsive anger, and isolation from others. It would take considerable time, energy, and skill to change this pattern.

A more immediate path away from gratuitous warfare would be to insist on equality between men and women in military service and combat. In terms of the thesis of this chapter, sexism may be the most important cause of aggression by nations, since it preserves the prejudice of male superiority. The same can be said about discrimination against male gays by the military. It is possible that no amount of legal rulings may be able to overcome this kind of discrimination. There is at least one feminist group supporting equal military service for men, women, and gays, established at The Minerva Center in DePaul University. This group also publishes a journal, *Minerva*.[3]

It also might be practical to use the difference between men and women in our political structures. It is possible that electing/appointing women to high office, rather than men, might be a step, on the average, of slowing down the leap into war and violence. There are exceptions, of course, like Margaret Thatcher, who manipulated collective emotions as skillfully as any man. But most women are at least somewhat less easy with this kind of exploitation than our present leaders, hypermasculine men. Women also would be less trigger happy than men, who have a tendency to fight first and ask questions later.

In her article "Let Them Eat War" (2004), Arlie Hochschild has proposed that large numbers of working-class men support the Bush regime, even though its policies are against the interests of their class. She argues that the reason for their support is emotional, rather than economic. They admire, and wish to emulate Bush's style of meeting threat with aggression rather than with negotiation and compromise. His hypermasculine, violent style is a reaffirmation of their own. It would appear that this style is so central to their identity that it overrides their economic interests.

Each of the initiatives proposed here may be only one step toward controlling violence. Having a majority of leaders be women, rather then men, for instance, seems a long way away. In *Lysistrata,* a drama from ancient Greece, women joined together to deny sex to men who fought. Perhaps modern women might take note as far as not only lessening war directly, but also indirectly, to encourage men to vote for women, or at least, less arrogant leaders. We don't want leaders who engage in what Goffman has called "character contests" with other leaders, but leaders who take a crisis as an opportunity to do what Taylor and her colleagues (2000) call "tend and befriend."

Notes

1. This reference was suggested to me by George Gonos.

2. There is by now a literature linking masculinity to aggression and violence. See Bowker 1998; Craig 1992; Gibson 1994; Hatty 2000; and Morgan 2001.

3. Sharon Hoshida called this group to my attention.

CHAPTER **11**

A Theory of Runaway Nationalism

THE IDEA OF ETHNOCENTRISM provides a first step toward understanding fervent nationalism, but doesn't spell out the details. It is also static, with no indication of the dynamics of collective behavior. How can we understand the extremes of the "us versus them" mentality? A theory of alienation is outlined, focusing on emotional/relational dynamics. Blind loyalty and identification with one's nation seems to be a form of infatuation, rather than genuine love. Similarly, hatred of supposed enemies could be a defense against shame and alienation. Both of these propositions depend on demystifying the vernacular meanings of love and hate. Infatuation and hidden shame are also key components in hypermasculinity, a pattern that dominates national and world politics. It appears that gratuitous collective violence is an outcome of bimodal alienation (engulfment within groups, isolation between them). These ideas suggest a Goffmanian world of insecurity at the level of relationships within and between nations and other groups in conflict. Several reforms that might counter these processes are suggested.

Building on the earlier chapters, this one applies the Web approach (Phillips et al. 2002) and my own part/whole method (Scheff 1997c) to propose emotional/relational origins of world conflict. Combining these two approaches involves: (1) Using my own experiences as background; (2) defining the research problem with highly abstract concepts; and (3) moving up and down the conceptual ladder of abstraction between concrete situations and social structure/process. This scheme may be seen as the next step in Goffman's attempt to free ourselves from entrapment in the vernacular words, images, and ideas of everyday life that maintain the status quo.

My father was an immigrant from Lithuania. My mother's parents were from Russia. Both of my parents were Roosevelt Democrats, and proud of their country. My mother recited patriotic poems:

> Lives there a man with soul so dead
> Who to himself he hath not said
> This is my own, my native land?

They never quite bought the idea of "my country, right or wrong," but many of our neighbors did. This idea is now epidemic in the United States, and in many other states and ethnic groups.

At the present time there is a thread of blind loyalty in the United States supporting the rank opportunism of the Bush regime. It is difficult to understand it strictly in terms of political economy. As Arlie Hochschild (2004) has pointed out, the majority of Bush's supporters are working-class; their economic interests are not served by Bush. One needs to consider how worldviews are constructed, especially what Bernard Phillips (Phillips et al. 2002) calls "stratified worldviews." How can we explain the loyalty of Bush's many supporters, as against the views of his detractors, which is most of the world?

Toward a Theory of Nationalism

Most contemporary discussions of blind nationalism and violence are entirely descriptive (see, for example, Kressel 2002). Psychological explorations of collective "evil" are also largely descriptive, even though they refer to the most basic component of ethnocentrism, the "us versus them" attitude. Both Roy Baumeister (1997) and Ervin Staub (2003) have written about collective violence, but lack an explicit theory of individual and collective dynamics.

A first step into a dynamic theory of nationalism is suggested by Durkheim's (1915) idea that any enduring religion requires the interplay between belief, on the one hand, and ritual, on the other. He proposed that the elemental basis for religion is the reciprocal relation of belief to ritual, and vice versa. Belief leads to ritual, and ritual to belief, in a self-perpetuating loop. Organized religions can be viewed as social systems arising out of the interaction between belief and ritual, ideas and actions.

Viewing religion as a social system can further understanding of blind allegiance to nations or ethnic groups. But more detail will be needed. In particular, we need to understand how blind nationalism is generated not only in the world of ideology and action, but also in the emotional/relational world (ERW). How is nationalism forged out of belief, ritual, emotion, and relationships?

Benedict Anderson (1991) has suggested that a nation is an "imagined community." Although he doesn't develop the idea, this phrase suggests what might be seen as an anomaly. We all know many people personally, our neighbors and work associates and members of our own families.

Yet we may identify with, and will lay down our lives to protect the millions of fellow citizens who we not only don't know, but have never met and will never meet. For reasons that will be considered below, it may be much easier to identify with imagined people you don't know than real ones that you do.

The social theory of G.H. Mead (1934) and recent discussions of infatuation may be the next steps toward further understanding. Mead argued that the self is social, a response to a community that is, in great part, imagined. The core of this theory is what he called "taking the role of the other," by which he meant viewing a situation not only from our own point of view, but also from the point of view of the other(s). His concept of "the generalized other" makes it clear that role-taking refers not only to people that we know, but also to those that we only imagine. Although Mead didn't explicitly discuss the possibility of identifying with the imagined other, his theory implies it.

One example of an imagined point of view that one might identify with is posterity: one imagines what future generations might think of one's self, and judges one's self from that point of view. A more common example of generalization of the other would be for a white person to imagine the point of view of all other whites, and identify with that imagined point of view. The only step remaining for forming an "us versus them" mentality would be to idealize the one at the expense of the other.

Imagining the point of view of the other(s) occurs not only in nationalism, but is a commonplace requirement of everyday life for everyone. Since ordinary language is extremely ambiguous, one must take the point of view of the other in order to understand even fairly simple statements. A crucial part of the context of any message is the point of view of the person(s) from whom one received the message. As Cooley (1922) said, "We live in the minds of others without knowing it ..." But the "us versus them" mentality requires not only imagining points of view of two communities, but also identifying with one and rejecting the other. When a friend complained to one of my relatives about our careless destruction in Iraq and the death or injury of many of its people, my relative said, "Better them than us."

One problem with Mead's scheme is that he didn't worry about variability in the accuracy with which we imagine the point of view of the other(s). His theory seems to imply accuracy, which can't possibly be always, or even, typically, true. I will return to this issue below, in the discussion of infatuation and voter education. The other issue that will be pursued here, more extensively than the issue of accuracy, will be the emotional aspects of role-taking. Neither Mead nor Anderson has anything to say about emotions. This chapter will suggest that they play a dominant part in the kind of identification and rejection that leads to aggression.

Most discussions of nationalism give little or no attention to the role of emotions. For example, it has been argued that military service simply involves the meeting of one's obligations, as in any other institution (Hinde and Watson 1994). The willingness of soldiers to die for others is simply normative. It is probably true that much of what goes on in the human world can be explained in this way: we merely follow the rules. Perhaps this kind of explanation is best for understanding the everyday world. But it is also true that every day some rules are broken or ignored. And in times of change or crisis, all rules may be ignored. Without invoking the emotional/relational world, it is difficult to understand the fervor of nationalism. Untold millions of people have gratuitously laid down their lives, and taken the lives of others, in the name of their nation or other imagined communities.

Such willingness is understandable when it is quite clear that one's group is in danger because of a threat by another group. But current and past history suggests that most citizens support killing and being killed purely on speculation, even without plausible evidence of threat. The war on Iraq is one instance, and World War I, which commenced without any real attempt at peacemaking, and with little immediate threat (Scheff 1994), is another.

Few people would be willing to die for their neighborhood, county, state, or trade or professional association. My own professional association is the American Sociological Association (ASA). Although I have been laying down dollars every year for many years in order to belong, I wouldn't kill to avoid a hostile takeover by another discipline. The ASA may have a few such members, disciplinary patriots. For the rest of us, words, yes, but not bombs and bullets.

There is another, much smaller type of group that may demand blind loyalty, the immediate family. An earlier chapter (Chapter 9) illustrated this dynamic. In conflict-ridden families, the child will often identify with and idealize one parent, and vilify the other. This pattern is particularly prevalent in, but not limited to families of divorced parents. This chapter proposes that infatuation and shame/rage are the key elements of the social and psychological dynamics shared by conflictful families, gangs, aggressive nations, and ethnic groups.

Infatuation and Hatred

To begin to understand the social/psychological dynamics of fervent nationalism, it will be necessary to understand what is meant by *love of country*, on the one hand, and *hatred* of its supposed enemies, on the other. These terms, in vernacular usage, may not be as simple and straightforward as they seem. They can be used as mystifications that both distort and hide the nature of the emotional/relational world.

The use of ordinary words, rather than well-defined concepts, is a pressing problem in all of social science. For example, there have been a vast number of studies of *alienation* and of *self-esteem* that assume these words need not be defined. Although there are many, many standardized scales for measuring alienation and self-esteem, there have been few attempts to decide, conceptually, what it is that these scales are supposed to be measuring.

To this day, most key concepts in social science are quite ambiguous. Some of them, such as alienation and self-esteem, may involve too many potentially orthogonal meanings (such as individual, relational, cognitive, and emotional dimensions) to be measured by a single instrument. Others, such as irrationality or context, for example, may be mere residual categories, conceptually empty boxes, because they encompass the enormously wide variety of different kinds of things that remain after their polar opposite has been explored in detail. Chapter 5 has proposed a concept of the idea of context, which turns out to be massively complex.

Ambiguity in the Meaning of Love

As indicated in Chapter 7, the word *love* provides a vivid example of the first kind of ambiguity, a kind of umbrella word that encompasses many different facets. Since "love" of country is the central idea of patriotism, this chapter will continue the exploration of the meaning of love, so as to clearly differentiate love and infatuation.

According to Harold Bloom (1998, 549), Aldous Huxley suggested "we use the word love for the most amazing variety of relationships, ranging from what we feel for our mothers to what we feel for someone we beat up in a bordello, or its many equivalents."

The comment about beating someone up out of love is probably not an exaggeration. A recent set of experiments suggests that subjects' condemnation of murder is softened if they are told that it was caused by jealousy (Puente and Cohen 2003). These subjects seem to entertain the idea that one can love someone so much that one injures or even kills them, loving them to death.

Robert Solomon (1981, 3–4) elaborates on the broad sweep of the word *love*:

> Consider … the wealth of meticulous and fine distinctions we make in describing our feelings of hostility: hatred, loathing, scorn, anger, revulsion, resentment, envy, abhorrence, malice, aversion, vexation, irritation, annoyance, disgust, spite and contempt, or worse, "beneath" contempt. And yet we sort out our positive affections for the most part between the two limp categories, "liking" and "loving." We distinguish our friends from mere acquaintances and make a ready distinction between lovers and friends whom we love "but not that way." Still, one and the same

word serves to describe our enthusiasm for apple strudel, respect for a distant father, the anguish of an uncertain romantic affair and nostalgic affection for an old pair of slippers.

In modern societies the broad use of the word *love* may defend against the painful absence of true intimacy and community. The idea seems to be that *any* kind of relationship that has positive elements in it, even if mixed with extremely negative ones, can be named *love*.

What Does Love Mean?

One place to seek definitions is the dictionary. In the English language, unabridged dictionaries provide some *two dozen* meanings for love, most of them applicable to romantic or other human relationships. These are the first two meanings in the *American Heritage Dictionary* (1992):

> 1. A deep, tender, ineffable feeling of affection and solicitude toward a person, such as that arising from kinship, recognition of attractive qualities, or a sense of underlying oneness.

> 2. A feeling of intense desire and attraction toward a person with whom one is disposed to make a pair; the emotion of sex and romance.

These two definitions are of great interest, because they touch upon several complexities. Particularly daunting is the idea that love is ineffable (indescribable). I can sympathize with this idea because genuine love seems to be quite complex. Both popular and scholarly accounts flirt with the idea that one of the crowning qualities of love is that it is mysterious and therefore indescribable.

Contradicting this idea, Chapter 7 developed a definition of love, both in its romantic and non-romantic forms, that might be used instead of the vernacular word, which contains three components. Two are physical: sexual attraction and attachment. One is cognitive/emotional: attunement (balanced mutual awareness between self and other). My definition of non-romantic love omits sexual attraction, but involves the other two "A's," attachment and attunement.

This definition of the attunement component is based on an earlier approach by Solomon known as *shared identity* (Solomon 1981, xxx; 1994, 235): "... love [is] shared identity, a redefinition of self which no amount of sex or fun or time together will add up to.... Two people in a society with an extraordinary sense of individual identity mutually fantasize, verbalize and act their way into a relationship that can no longer be understood as a mere conjunction of the two but only as a complex ONE."

Although Solomon doesn't use terms like *mutual awareness* or *intersubjectivity,* they are clearly implied. In passing, he also implies another aspect of what I would call genuine love, that one's individual identity is held in balance with identifying with the other(s). One's own autonomous self is valued no more than the other(s), but also no less. It is this feature that differentiates between true solidarity and engulfment. The implication is that moments of unity with the other(s) are, in the long run, balanced against moments of individual autonomy.

This idea is implied in the poem, "To Have without Holding," by Marge Piercy (1980), already quoted at greater length in Chapter 7:

> Learning to love differently is hard / It hurts to thwart the reflexes / of grab, of clutch; to love and let / go again and again / as we make and unmake in passionate / diastole and systole the rhythm, of our unbound bonding, to have / and not to hold, to love / with minimized malice, hunger / and anger moment by moment balanced. . .

The poem comes very close to making explicit the moment-by-moment dance of togetherness and separateness that constitutes genuine love/solidarity.

This idea can be used to distinguish love from look-alikes, such as infatuation and engulfment. What most patriots profess to be love of their country lacks the perquisite of balanced shared identity, but is closer to being infatuation. Similarly, what is called hatred of national enemies could be a gloss on a complex process of hiding feelings of inadequacy and alienation under the cover of "pride" in one's country, as will be discussed below. The meanings of love and pride are so ambiguous in ordinary language that that they can easily be used in the service of defensive maneuvers like denial and projection.

Genuine love requires detailed knowledge of the other(s). Having only an image of the other's appearance, say, or some other single quality, is not love but infatuation. In this sense, it is not possible to actually love a celebrity who one has never met, and whose real life and character are unknown. If one were to ever get a chance to know the actual person, "love" might receive a rude shock. The star who seemed wonderful from a distance might turn out to be, at best, a mere mortal person like the rest of us, rather than a god or goddess. Genuine love means loving warts and all, not just admiring best features from afar.

Love is distinguishable from infatuation, which is mostly about the lover, rather than the love object or the relationship, since infatuation is self-generated fantasy. Collective infatuation is not only self-generated, but also socially amplified. Nations, like fan clubs, can whip their participants into an ecstasy of adoration. Unlike fan clubs, nations also do the opposite, amplifying individual negative feelings into orgies of hatred and rage.

Both individual and collective infatuation can be an enormously arrest-
ing, intense experience. The idealization of a mere image of the other(s),
unlike genuine love, has no reality check, and therefore can spiral toward
infinity. The great, never-ending stream of poetry of romantic infatuation
bears witness to the infinitely intense experience of the "lover":

> For should I see thee a little moment,
> Straight my voice is hushed;
> Yea, my tongue is broken, and
> Through me
> 'Neath the flesh, impalpable fire
> Runs tingling;
> Nothing sees mine eyes, and a
> Voice of roaring
> Waves in my ear sounds;
> Sweat runs down in rivers, a
> Tremor seizes
> All my limbs, and paler than
> Grass in autumn,
> Caught by pains of menacing
> Death, I falter,
> Lost in the love-trance.

In the last line, Sappho calls her ecstasy/nightmare a "love-trance." But
I would call it, at the risk of seeming a killjoy, an infatuation-trance. Although this particular poem was written over 2,500 years ago, similar
sentiments can be found in current pop song lyrics on the Top 40, but
much less beautifully expressed.

Similarly intense feelings of infatuation form the dominant emotion
in the propaganda of any nation preparing for war. One clear example
occurred in the patriotic novels, lyrics, and poetry of France during the
period between wars with Germany (1871–1914; Scheff 1994). Most
exiguous was the "military poetry" of the right-wing extremist Paul de
Roulede. His *Songs of a Soldier* (1872) gushed passionate "love" for the
glory of France, and demanded revenge on Germany as necessary for the
honor of France. It went through an unprecedented 83 editions by 1890,
making it one of the most popular books ever published in France.

The infatuation-trance of blind patriotism is like the naked trust that
small children have for their parents. In the early years of their life, at
least, most children form an idealized image of their parents as authorities
who can do no wrong, like gods on earth. It appears that many adults,
whether or not they retain this nursery image of the actual parent, transfer
it to their government. It is very difficult to overcome such an image, no
matter the mounting evidence that it is untrue.

After 9/11, some of my colleagues were asking, "Why do they hate
us?" But if I answered by pointing to the machinations of our government

over the last fifty years in the Middle East and the slaughter and mayhem that resulted, they rapidly lost interest. They didn't want to hear, with no concern even with whether what I said was true or not.

Collective Hatred and Rage

Collective hatred, like collective "love," can achieve much higher levels of intensity than that of individuals, but the spiral is much more hidden and complex. To understand this process, it seems to be necessary to forego everyday, vernacular explanations. I propose that "hatred" is the commonly used word for hidden vulnerable emotions, particularly grief, fear, and shame. One elemental source of hatred may be the shame of not belonging, forming groups that reject the group(s) supposedly rejecting them. As indicated in Chapter 8, the culture of such groups generates *techniques of neutralization* that encourage hatred and mayhem. At the level of individuals, there is rage generated by threatened or damaged bonds. There are also social and cultural spirals that give rise to collective hatred and rage.

Shame and Hate

As already indicated, rage seems to be a composite affect, a sequence of two elemental emotions, shame and anger. This idea has been advanced by other authors, notably Heinz Kohut (1971) and Helen Lewis (1971). Kohut proposed that violent anger of the kind he called "narcissistic rage" was a shame/anger compound. Lewis suggested that shame and anger have a deep affinity, and that one can find indications of unacknowledged shame occurring just prior to any episode of intense hostility.

This sequence has been shown in many transactions during psychotherapy sessions by Lewis (1971), in four marital quarrels by Retzinger (1991), and in Hitler's writings and speeches (Scheff 1994). Retzinger demonstrated that prior to each of the sixteen episodes of angry escalation in her cases, there had been first an insult by one party, indications of unacknowledged shame in the other party, and finally intense hostility in that party. This sequence can be seen as the motor of violence, since it connects the intense emotions of shame and anger to overt aggression.

Although there has been little research focused explicitly on pure, unalloyed anger, indications from the studies of discourse by Lewis (1971), Retzinger (1991), and my own work (such as Scheff 1990) suggest that pure anger is rare and unlikely to lead to violence or even social disruption. On the contrary, anger by itself is usually brief and instructive. A person who is frustrated and unashamed of her anger is mobilized to tell what is going on, and to do what is needed, without making a huge scene.

In my own case, I can testify that most of my experiences of anger have involved shame/anger, either in the form of humiliated fury, or in a more passive form, what Labov and Fanshel (1977) call "helpless anger." Both of these variants are long-lasting and extremely unpleasant, especially for me. Shame-induced anger is unpleasant while happening, and even more unpleasant when it is over, since I inevitably feel foolish and out of control.

But in the very few episodes of what seems to have been, in retrospect, pure anger, the experience was entirely different. I did not raise my voice, nor did I put anyone down or engage in any other kind of excess. I simply told my view of what was going on directly, rapidly, and with no calculation or planning. I was overcome with what might be called "machine-gun mouth." Everyone who was present at one of these communications suddenly became quite respectful. I didn't feel out of control, even though my speech was completely spontaneous; on the contrary, I was wondering why I had not had my say before. It would seem that anger without shame has only a signal function, to alert self and others to one's frustration.

When anger has its source in feelings of rejection or inadequacy, and when the latter feelings are not acknowledged, a continuous spiral of shame/anger may result, which may be experienced as hatred and rage. Rather than expressing and discharging one's shame through laughter ("Silly me" or "Silly us"), it is masked by rage and aggression. One can be angry that one is ashamed, and ashamed that one is angry, and so on, working up to a loop of unlimited duration and intensity. This loop may be the emotional basis of lengthy episodes or even life-long hatred that seems intense beyond endurance.

Chapter 10 proposed that physical aggression or complete withdrawal is a common component of hypermasculinity, which in turn has social/emotional bases: (1.) no affectional attachments; (2.) a single overarching obsession; and (3.) complete repression of shame. Only to the extent that all three of these conditions are fully met is silence or destructive violence likely. Calley's and Hitler's biographies suggest how completely episodes from their lives illustrate all three of these conditions. Although women with this pattern would be as likely as men to commit or condone violent acts, men appear to qualify much more frequently and fully than women.

Most men are trained from early childhood to suppress all vulnerable emotions, especially fear, grief, and shame. Parents and male children usually confound fear with cowardice, and grief and shame with weakness. After thousands of episodes of intentional suppression, men learn to numb out these feelings automatically. In terms of the theory proposed here, the repression of shame is the core process in hypermasculinity, because it numbs out both fear and conscience. Killing or maiming other humans would be intensely painful if the automatic shame response were still in play.

In "Let Them Eat War," Hochschild (2004) suggests a similar mechanism of defense to explain why working-class men, against their economic interests, support our cowboy president. She argues that Bush covers his own fears and other vulnerable emotions by aggressive action, a pattern that these males also follow or would like to. This analysis points to a key issue in understanding how reactionary leaders generate support among their followers (as was the case with Hitler's appeal to the Germans). Their appeal is largely social and emotional, rather that economic or ideological.

Collective hatred and violence seems to depend on the suppression of other vulnerable emotions, not just shame. Vamik Volkan (2004) has made a convincing case that the most lethal violence is caused by the humiliation of groups that have suppressed collective grief. Many groups, he notes, have what he calls "chosen traumas," a historical episode of massive loss. For example, he shows that the chosen trauma of the Serbs, their loss of the Battle of Kosovo in 1389, has taken on such a great symbolic/emotional value that reference to it is needed to understand the tragedies in Bosnia in 1992 and Kosovo in 1999 (2004, 50).

Particularly relevant to the understanding of mass violence is Volkan's idea that chosen traumas may give rise to collective feelings of entitlement to revenge. He also makes the connection between collective and individual emotions:

> ... serious threats to large-group identity, such as shared helplessness and humiliation, are perceived by members of that large group as *individually* wounding and *personally* endangering: they induce a collective response of anxiety or terror ... (2004, 33)

This linking of personal and collective responses makes sense to me in terms of responses to 9/11 that I have seen in persons close to me. Out of my large extended family, only two persons reacted in this way. But their response exactly illustrates Volkan's point; they went into an aggressive funk, continually declaring their hatred of "the enemy" and their love for their country. They exhibit blind trust for the present Bush regime, in exactly the way that Volkan proposes.

My own initial reaction to 9/11 was also extreme, but in a different way. Rather than an aggressive funk, I went into a depressive one. After watching the assault on the Towers on TV many times, I fell into a trance-like state. This state persisted even after I finally turned off the TV. On the next day, however, a different kind of episode occurred that lifted me out of depression.

As I was driving in my car, I heard radio interviews of survivors from the World Trade Center. I noticed that several of them mentioned that when they were running down the stairs to escape, they were quite surprised to see policemen and firemen running up the stairs. As it turned out, some of these men sacrificed their own lives trying to help others escape.

After turning off the radio, as I was thinking of the courage of these men, I burst into tears. I cried for a long time, convulsively, like a baby. After the cry, I felt like I was myself again.

What happened? My interpretation is that seeing the Towers fall had left me in a state of helpless humiliation, grief, and fear. Like most men, I was unable to manage these particular emotions since at some level, I am still ashamed of them. So I suppressed them, leading to my funk. But I felt pride when I identified with the brave men who sacrificed their lives helping others. The pride countered my shame, leading to an episode of effective mourning. A comparison of my episode, and the failure to mourn by my two in-laws, illustrates Volkan's idea about the importance of unresolved grief and shame in collective responses to trauma

Chapter 8 described how *bimodal alienation* (isolation between, and engulfment within groups) generates violence. Members of each group are distant from the other group, but are infatuated with each other, to the point that they give up important parts of themselves in order to be completely loyal to the group. A very wealthy and influential person in my local community said to me: "I am a patriot. When my country wants something, I give it, no questions asked." I said, "Suppose you have doubts?" He said, "Not possible. My country comes first." Idealizing the nation means suppressing one's thoughts and feelings, producing the principle of *obrigkeit* (blind loyalty and obedience). Bimodal alienation (isolation between groups and engulfment within them) may be the fundamental condition for intergroup conflict.

Practical Applications of Theory

How can spirals of unresolved grief, unacknowledged shame, and anger that lead to hatred be avoided or slowed when they are occurring? One answer may lie in the direction of effective mass mourning and acknowledgment of shame. Acknowledgment, however, does not refer to merely verbal acknowledgment, as in the routine confessions in Alcoholics Anonymous and its spin-offs. Unfortunately, there have been very few discussions of this issue. Acknowledgment is one of those terms, like "working through" in psychoanalysis, that play a central role in professional discourse, but are seldom defined or even illustrated through concrete examples.

This discussion points toward several paths for conciliation between belligerent groups. My theory of protracted conflict suggests that the foremost cause is mass alienation within and between the groups. Any steps that would decrease mass alienation would lessen the potential for conflict. Some examples follow.

An earlier essay on alienation (Scheff 1997a, Ch. 4) proposed that teachers need to be retrained to be aware of the way in which they reject working-class and minority students. I also suggest classes on family relations that would help young people form stable families. Also in that chapter I recommend reform for welfare programs to lessen rejection and shame. Young men form the bulk of combatants for intergroup and international conflict. If they could be better integrated into work or welfare, school, and family, they would be less vulnerable to pressure to fight an external, and often what amounts to an, imagined enemy.

At a more general level, it may be necessary to pursue reforms that could make the sentiments that the majority hold for their country less like infatuation and more like love, warts and all. And the sentiments that they hold toward the enemy less like blind hatred and more like understanding or at least objectivity. Most supporters of the Iraq war don't know where it is, much less the history of U.S. interference. Perhaps they don't want to know. But in any case, one reform that might help would be the requirement that citizens pass an examination before being allowed to vote.

Getting knowledge relevant to the major issues of the day is not easy, even for a scholar. One problem is the complexity and depth of many of the issues. Another is the poor job the mass media do. Can relevant knowledge be made available to every one?

Can knowledge for public consumption be presented in a format that would result in easy access, yet could lead toward understanding? A wonderful model for such a format is available online for film reviews on the website www.metacritic.com. For virtually all films of the last three or four years, there are a large number of reviews (20–120) for *each* film. The website is designed remarkably well, enabling a quick look at opinion on films expressed as average rating, a crucial sentence from each review, and, finally, the opportunity to read all of the reviews in their entirety.

By seeing the wide range of critical opinion, the average reader might rapidly come to an adequate judgment of the film. Seeing how the experts agree and, especially, how they disagree, gives the reader the possibility of what might be called binocular judgment (seeing an issue from many points of view, rather than just one). With this kind of material, the reader is in a position to form her/his own opinion.

A similar format for expert opinion on political and social matters could be made available in order to help citizens prepare to take their voter's examination. Such a reform, along with those mentioned above, and others might move us back toward a democracy based on genuine love of country, rather than blind infatuation.

Conclusion

Given the breadth of a theoretical approach encompassing both macro and micro elements, I employed the Web/part/whole approach to the scientific method in order to confront complexity. In this way, I sought to link abstract concepts like nationalism and alienation with specific emotions like infatuation, shame, fear, and rage, and with specific types of alienated relationships. In addition, I was able to apply my arguments in order to make suggestions for confronting protracted hatred and violence.

CHAPTER 12

Conclusion

THIS CHAPTER SUMMARIZES the main points made in this book, and their implications for future studies. What can we learn from Goffman's work, the way he went about it, and from his life? In particular, what were his main areas of concern, achievements, shortcomings, and omissions? Some of my own work has been used to show extensions of his ideas, and also to overcome his shortcomings and omissions. Goffman's emphasis on trope clearing and mine on concept development offer a new route for studying the human condition.

Goffman went quite far in deconstructing assumptive worlds, taken-for-granted conventional views of what is thought to be reality. He also provided a counter-world, based on a new lexicon for describing the social world. Although Goffman didn't make it explicit, his work continually suggests the idea that human beings and their societies are much more complex then we usually assume. Finally, his lexicon and his application of it to concrete examples open up a whole arena of behavior and experience that is virtually invisible in modern societies—the emotional/relational world (ERW).

Goffman's primary achievement was creating a new vocabulary and a point of view to describe the social world. His lexicon was extensive enough to jolt many readers out of some of their most basic assumptions about what it means to be a human being. Reading Goffman's work, in this respect, can be equivalent to living in another culture long enough to see one's own culture and/or one's self in a new way. Another similar experience, closer to home, is to lose one's self in the novel of a master like Proust, or any other extraordinary book that opens up a new and hitherto unfamiliar world to the reader. Readers of Proust have remarked that in describing his own childhood, he was also describing theirs. Goffman has a similar effect on many of his readers.

Goffman realized, as did Schutz and Gouldner, that most people, including social scientists, live in "the world of everyday life," taking it for granted as if it were the only possible world. Goffman's work brings into living color the importance of Phillips's focus on stratified worldviews, suggesting the way in which culture continually controls our daily life. If social science is going to do more than continually rediscover and confirm the status quo, it must be liberated from that straitjacket.

Goffman had some success in deconstructing specific elements in the assumptive world of modern societies. His greatest success was to make visible an aspect of human existenence that has become dim in ur-ban/industrial societies, the ERW. In modern societies, attention is almost entirely riveted on the material world and, with respect to our selves and our fellows, cognition and behavior. Relationships and emotions lead only a shadow life in our scheme of the world.

The philosopher Wittgenstein had argued that ordinary language is sufficient for solving some problems, but is grossly inadequate for solving others. He went so far as to state that the use of the ordinary language lexicon in some areas is the reason that problems in that area are insoluble. One is entrapped in erroneous assumptions because they are embedded in ordinary language.

This idea was just a devout prayer for Wittgenstein, because he didn't get very far in demonstrating how useful it might be. In this respect, Goff-man's work is an answer to Wittgenstein's prayer. Goffman was devoted to the development of a new lexicon for the hitherto shadowy world of social interaction. He somehow sensed that, in the English language at least, it is virtually impossible to describe the structure/process of interaction in ways that don't merely confirm and justify it. The way that each of us is socialized leads us to that impression, and our relationships, emotions, and the very language we use continually reaffirm it.

As already indicated, the languages of modern societies, especially English, spotlight the material world, behavior, and cognition. At the same time, they tend to edit out of existence emotions and social re-lationships. Even if one wishes to reinsert emotions and relationships into descriptions, it's an uphill battle. The emotion and relationship lexicons in the languages of modern societies are confused and con-fusing. Chapters 3 and 4 described how narrowly shame is defined in English, as compared to other languages. Chapters 7 and 8 show an opposite tendency toward love and hate in English: they are defined so broadly as to be almost meaningless.

All of these confusions in the emotion lexicon function in the same way, to cover over relationship difficulties, especially disconnection and alienation. Shame is defined so narrowly as being extremely negative that we tend not to notice its everyday versions. Love is defined so broadly that it is used to deny subtle, and in some instances, flagrant kinds of alienation.

The underlying assumption about emotions and relationships in Eng-lish-speaking societies is that they are *unimportant* relative to the material world, behavior, and cognition. They don't matter, so why bother to even notice them? This is the trope for our time, analogous to the idea in the ancient world that the earth was the center of the solar system. Until this trope was cleared, the science of astronomy was literally impossible.

Enter Goffman, giant-killer, trope-clearer. His studies of social interaction bring into the foreground the idea opposite to the ruling trope. The ERW is of critical importance because we spend much of our lives, like fish in water, swimming in relationships and emotions. Worse yet, we spend an enormous amount of time and energy knocking ourselves out trying to act cool, as if the ERW doesn't exist. This latter work, clearing our tracks of involvement in the ERW, probably requires more effort than the emotional/relational work itself. No matter how many specialized theories and studies using experiments, standardized scales, and sample surveys, a science of social psychology will be impossible until the ruling trope is identified and cleared.

Goffman's main ideas, such as impression management and character contests, go beneath the surface of social interaction and consciousness into the hidden realms of vicissitudes and quality of relationships and their accompanying emotions. In this shadowy world, he savagely attacked individualistic ideas of the self, psychiatry, femininity, and, inadvertently, masculinity. His examples of what at first glance seem to be commonplace interactions expose their complexity, the details of our everyday experience that we usually ignore. Since the assumptions of everyday life simplify the fine details, Goffman complicated.

With respect to the idea of the looking-glass self, Goffman not only provided many, many examples from everyday life of its workings, but also took the idea further than Cooley did. Cooley's version considered only three steps: imagining the other's view of self, the other's judgment of that view, and finally, the pride or shame that resulted. His version implies that one simply accepts the resultant pride or shame willy-nilly.

But Goffman's work implies a fourth, vitally important step: how one manages the feelings that result. He suggests that most of the time, we try to avoid them, just as we initially try to manage the view that the other takes. Emotion management is a vital part of impression management. Goffman's idea of the cult of masculinity provides an example of both types of management: boys learn to manage the impression they make on others as masculine by suppressing the emotions that are assumed to be signs of weakness, the "vulnerable emotions," and by exaggerating the emotion taken to be a sign of strength, anger. As suggested in Chapter 10, this particular type of impression and feeling management may be a crucial component of the processes leading to either withdrawal or violence. First noticing, then, by implication, linking the two types of management is one of many examples of Goffman's penchant for complicating rather than simplifying representations of human life.

Another example of complexity that can be read into Goffman's work is the idea of subjective and intersubjective *context*. Chapter 5 discussed the possibility that in his most difficult book, *Frame Analysis,* Goffman was moving toward an explicit model of the structure of context. His approach seems to be so complex that it might require mathematical notation in order to avoid vertigo if we are to portray intensely repetitive (iterative) processes.

My analysis of family systems using reports of dialogues in Chapter 9 follows Goffman's approach by using many concrete examples to vivify general ideas. The results also seem to support Goffman's highly critical view of relationships in our society. Reasoning from the reported dialogues, most of the families in my study appear to be dysfunctional, or at least to use impoverished modes of communication. For example, the frequent report made by many students that they were very close to one of their parents often seemed to be based on rejection of the other parent, an "us versus them" configuration on the smallest possible scale.

Of course the study doesn't prove anything, since my method was not systematic. It is possible that the impression of family dysfunction and disconnection conveyed by the dialogues is merely a sampling artifact, or some other aspect of the procedures I used. Still, it was striking how virtually all the dialogues suggested poor communication practices, and particularly how elementary the mistakes and misunderstandings were. Particularly glaring was my impression that almost all the students felt harassed or unappreciated by at least one parent, and that, unknown to the student reporters, the dialogues also suggested that the students were also part of the problem, harassing and not appreciating their parents in turn.

Using the fine details of actual dialogue as a way of considering a problem is not limited to the interpersonal level. My earlier (1994) studies of the origins of World War I and of Hitler's appeal to the Germans were both too long to include in this volume. To get some foothold on the causes of WWI, I analyzed popular poetry and exchanges of letters between heads of state immediately prior to the beginning of the war. To approach the problem of Hitler's appeal, I investigated details from Hitler's biography, speeches, and writings.

Both the detailed and conventional sources of evidence suggested interpretations that run counter to received wisdom. In the case of WWI the principle cause seems to have been the French leadership and public's desire for revenge for their defeat in the Franco-German War (1871). A similar thread can be found in Hitler's appeal to the Germans. His biography, writings, and speeches, and the public response, suggest that his main appeal was as an agent of vengeance for the defeat in WWI, and for what the public saw as gross injustice in the way they were treated after the peace.

I believe that the basic thrust of both of these studies is still correct, but given Volkan's approach to collective violence (2004), and my own recent work on hypermasculinity, summarized in Chapter 10, I would modify some of the details. I think now that the unacknowledged emotions driving gratuitous violence should include not only anger and shame, but all three of the "vulnerable emotions," which would mean adding grief and fear.

Volkan's earlier work focused on the failure to mourn (giving rise to what has been called *unresolved grief br*) as the major cause of collective violence. In the 2004 volume he adds humiliation, and by implication, the acting out of anger. A common thread in the instigation of wars is that instead of mourning their losses (of wars, lives, territory, etc.) leaders and the public mask their grief and shame with angry aggression. This proposition may help explain not only the instances of WWI and Hitler's appeal, but also the U.S. response to 9/11 (in Volkan's apt phrase, our "chosen trauma").

However, both my earlier work and Volkan's leaves out the third of the vulnerable emotions, fear. I think that self-amplifying loops of fear are usually causal agents in collective violence. It appears that prior to WWI, the Germans feared being overrun by the powerful coalition of France, Russia, and England, just as those countries feared the power of the German army and the expansive designs of the German leaders. Each side took steps to protect itself against the other, which resulted in further fear, and further preparation, and so on, round and round. The cycle of fear breeding fear gave rise to a level of emotional tension so high as to make war seem inevitable. To complicate matters further, the fear cycle interacted with a similar loop of shame: each country's actions insulting the other through its retaliatory moves.

Given the unbearably high level of tension in the Europe of 1914, why was there virtually no attempt at negotiations? The assassination of Archduke Franz Ferdinand in the Balkans precipitated the war, but it could have much more reasonably been a call to the negotiation table. It seems to me that this issue might remain an enigma to historians unless we consider the results of hypermasculinity on emotion management, and therefore on behavior.

The style of emotion management of the leaders of the belligerent nations, all men, was to disown all of the emotions they and the public were feeling, especially fear, shame, and grief, in favor of an aggressive stance toward "the enemy." Volkan's theory (2003) suggests one of the consequences of this kind of emotion management, what he calls "collective regression." That is, ordinarily sensible adults become irrational. This note is often caught inadvertently in patriotic poems. The following excerpt from "The Charge of the Light Brigade" (1880) provides an example:

> Forward, the Light Brigade!
> Was there a man dismayed?
> Not tho' the soldiers knew

Someone had blundered:
Theirs was not to make reply,
Theirs was not to reason why,
Theirs was but to do and die...

Tennyson was not complaining about the idiocy of men charging directly into enemy fire waving sabers, but displaying his patriotic fervor for the heroes of the Crimean War. Notice how the men's disinterest in someone having "blundered" recalls the shades of the U.S. public's lack of interest in disclosures about 9/11 and the launching of the Iraq war.

Limitations and Omissions in Goffman's Work

Some of Goffman's attempts to reconstruct our views of the social world are evocative, but overall less successful. His ideas about the social nature of the self seem incomplete, since they rule out, by fiat, many aspects of the psychology of the individual person. In this respect his work is at the opposite pole from academic and most clinical psychology. In current psychological work, the social aspects of human life usually get lost. What seems to be necessary is the integration of these two perspectives, rather than having each continue in isolation from the other.

Goffman's extensive treatment of the social institution of mental illness provides another example of this problem. Like the labeling theory of mental illness, Goffman's work points to only one layer of the onion—one of the sub-systems that generate conformity to the residual rules, on the one hand, and deviance, on the other.

Similarly, Goffman took a long first step toward integrating emotions into the study of the human condition, particularly the emotion of shame/embarrassment, and in passing, disgust. However, his purview didn't include most of the other emotions, such as love, hate, joy, grief, fear, and anger. Similarly, his commentary on relationships, and most of his examples, covered a wide range of the insecurity and disconnectedness of everyday life, but not the opposite realms of secure bonds and moments of connection.

The main focus of Goffman's work was usually interpersonal, it didn't explore the linkages between the microworld of interaction and large-scale collective process. His analyses of the make-up of the self, total institutions, and gender provide hints in this direction, but are neither explicit nor systematic. The later chapters of this book take up this challenge by applying the idea of the looking-glass self and impression/emotion management to the generation of collective violence. These chapters suggest how the micromanagement of emotions and impressions that produce hypermasculinity and blind patriotism might be repeated, much amplified, in the relationships between nations and ethnic groups.

In order to examine possible links between interpersonal and group conflict, it may be necessary to venture into areas that Goffman didn't enter. For example, we may need to reexamine many taken-for-granted assumptions about the nature of love, hate, and the bonds between persons and between groups. The vernacular meanings of these words are tropes that function to preserve the status quo. The later chapters in this book examine how defining love, hate, shame, and bonds as concepts might cast light on the meaning of masculinity, nationalism, and more generally on alienation and solidarity in large groups.

To extend the main contours of Goffman's work on the interaction order to large groups, it may be necessary to imitate his practice of using many, many concrete examples to explore abstract ideas. Typical studies of group structure/process fail, it seems to me, because they do one or the other, but not both. Most historical, demographic, and indeed, quantitative work in general tends to be mostly descriptive, providing details, but with little attempt to relate to general ideas. Vast amounts of research effort, for example, are spent on sample surveys that have little or no theoretical framework.

On the other hand, virtually all theoretical studies eschew concrete particulars. The work of G.H. Mead is a clear example. Even Cooley, who provided the occasional concrete example, usually wrote abstractly about general ideas, like the looking-glass self. It was Goffman who brought Cooley's idea to life, because of his extensive use of examples in highly varied situations. In particular, it was his many examples that provided the incentive for conceptualizing a fourth step, the management of emotions. This idea, in turn, provides a path into the vast and confusing world of collective conflict, and the role of hypermasculinity and blind patriotism in gratuitous violence.

The primary key to Goffman's success, it seems to me, was his reliance on intuition for observing and describing human experience. In this way he was able to first select and then utilize many varied concrete instances in order to develop new and original general ideas. In this way, he avoided premature systematization and premature specialization. His method, in a manner of speaking, was to have no method, or at least no systematic and/or highly specialized method.

As mentioned earlier, one vexing problem with using Goffman's work is that not only did he have no organized method for dealing with substantive issues, but also that his writing itself lacked sufficient organization. In a somewhat indirect way, the absence of reflexiveness, of self-reference, might be related to this problem. What commentators have seen as Goffman's modesty about himself, the absence of autobiographical detail in his work, may have contributed to the difficulty readers have with understanding his writing.

Reflexive writing, since it is self-referential, encourages one to view one's writing from the viewpoint of the reader. How will these comments about self appear to a reader? Following from the discussion of looking-glass self dynamics in Chapters 3 and 7, moving between the viewpoint of self and other in a balanced way might be the key to being both original and understandable.

Like many highly creative writers, Goffman's writing may have been unbalanced in this respect. He was so caught up in expressing his unique vision of the world that he had trouble seeing it from the point of view of the other. This unbalance seems to me to be the main reason that he seldom provides even a single recognizable thesis for any of his studies, let alone repeats it at various levels of abstraction/concreteness.

One of the goals of this book has been the attempt to name central theses for some of Goffman's studies. For this purpose, in addition to careful re-readings of his work, I have also inserted some aspects of Goffman's life. I have tried to understand relevant parts of his life in my argument about his work, and in that way make up for his own failure to do so. It seems to me that examining these aspects has helped me identify key theses in his studies, or at least reassure me that I was on the right track.

Even if Goffman's theses are finally understood, there still remains a final hurdle. Being a trope-clearer, his theses represent an affront to current social and behavioral science. As has been pointed out many times, Goffman has nothing to offer to what is often taken to constitute these fields: systematic theory, method, and data, usually in some highly specialized discipline or sub-discipline, because his attention is elsewhere.

The problem with premature systematization/specialization is that it makes it virtually impossible for the researcher to use his or her intuitive understanding. Commitment to an abstract theory, systematic method, type of data, discipline, or sub-discipline at the very beginning of a project virtually rules out important findings. Why is that?

Commitment to one narrow approach weds one to the assumptive world of our society, and therefore to maintaining the status quo. In being systematic in one narrow way, one may be countering one particular trope, but at the same time, one is virtually forced to accept all the other ruling tropes. Systematic and/or discipline-bound studies settle, by and large, for conventional tropes, rather than exploring the prior issue: What new *concepts* are relevant to my particular study? The primary issue for all the social and behavior sciences at this point is still conceptual: how can I define my particular problem in a way that uses at least one clearly defined concept?

No matter how systematized the theory, method, and data, studying a trope is the road to catastrophe. The vast expenditure of time and effort on self-esteem research, using standardized scales, is an example. As discussed in an earlier chapter, this massive effort has had nothing but trivial results. The basic problem has been the failure of any of the thousands of studies to define what they mean by self-esteem. As previously mentioned, this trope confounds at least four independent components: predispositional, social, cognitive, and affective elements. Until this confound is clarified, no progress can be made.

Although not on so vast a scale, most systematic studies have followed a similar path. For example, the idea of alienation plays a central role in many theories of society, and has been studied extensively with standardized scales. Yet in spite of Seeman's demonstration years ago of the many meanings attributed to this idea, alienation remains a trope like most of the other basic ideas in the social and behavioral sciences.

As already indicated, another example of premature specialization is the way both sociological and psychological studies of suicide are mesmerized into disciplinary, rather than interdisciplinary approaches. Each of the disciplines is justifiably proud of the advances that mono-disciplinary approaches have made, so they keep repeating them with virtually no further advances. It appears that the need for integration in the approaches to understanding suicide is a bitter pill, but it must be swallowed.

Given the primitive state of human research and scholarship, what steps can we take that might lead us forward? Goffman's work is suggestive in this respect. Most areas of study still need trope-clearing, prior to attempts at systematization.

1. The first step toward formulating a problem should be conceptual, and therefore intuitive. Do not commit to some particular format of investigation beforehand.

2. Become intimately acquainted with the sites of your problem, firsthand. It is OK to have assistants, but you yourself must be one of the investigators, rather than an absentee landlord.

3. Investigate the problem reflexively. That is, seek to identify and clarify the way in which your own personal background and motives are relevant.

4. Also try to keep in mind the opposite pole, an application to the real world that your solution might have, should you find it. Then, formulate a study that is also unrelated to self, but to a problem in the world outside of self.

5. Clearly define at least one concept that will be the focus. Try to define the problem in terms of at least one, and preferably two concepts. This is the step that Goffman never quite completed, and that limits the usefulness of his work.

6. When you began to get promising preliminary results with the initial formulation of the problem, seek to systematize your approach as far as possible. The sign that you have reached the limit of systematization is usually simplification. When your approach begins to lose touch with complexity, you have gone too far.

My own work (1997c) on part/whole analysis is a beginning attempt to systematize and integrate Goffmanian and other approaches. Concrete situations, especially those that have been mechanically recorded, and are therefore exasperatingly verbatim, provide the parts that can then be explored using general ideas. For example, I have based much of my work on collective conflict on the earlier, extremely detailed studies of unacknowledged shame in psychotherapy sessions by Helen Lewis (1971) and marital quarrels by Retzinger (1991). The intuitive analysis of the least parts of interaction, the words and gestures, seems to be necessary to deconstruct ruling tropes and reconstruct new ones. Part/whole analysis of this kind may breathe new life into social science.

Combining part/whole analysis and the Web approach involves three steps that Phillips and I agree on: (1) reflexiveness: using the researcher's own experiences as background; (2) defining the research problem around at least one clearly defined concept; and (3) moving up and down the conceptual ladder of abstraction between concrete situations on the one hand, and theory and social structure/process, on the other. The blending of the two approaches into one should serve to balance the tendency of the Web approach toward the abstract and of part/whole analysis toward the concrete. The new scheme may be the next step in line with Goffman's attempt to free ourselves from entrapment in the vernacular words, images, and ideas of everyday life.

References

Abbott, Andrew. 2001. *Chaos of Disciplines.* Chicago: University of Chicago Press.

———. 2004. *Methods of Discovery: Heuristics for the Social Sciences.* New York: Norton.

Alverez, Alexander. 1997. Adjusting to Genocide: Techniques of Neutralization and the Holocaust. *Social Science History* 21: 139–78.

Anderson, Benedict. 1991. *Imagined Communities.* London: Verso.

Austin, J.L. 1965. *How to Do Things with Words.* Oxford: Oxford University Press.

Baptista, Luiz Carlos. 2003. Framing and Cognition. Chapter 8 in Javier Trevino (ed.), *Goffman's Legacy,* pp. 197–215. Lanham, MD: Rowman & Littlefield.

Bartlett, Frederic. 1932. *Remembering.* Cambridge: The University Press.

Baumeister, Roy. 1997. *Evil: Inside Human Violence and Cruelty.* New York: W.H. Freeman.

Baumeister, Roy F., and Mark R. Leary, 2000. The Need to Belong: Desire for Interpersonal Attachments as a Fundamental Human Motivation. In E. Tory Higgins and Arie W. Kruglanski (eds.), *Motivational Science: Social and Personality Perspectives,* pp. 24–49. Philadelphia: Taylor & Francis.

Belknap, Michael B. 2002. *The Vietnam War on Trial.* Lawrence: University Press of Kansas.

Benedict, Ruth. 1946. *The Chrysanthemum and the Sword.* New York: Houghton Mifflin.

Benford, Robert D., and David A. Snow. 2000. Framing Processes and Social Movements: An Overview and Assessment. *Annual Review of Sociology* 26: 11–39.

Bennett, Alan. 2000. Cold Sweat. In Gary Fine and Greg Smith (eds.), *Erving Goffman,* vol. 1–4. London: Sage. (Article originally published in 1994.)

Billig, Michael. 1999. *Freudian Repression: Conversation Creating the Unconscious.* Cambridge: Cambridge University Press.

Bloom, Harold. 1998. *Shakespeare: The Invention of the Human.* New York: Riverhead Books.

Blumer, Herbert. 1986. *Symbolic Interactionism.* Berkeley: University of California Press.

Boswell, James. 1961. *Journal of a Trip to the Hebrides.* New York: McGraw-Hill.

Bowen, Murray. 1978. *Family Therapy in Clinical Practice.* New York: Jason Aaronson.

Bowker, L.H. (ed.). 1998. *Masculinities and Violence*. Newbury Park, CA: Sage.

Braithwaite, J. 1989. *Crime, Shame, and Reintegration*. Cambridge: Cambridge University Press.

Breggin, Peter. 1991. *Toxic Psychiatry: Why Therapy, Empathy, and Love Must Replace the Drugs, Electroshock, and Biochemical Theories of the "New Psychiatry."* New York: St. Martin's Press.

Bromberg, N., and V. Small. 1983. *Hitler's Psychopathology*. New York: International Universities Press.

Broucek, Francis. 1991. *Shame and the Self.* New York: Guilford.

Brown, Penelope, and Stephen C. Levinson. 1987. *Politeness: Some Universals in Language Usage*. New York: Cambridge University Press.

Bruner, Jerome. 1983. *Child's Talk*. New York: Norton.

Bullock, A. 1964. *Hitler, a Study in Tyranny*. New York: Harper and Row.

Burns, Tom. 1992. *Erving Goffman*. London: Routledge.

Cahill, Thomas. 1995. *How the Irish Saved Civilization*. New York: Doubleday.

Calley, William Laws. 1971. *Lieutenant Calley: His Own Story* (as told to John Sack). London: Hutchinson and Co., Cambridge University Press.

Canfield, John. 1990. *The Looking-Glass Self.* New York: Praeger.

Carrere, S., K. T. Buehlman, J. A. Coan, J. M. Gottman, and L. Ruckstuhl. 2000. Predicting Marital Stability and Divorce in Newlywed Couples, *Journal of Family Psychology* 14(1), January, 1–17.

Chenail, Ronald. 1995. Recursive Frame Analysis. *The Qualitative Report* 2(2), October.

Cicourel, Aaron. 1992. The Interpenetration of Communicative Contexts. Chapter 11 in Alessandro Duranti and Charles Goodwin (eds.), *Rethinking Context*, pp. 291–315. Cambridge: Cambridge University Press.

Clark, Herbert H., and Catherine R. Marshall. 1981. Definite Reference and Mutual Knowledge. In A.K. Joshi, B.L. Webber, and I.A. Sag (eds.), *Elements of Discourse Understanding*, pp. 10–63. Cambridge: Cambridge University Press.

Clark, Ramsey. 1994. *The Fire This Time: U.S. War Crimes in the Gulf.* Emeryville, CA: Thunder's Mouth Press.

Collins, Randall. 1980. Erving Goffman and the Development of Modern Social Theory. In Jason Ditton (ed.), *The View from Goffman*, pp. 170–209. New York: St. Martin's Press.

———. 1990. Violent Conflict and Social Organization: Some Theoretical Implications of the Sociology of War. *Amsterdams Sociologisch Tijdschrift* 16, 63–87.

———. Forthcoming *Violent Conflict: A Micro-Sociological Theory.*

Cooley, Charles H. 1922. *Human Nature and the Social Order.* New York: Scribner's.

Craig, S. (ed.). 1992. *Men, Masculinity, and the Media*. Newbury Park, CA: Sage.

Craik, Kenneth. 1943. *The Nature of Explanation*. Cambridge: The University Press.

Darwin, Charles. 1872 (1998). *The Expression of the Emotions in Men and Animals* (Paul Ekman, ed.). London: John Murray.

Davidson, Donald. 2001. *Inquiries into Truth and Interpretation,* 2nd ed. Oxford: Clarendon Press.

Davidson, E. 1977. *The Making of Adolf Hitler.* New York: Macmillan.

Davis, Murray S. 1975. Review of "Frame Analysis: An Essay on the Organization of Experience." *Contemporary Sociology* 4(6), 509-603.

Demos, E. Virginia. 1995. *Exploring Affect: The Selected Writings of Silvan S. Tomkins.* Cambridge: Cambridge University Press.

Ditton, Jason (ed.). 1980. *The View from Goffman.* New York: St. Martin's Press.

Doka, K., and T. Martin. 1998. Masculine Response to Loss. *Journal of Family Studies* 4, 143-58.

Douglas, Mary. 1966 (2002). *Purity and Danger.* London: Routledge.

Drew, Paul, and Anthony Wootton (eds.). 1988. *Erving Goffman: Exploring the Interaction Order.* Cambridge: Polity.

Durkheim, Emile. 1915. *Elementary Forms of the Religious Life.* Glencoe, IL: Free Press.

Edelmann, Robert J. 1987. *The Psychology of Embarrassment.* Chicester: Wiley.

Ekman, Paul, W. Friesen, and Phoebe Ellsworth. 1972. *Emotion in the Human Face.* New York: Pergamon.

Elias, Norbert. 1939 (1978, 1982, 1983). *The Civilizing Process,* vol. 1-3. New York: Pantheon.

———. 1996. *The Germans: Power Struggles and the Development of Habitus in the Nineteenth and Twentieth Centuries.* Cambridge: Polity.

———. 1998. *On Civilization, Power, and Knowledge.* Chicago: University of Chicago Press.

Elias, N., and John Scotson. 1965. *The Established and the Outsiders.* London: Frank Cass.

Entman, Robert M. 1993. Framing: Toward Clarification of a Fractured Paradigm. *Journal of Communication* 43(4), 51-58.

Erikson, Erik. 1950. *Childhood and Society.* New York: Norton.

Evans, Bertrand. 1960. *Shakespeare's Comedies.* London: Oxford University Press.

Everett, Arthur. 1971. *Calley.* New York: Dell.

Fergus, K.D., and D.W. Reid. 2001. The Couple's Mutual Identity: A Systemic-Constructivist Approach to the Integration of Persons and Systems. *Journal of Psychotherapy Integration* 11, 385-410.

Fine, Gary, and Greg Smith (eds.). 2000. *Erving Goffman,* vol. 1-4. London: Sage.

Freud, Sigmund. 1905. Three Essays on the Theory of Sexuality. In *Standard Edition,* vol. 7, pp. 135-244. London: Hogarth Press.

———. 1927. The Future of an Illusion. In *Standard Edition,* vol. 21. London: Hogarth Press.

Freud, Sigmund, and J. Breuer. 1895 (1966). *Studies on Hysteria.* New York: Avon.

Gamson, William A. 1975. Review of "Frame Analysis" by Erving Goffman. *Contemporary Sociology* 4, 603-7.

Geertz, Clifford. 1973. *The Interpretation of Cultures.* New York: Basic Books.

————. 1983. *Local Knowledge*. New York: Basic Books.

Gergen, Kenneth. 1996. Postmodern Culture and the Re-visioning of Alienation. In Felix Geyer (ed.), *Alienation, Ethnicity, and Postmodernism*, pp. 117–26. Westport, CT: Greenwood.

Gibson, J.W. 1994. *Warrior Dreams*. New York: Hill and Wang.

Giddens, Anthony. 1988. Goffman as Systematic Social Theorist. Chapter 9 in Paul Drew and Anthony Wootton (eds.), *Erving Goffman: Exploring the Interaction Order*, pp. 250–79. Cambridge: Polity.

Gilbert, G. 1950. *The Psychology of Dictatorship*. New York: Ronald.

Gilligan, James. 1997. *Violence: Reflections on a National Epidemic*. New York: Vintage.

Gitlin, Todd. 1980. *The Whole World Is Watching: Mass Media in the Making and Unmaking of the New Left*. Berkeley: University of California Press.

Goddard, Harold. 1951. *The Meaning of Shakespeare*. Chicago: University of Chicago Press.

Goffman, Erving. 1952. On Cooling the Mark Out. *Psychiatry* 15(4 November,), 451–63.

————. 1955. On Face-Work: An Analysis of Ritual Elements in Social Interaction. *Psychiatry: Journal of Interpersonal Relations* 18(3), 213–31.

————. 1956. Embarrassment and Social Organization. *American Journal of Sociology* 62, 264–71.

————. 1958. The Characteristics of Total Institutions. In *Symposium on Preventive and Social Psychiatry* (April 15–17, 1957). Washington, DC: Walter Reed Army Institute of Research.

————. 1959. *Presentation of Self in Everyday Life*. New York: Anchor.

————. 1961a. *Asylums*. New York: Anchor.

————. 1961b. *Encounters*. Indianapolis: Bobbs-Merrill.

————. 1963a. *Behavior in Public Places*. New York: Free Press.

————. 1963b. *Stigma*. Englewood Cliffs, NJ: Prentice-Hall.

————. 1964. The Neglected Situation. *The American Anthropologist* 66(6, part 2), 133–36.

————. 1967. *Interaction Ritual*. New York: Anchor.

————. 1969. *Strategic Interaction*. Philadelphia: University of Pennsylvania Press.

————. 1971. *Relations in Public*. New York: Basic Books.

————. 1974. *Frame Analysis*. New York: Harper.

————. 1979. *Gender Advertisements*. London: Macillan.

————. 1981. *Forms of Talk*. Philadelphia: University of Pennsylvania Press.

————. 1983a. Felicity's Condition. *American Journal of Sociology* 89(1), 1–53.

————. 1983b. The Interaction Order. *American Sociological Review* 48, 1–17.

Gottschalk, Louis. 1995. *Content Analysis of Verbal Behavior*. Hillsdale, NJ: Lawrence Erlbaum Associates.

Gottschalk, Louis, C. Winget, and G. Gleser. 1969. *Manual of Instruction for Using the Gottschalk-Gleser Content Analysis Scales*. Berkeley: University of California Press.

Goudsblom, Johann. 1977. Responses to Elias's Work in England, Germany, the Netherlands, and France. In Peter Gleichmann (ed.), *Human Figurations*. Amsterdam: Sociologische Tijdschrift.

Gouldner, Alvin W. 1970. *The Coming Crisis of Western Sociology.* New York: Basic Books.

———. 1972. The Politics of the Mind: Reflections on Flacks' Review of *The Coming Crisis of Western Sociology. Social Policy* 5, March/April, 13-21, 54-58.

Greenshaw, Wayne. 1971. *The Making of a Hero; The Story of Lieut. William Calley Jr.* Louisville: Touchstone.

Gronfein, William. 1999. Mental Illness and the Interaction Order in the Work of Erving Goffman. In Greg Smith (ed.), *Goffman and Social Organization: Studies in a Sociological Legacy.* London: Routledge.

Hammer, Richard. 1971. *The Court-Martial of Lt. Calley.* New York: Coward, McCann & Geoghegan.

———. 1992. Talk about Embarrassment: Exploring the Taboo-Denial-Repression Hypothesis. *Symbolic Interaction* 15, 203-25.

Hatty, S. 2000. *Masculinities, Violence, and Culture.* Newbury Park, CA: Sage.

Heath, Christian. 1988. Embarrassment and Interactional Organization. In Paul Drew and Anthony Wootton (eds.), *Erving Goffman: Exploring the Interaction Order,* pp. 136-60. Cambridge: Polity.

Heinz, Walter. 1992. Changes in the Methodology of Alienation Research. In Felix Geyer and Walter Heinz (eds.), *Alienation, Society, and the Individual,* pp. 213-21. New Brunswick, NJ: Transaction.

Hersh, Seymour M. 1970. *My Lai 4: A Report on the Massacre and Its Aftermath.* New York: Random House.

Hinde, Robert, and H. Watson (eds.). 1994. *War, a Cruel Necessity? The Bases of Institutionalized Violence.* London: I.B. Tauris.

Hitler, A. 1943 (1927). *Mein Kampf.* Boston: Houghton Mifflin.

Hochschild, Arlie. 2004. Let Them Eat War. *European Journal of Psychotherapy, Counseling & Health* 6(3), December, 1-10.

———. 1983. *The Managed Heart.* Berkeley: University of California Press.

Horney, Karen. 1950. *Neurosis and Human Growth.* New York: Norton.

Horowitz, Mardi. 1981. Self-righteous Rage. *Archives of General Psychiatry* 38, 1233-38.

Howard, Rhoda E. 1995. *Human Rights and the Search for Community.* Boulder: Westview.

Hymes, Dell. 1984. On Erving Goffman. *Theory and Society* 13(5), 621-31.

Kardiner, Abraham. 1939. *The Individual and His Society.* New York: Columbia University Press.

Karls, James, and Karin Wandrei (eds.). 1994. *Person-in Environment System: The PIE Classification System for Social Functioning Problems.* Washington, DC: National Association of Social Workers Press.

Katz, Jack. 1999. *How Emotions Work.* Chicago: University of Chicago Press.

Kaufman, Gershen. 1989. *The Psychology of Shame.* New York: Springer.

Kaufman, Gershen, and Lev Raphael. 1984. Shame as Taboo in American Culture. In Ray Browne (ed.), *Forbidden Fruits: Taboos and Tabooism in Culture,* pp. 57-64. Bowling Green: Bowling Green University Press.

Keltner, Dacher, and B.N. Buswell. 1997. Embarrassment: Its Distinct Form and Appeasement Functions. *Psychological Bulletin* 122, 250-70.

Kirsch, Irving, Thomas Moore, Alan Scoboria, and Sarah Nicholls. 2002. The Emperor's New Drugs: An Analysis of Antidepressant Medication Data

Submitted to the U.S. Food and Drug Administration. *Prevention and Treatment* 5(July), 1–11.

Koenig, Thomas. 2004. Reviews of Frame Analysis. www.lboro.ac.uk/research/mmethods/resources/links/frames.

Koenigsberg, Richard A. 2005. Virility and Slaughter. home.earthlink.net/~library ofsocialscience/online_pubs.htm.

Koestler, Arthur. 1959. *The Sleepwalkers*. New York: Grosset and Dunlap.

——. 1967. *The Act of Creation*. New York: Dell.

Kohut, Heinz. 1971. Thoughts on Narcissism and Narcissistic Rage. *The Search for the Self*, pp. 77–108. New York: International Universities Press.

Kressel, Neil. 2002. *Mass Hate*. Boulder: Westview.

Krystal, Henry. 1988. *Integration and Self-healing: Affect, Trauma, Alexithymia*. Hillsdale, NJ: Analytic Press.

Kubizek, A. 1955. *The Young Hitler I Knew*. Boston: Houghton Mifflin.

Kundera, Milan. 1995. *Testaments Betrayed*. New York: Harper Collins.

Labov, William, and David Fanshel. 1977. *Therapeutic Discourse: Psychotherapy as Conversation*. New York: Academic Press

Laing, Ronald D. 1960. *The Divided Self*. London: Tavistock.

——. 1967. *The Politics of Experience*. New York: Ballantine.

Laing, Ronald D., and Aaron Esterson. 1964. *Sanity, Madness and the Family*. London: Tavistock.

Laing, R. D., H. Phillipson, and A. Lee. 1966. *Interpersonal Perception*. New York: Springer.

Lansky, Melvin. 1992. *Fathers Who Fail: Shame and Psychopathology in the Family System*. Hillsdale, NJ: Analytic Press.

——. 1995. *Posttraumatic Nightmares*. Hillsdale, NJ: Analytic Press.

Leary, Mark, and Roy Baumeister. 2000. The Nature and Function of Self-Esteem: Sociometer Theory. In Mark Zanna (ed.), *Advances in Experimental Social Psychology*, vol. 32, pp. 1–62. San Diego: Academic Press.

Lefebvre, Vladimir. 1977. *The Structure of Awareness: Toward a Symbolic Language of Human Reflexion*. Newbury Park, CA: Sage.

Lemert, Charles. 1997. Goffman. In Charles Lemert and Ann Branaman (eds.), *The Goffman Reader*, pp. ix–xlviii. Oxford: Blackwell.

Lemert, Edwin. 1951. *Social Pathology*. New York: McGraw-Hill.

——. 1962. Paranoia and the Dynamics of Exclusion. *Sociometry* 25, 2–20.

Levine, Peter. 1997. *Waking the Tiger: Healing Trauma*. Berkeley, CA: North Atlantic Books.

Lewis, Helen. 1971. *Shame and Guilt in Neurosis*. New York: International Universities Press.

Lewis, Michael. 1995. Embarrassment: The Emotion of Self-Exposure and Evaluation. In June Tangney and Kurt Fischer, *Self-Conscious Emotions*, pp. 210–11. New York: Guilford.

Lofland, John. 1980. Early Goffman: Style, Structure, Substance, Soul. In Jason Ditton (ed.), *The View from Goffman*, pp. 24–51. New York: St. Martin's Press.

——. 1984. Erving Goffman's Sociological Legacies. *Urban Life* 13(1), 7–34. Reprinted in Gary Fine and Greg Smith (eds.), 2000, *Erving Goffman*, vol. 1, pp. 156–78. London: Sage.

Lynd, Helen 1958. *Shame and the Search for Identity*. New York: Harcourt Brace.

Mannheim, Karl. 1936. *Ideology and Utopia.* London: Routledge and Kegan Paul.

———. 1951. *Man and Society in an Age of Reconstruction; Studies in Modern Social Structure.* New York: Harcourt Brace.

Manning, Peter. 1980. Goffman's Framing Order: Style as Structure. In Jason Ditton (ed.), *The View from Goffman,* pp. 252–84. New York: St. Martin's Press.

Manning, Philip. 1992. *Erving Goffman and Modern Sociology.* Cambridge: Polity.

Mead, George H. 1934. *Mind, Self, and Society.* Chicago: University of Chicago Press.

Metge, Joan. 1986. *In and Out of Touch: Whakamaa* [bond affect] *in Cross Cultural Perspective.* Wellington, NZ: Victoria University Press.

Miller, A. 1983. *For Your Own Good.* New York: Farrar, Straus, Giroux.

Miller, Rowland S., and June P. Tangney. 1994. Differentiating Embarrassment and Shame. *Journal of Social and Clinical Psychology* 13, 273–87.

Miller, William. 1993. *Humiliation.* Ithaca: Cornell University Press.

———. 1997. *The Anatomy of Disgust.* Cambridge: Harvard University Press.

Minerva Center. www.minervacenter.com.

Morgan, R. 2001. *The Demon Lover: The Roots of Terrorism.* New York: Washington Square Press.

Morrison, Andrew. 1989. *Shame: The Underside of Narcissism.* Hillsdale, NJ: Analytic Press.

Nagel, Thomas. 1979. Sexual Perversion. Chapter 4 in his *Mortal Questions.* Cambridge: Cambridge University Press.

Nathanson, Donald. 1992. *Shame and Pride.* New York: Norton.

Neisser, Ulrich. 1976. *Cognition and Reality.* New York: W.H. Freeman.

Newman, Kathryn. 2004. *Rampage.* New York: Basic Books.

Nietzsche, Frederick. 1887 (1967). *Geneology of Morals.* New York: Vintage.

Norwood, Robin. 1985. *Women Who Love Too Much.* New York: Pocket.

Oates, Joyce Carol. 1974. *New Heaven, New Earth.* New York: Vanguard Press.

O'Connell, Sanjida. 1998. *Mindreading: An Investigation into How We Learn to Love and Lie.* New York: Doubleday.

Oromaner, Mark. 2000. Erving Goffman and the Academic Community. Chapter 10 in Gary Fine and Greg Smith (eds.), *Erving Goffman,* vol. 1, pp. 114–19. London: Sage.

Parkes, Colin. 1998 (1988). *Bereavement: Studies of Grief in Adult Life,* 3rd ed. Madison, CT: International Universities Press.

Parsons, T., and E. Shils. 1951. *Toward a General Theory of Action.* Cambridge: Harvard University Press.

PBS. n.d. *The American Experience: Vietnam.* http://www.pbs.org/wgbh/amex/vietnam/trenches/mylai.html.

Phillips, Bernard S. 1988. Toward a Reflexive Sociology. *The American Sociologist* 19(Summer), 138–51.

———. 2001. *Beyond Sociology's Tower of Babel: Reconstructing the Scientific Method.* New York: Aldine de Gruyter.

Phillips, Bernard, Harold Kincaid, and Thomas J. Scheff (eds.). 2002. *Toward a Sociological Imagination: Bridging Specialized Fields.* Lanham, MD: University Press of America.

Piercy, Marge. 1980. *The Moon Is Always Female.* New York: Random House.

Posner, Judith. 2000a. Erving Goffman: His Presentation of Self. Chapter 9 in Gary Fine and Greg Smith (eds.), *Erving Goffman,* vol. 1, pp. 99–113. London: Sage.

———. 2000b. Rebuttal to Oromaner Paper. Chapter 11 in Gary Fine and Greg Smith (eds.), *Erving Goffman,* vol. 1, pp. 120–21. London: Sage.

Psathas, George. 1980. Early Goffman and the Analysis of Face-to-Face Interaction. Chapter 2 in Jason Ditton (ed.), *The View from Goffman,* pp. 52–79. New York: St. Martin's Press.

Puente, Sylvia, and Dov Cohen. 2003. Jealousy and the Meaning of Love. *Personality and Social Psychology Bulletin* 29, 449–60.

Quine, William. 1979. A Postscript on Metaphor. In S. Sacks (ed.), *On Metaphor,* pp. 159–164. Chicago: University of Chicago Press.

Retzinger, S.M. 1989. A Theory of Mental Illness. *Psychiatry* 52, 325–35.

———. 1991. *Violent Emotions: Shame and Rage in Marital Quarrels.* Newbury Park, CA: Sage.

———. 1995. Identifying Shame and Anger in Discourse. *American Behavioral Scientist* 38, 541–59.

Riggins, Stephen (ed.). 1990. *Beyond Goffman.* Berlin: Mouton de Gruyter.

Rogers, Mary. 1980. Goffman and Power. Chapter 4 in Jason Ditton (ed.), *The View from Goffman,* pp. 100–133. New York: St. Martin's Press. A later version can be found in The Personal Is Dramaturgical (and Political): The Legacy of Erving Goffman. Chapter 2 in Javier Trevino (ed.), 2003, *Goffman's Legacy,* pp. 71–85. Lanham, MD: Rowman & Littlefield.

Sabini, Joseph, B. Garvey, and A.L. Hall. 2001. Shame and Embarrassment Revisited. *Personality & Social Psychology Bulletin* 27, 104–17.

Satir, Virginia. 1972. *Peoplemaking.* Palo Alto, CA: Science and Behavior Press.

Scheff, Thomas. 1966 (1999). *Being Mentally Ill.* Chicago: Aldine Press.

———. 1967. Toward a Sociological Model of Consensus. *American Sociological Review* 32(February), 32–46.

———. 1979 (2000). *Catharsis in Healing, Ritual, and Drama.* New York: iUniverse.

———. 1984. The Taboo on Coarse Emotions. *Review of Personality and Social Psychology,* June, 146–69.

———. 1986. Toward Resolving the Controversy over "Thick Description." *Current Anthropology* 27, 408–9.

———. 1987. Interminable Quarrels: A Case Study of a Shame/Rage Spiral. In Helen B. Lewis (ed.), *The Role of Shame in Symptom Formation,* pp. 109–50. Patterson, NJ: LEA.

———. 1988. Shame and Conformity: The Deference/Emotion System. *American Sociological Review* 53(June), 395–406.

———. 1989. Cognitive and Emotional Conflict in Anorexia: Reanalysis of a Classic Case. *Psychiatry* 52, 148–56.

———. 1990. *Microsociology: Discourse, Emotion and Social Structure.* Chicago: University of Chicago Press.

———. 1994. *Bloody Revenge: Emotions, Nationalism, War.* Boulder: Westview.

———. 1995. Conflict in Family Systems: The Role of Shame. In June Tangney and Kurt Fischer (eds.), *Self-Conscious Emotions,* pp. 383–412. New York: Guilford.

———. 1997a. Alienation, Nationalism, and Inter-ethnic Conflict. (Unpublished ms.)

———. 1997b. Local Peacemaking through "Community Conferences." (Unpublished ms.)

———. 1997c. *Emotions, the Social Bond, and Human Reality.* Cambridge: Cambridge University Press.

———. 1999. *Being Mentally Ill,* 3rd ed. New York: Aldine de Gruyter.

———. 2000. Shame and the Social Bond. *Sociological Theory* 18, 84-98.

———. 2002. Working Class Emotions and Relationships: Secondary Analysis of Sennett and Cobb, and Willis. In Bernard Phillips, Harold McKinnon, and Thomas Scheff (eds.), *Toward a Sociological Imagination: Bridging Specialized Fields,* pp. 263-92. Lanham, MD: University Press of America.

———. 2003a. Shame in Self and Society. *Symbolic Interaction* 26(2), 239-62.

———. 2003b. Male Emotions and Violence: A Case Study. *Human Relations* 56, 727-49.

———. 2003c. The Goffman Legacy: Deconstructing/Reconstructing Social Science. In Javier Treviño (ed.), *Goffman's Legacy,* pp. 50-70. Lanham, MD: Rowman & Littlefield.

———. 2004. Hatred as a Shame/Rage Construct. In Christopher Frost (ed.), Special Issue on Hatred. *Humanity and Society* 28, 24-39.

———. 2005. Looking-Glass Self: Goffman as Symbolic Interactionist. *Symbolic Interaction* 28(2), 147-66.

Scheff, T.J., with David Fearon, Jr., 2004. Social and Emotional Components in Self-Esteem. *Journal of the Theory of Social Behavior* 34, 73-90.

Scheff, T.J., and S. M. Retzinger. 1991. *Emotion and Violence: Shame and Rage in Destructive Conflicts.* Lexington, MA: Lexington. (Reprinted in 2000 by iUniverse.)

Schegloff, E. 1988. Goffman and the Analysis of Conversation. In Paul Drew and A. Wootton (eds.), *Erving Goffman: Exploring the Interaction Order,* pp. 89-135. Cambridge: Polity.

———. 1992. In Another Context. Chapter 7 in Alessandro Duranti and Charles Goodwin (eds.), *Rethinking Context.* Cambridge: Cambridge University Press.

Scheibe, Karl. 2000. *The Drama of Everyday Life.* Cambridge: Harvard University Press.

Scheler, Max. 1912 (1961). *Ressentiment.* Glencoe, IL: Free Press.

Schneider, Carl. 1977. *Shame, Exposure, and Privacy.* Boston: Beacon.

Schudson, Michael. 1984. Embarrassment and Erving Goffman's Idea of Human Nature. *Theory and Society* 13(5), 633-48.

Schutz, Alfred. 1962. *The Problem of Social Reality.* The Hague: M. Nijhoff.

Seeman, Melvin. 1975. Alienation Studies. *Annual Review of Sociology* 1, 91-124.

Sennett, Richard. 1980. *Authority.* New York: Alfred Knopf.

———. 2003. *Respect in a World of Inequality.* New York: W.W. Norton.

Sennett, R., and J. Cobb. 1972. *The Hidden Injuries of* Class. New York: Alfred Knopf.

Shanon, B. 1990. What Is Context? *Journal for the Theory of Social Behavior* 20, 158-66.

Sharkey, William. 2001. http://www2.hawaii.edu/~sharkey/embarrassment/ embarrassment_references.html.

Simmel, Georg. 1904. Fashion. *International Quarterly* X, 130-55. (Reprinted the same year in the *American Journal of Sociology* 62, 541-59.)

——. 1955. *Conflict and the Web of Group Affiliations.* Glencoe, IL: Free Press.

Smith, Greg (ed.). 1999. *Goffman and Social Organization: Studies in a Sociological Legacy.* London: Routledge.

Solomon, Robert. 1981. *Love: Emotion, Myth, and Metaphor.* Garden City, NY: Anchor Press/Doubleday.

——. 1994. *About Love: Re-inventing Romance for Our Times.* Lanham, MD: Littlefield Adams.

Speer, Albert. 1970. *Inside the Third Reich.* New York: Macmillan.

Sperber, Dan, and Deirdre Wilson. 1995. *Relevance.* Cambridge, MA: Harvard University Press.

Staub, Ervin. 2003. *The Psychology of Good and Evil.* Cambridge: Cambridge University Press.

Steiner, George. 1971. Review of Albert Speer's *Inside the Third Reich. New Yorker,* July 24, 70-75.

Stern, Daniel. 1977. *The First Relationship.* Cambridge: Harvard University Press.

Stierlin, H. 1976. *Adolf Hitler: A Family Perspective.* New York: Psychohistory Press.

Sykes, G., and D. Matza. 1957. Techniques of Neutralization: A Theory of Delinquency. *American Sociological Review* 22, 664-70.

Szasz, T.S. 1961. *The Myth of Mental Illness.* New York: Hoeber-Harper.

Tangney, June, and Rhona Dearing. 2002. *Shame and Guilt.* New York: Guilford.

Tangney, June, Rowland S. Miller, Laura Flicker, and Deborah H. Barlow. 1996. Are Shame, Guilt, and Embarrassment Distinct Emotions? *Journal of Personality and Social Psychology* 70, 1256-69.

Tavuchis, Nicholas. 1991. *Mea Culpa: A Sociology of Apology and Reconciliation.* Stanford: Stanford University Press.

Taylor, Graeme J., R. Bagby, and J. Parker. 1997. *Disorders of Affect Regulation: Alexithymia in Medical and Psychiatric Illness.* New York: Cambridge University Press.

Taylor, Shelley, et al. 2000. Biobehavioral Responses to Stress in Females: Tend-and-Befriend, not Fight-or-Flight. *Psychological Review* 107, 411-29.

Toiskallio, Kalle. 2000. Review of Goffman and Social Organization. In Craig Smith (ed.), *Acta Sociologica* 43 (2), 178-80.

Toland, J. 1976. *Adolf Hitler.* Garden City, NY: Doubleday.

Tomkins, Silvan. 1963. *Affect, Imagery, Consciousness. Volume II.* New York: Springer.

Travers, Andrew. 1997. Goffman. *Reviewing Sociology* 10(1), 1-2.

Treviño, Javier (ed.). 2003. *Goffman's Legacy.* Lanham, MD: Rowman & Littlefield.

Tronick, E., M. Ricks, and J. Cohen. 1982. Maternal and Infant Affect Exchange. In T. Field and A. Fogel (eds.), *Emotion and Early Interaction.* Hillsdale, NJ: Lawrence Erlbaum.

Volkan, Vamik. 2004. *Blind Trust: Large Groups and Their Leaders in Times of Crisis and Terror.* Charlottesville, VA: Pitchstone.

Von Raumer, Wilhelm. 1857. *The Education of Girls.* (Cited in Elias 1978).

Watzlawick, Paul, Jane Bevan, and Donald Jackson. 1967. *The Pragmatics of Human Communication.* New York: Norton.

West, Candace. 1996. Goffman in Feminist Perspective. *Sociological Perspectives* 39, 353-69.

Whitehead, Alfred North. 1962. *Science and the Modern World.* New York: Macmillan.

Williams, Robin. 1988. Goffman's Methods. In Paul Drew and Anthony Wootton (eds.), *Erving Goffman: Exploring the Interaction Order,* pp. 64-88. Cambridge: Polity.

Willis, Paul. 1977. *Learning to Labor.* New York: Columbia University Press.

Winkins, Yves. 1988. *Erving Goffman: Les Moments et Leurs Hommes.* Paris: Seuil/Minuit.

———. 2000. Baltasound as the Symbolic Capital of Social Interaction. In Gary Fine and Greg Smith (eds.), *Erving Goffman,* vol. 1, pp. 193-212. London: Sage.

Index